8·10·71

JAMES JOYCE'S DISUNITED KINGDOM

Tenet insanabile multos
Scribendi cacoethes et aegro in corde senescit.

Juvenal (*Satires* VII.51)

I am quite content to go down to posterity as a scissors and paste man for that seems to me a harsh but not unjust description.

James Joyce
(letter to George Antheil, 3 January 1931, *Letters*, I)

Nay, more, were I not all I was,
Weak, wanton, waster out and out,
There would have been no world's applause
And damn all to write home about.

James Joyce
('An Epilogue to Ibsen's Ghosts', 1934)

you have reared your disunited kingdom on the vacuum of your most intensely doubtful soul.

Finnegans Wake 188, 15-17

JOHN GARVIN

James Joyce's Disunited Kingdom

and the Irish Dimension

GILL AND MACMILLAN, DUBLIN
BARNES & NOBLE BOOKS, NEW YORK
a division of Harper & Row Publishers, Inc.

First published in 1976
Gill and Macmillan Limited
15/17 Eden Quay
Dublin 1
and in London through
association with the
Macmillan Publishers Group

Published in the U.S.A. 1977 by
Harper & Row Publishers, Inc.
Barnes & Noble Import Division

Gill & Macmillan SBN : 7171 0782 5
Barnes & Noble ISBN : 0-06-492331-2
Library of Congress Catalog Card Number : 76-19930

Printed in Great Britain by
Bristol Typesetting Co Ltd
Barton Manor, St Philips Bristol

For my wife and family
that they may see what I was at

Contents

ABBREVIATIONS

U	*Ulysses*
FW	*Finnegans Wake*
MBK	*My Brother's Keeper*
Diary	*The Dublin Diary of Stanislaus Joyce*

Page References

Where pagination is given without reference to a particular book, the references in Part I of this book are to *Ulysses* (Penguin edition), and in Part II to *Finnegans Wake*.

Introduction

IT has been found convenient to base Part I of this book on *Ulysses* and Part II on *Finnegans Wake* but both parts involve references to Joyce's earlier works with which the reader is presumed to be familiar. The general treatment has been greatly extended by reference to critical and biographical sources, notably Richard Ellmann's *James Joyce* and the contents of the three volumes of *James Joyce's Letters*.

Anything to be published about *Ulysses* more than fifty years after its original appearance should constitute a new and original contribution to its interpretation or explication. In the first part of this book, therefore, I have assumed knowledge by the reader of all authoritative exegeses and commentary published, and I offer my own interpretations as extensions of these. Many of the webs of interpretation that continue to be spun from the text tend to become ever more finedrawn and fanciful : I trust that what is now presented represents seminal material from which new themes and interpretations may be formulated. Such new material includes the symbolism of the Ashplant, the identification of the Narrator in 'Cyclops' with Simon Dedalus—that is, in effect, with James Joyce's father; the details of the case of the unfortunate policeman on whom Bloom's pen-name, Henry Flower, is based; a comparison of John F. Taylor's actual oration with Joyce's version in 'Aeolus', and a new interpretation of the role of Blazes Boylan *vis-à-vis* Bloom and Stephen. The fact that Willie Mulvey soldiered in Gibraltar is revealed for the first time and is shown to have influenced Joyce in locating Molly Bloom's early years in that exotic centre. My exegesis of *U* is also used as an indication of the progression of Joyce's art towards the composition of *FW*.

A full exegesis of the whole farraginous content of

Finnegans Wake should ideally involve the cooperation of numerous people of different skills. A septuagintal commission perhaps. My Irish terms of reference predetermined my basic attitude: in the hither-and-thithering waters of the text I saw here one feature and there another of a portrait of the artist and an intelligible series of relationships with the other principal characters considered *sub specie Hibernitatis*. These I have followed in the first three chapters of Part II, ('The Exile of Erin', 'Shem and Shaun', and 'Jaun and Yawn'), so as to produce a simple narrative in which every important statement or identification is supported by appropriate citations from the text. In the following chapters, 'The Trial of Festy King', 'Popes and Paschs', and 'Bruinoboroff', I have uncovered some basic sources for the themes of crime and punishment, theological controversy and battles long ago. In all these studies I concentrate on factual, verifiable sources and not on generalisations or semantic and linguistic abstractions.

In my explication of *Ulysses*, as well as in that of *Finnegans Wake*, I rely to a considerable extent on the facts of Joyce's life including those revealed in the three volumes of his *Letters* to illustrate or explain or discount particular portions of his artistic works, especially where I find them revealing a solipsistic trend. The public has become accustomed to accept Joyce's portraits of himself as courageous self-revelation. It is assumed that he is telling the whole truth, living his books and writing his life. This is how Joyce himself described his position to Gillet: 'when work and life make one, when they are interwoven in the same fabric'. When one disentangles that fabric and puts the fact and the fiction in juxtaposition, the process often reveals a more than legitimate bias in favour of the author. In these instances I allow Joyce to speak for, and sometimes to contradict, himself, remaining for my part, I trust, entirely objective and uncommitted.

I had originally intended to entitle this work *The Joyce Country*, a term which I had borrowed from geography to apply metaphorically to the basically Irish character of Joyce's writings, bearing in mind that Joyce had cut out just such a metaphorical enclave in this area for himself under Nora's influence and with the aid of Mangan's poetry (see my chapters on 'Festy King' and 'Popes and Paschs'). The title was used as a heading for a review of Messrs Campbell and Robinson's *A Skeleton Key to Finnegans Wake* under the name of Marcus MacEnery, a ghost of mine deputising for another ghost, Andrew Cass, then on vacation, which was published in *The Irish Times* on 13 September 1947. The intention was to emphasise that the basic theme of *Finnegans Wake*, its chief characters, its topography, its historical, literary and musical motifs, were nearly all of Irish, and generally of Dublin, origin and that the authors of the *Key*, while performing a valuable exercise in discovering the universalised themes and abstractions of decayed divinities and theogonies overlaid on the Irish foundation, were, when they neglected the latter, merely providing blue prints of the upper storeys of a structure resting on nothingness.

I do not have a copy of that review available for consultation as I write, but I find an extract from it in Marvin Magalaner and Richard M. Kain's *Joyce the Man, the Work, the Reputation*, New York University Press, 1956, which suits my present purpose. The relevant passage (p. 342) runs as follows:

> The reviewer of the *Key*, in *The Irish Times*, claimed that [a complete exegesis] would have to come from (1) an Irishman, (2) one suffering in Joyce's words from 'an ideal insomnia', (3) one afflicted with Joyce's malady, the dread *cacoethes scribendi.*

Magalaner goes on to quote the review: 'It is a nice speculation to consider what type of man, competent to undertake the labour of such an opus, would at the same time be satisfied with the limited and austere form of self-expression available from trailing the steps of the master with foot-notes.' (There are no footnotes in this book, but it is not, of course, the work of an Academic.)

My ghost or ghosts, whom I have long since put down with ashplants, would, I think, now admit that each specialist will find his own book in *Finnegans Wake*, the singer, musician, poet, historian, theologian, cosmologist, spiritualist, Egyptologist, medicine man and bibliophile, but they would still maintain that the fact that Joyce was a native of Dublin, Ireland, is fundamental to the form and content of his book and that it is essentially a work in which Irish themes and the Irish accent predominate.

Brian O'Nolan suggested that the 1947 article should have had the sub-title, 'The Twelve Puns', an allusion to The Twelve Pins, the collective name in English for a dozen peaks or bens (Irish *beann*, pl. *beanna*) in the mountain ranges of Connemara, adjoining the district known as Joyce's Country. Next, my friend, the late Donagh MacDonagh, borrowed the expression from me for some of his writings on Joyce and, finally, Professor Tindall of Columbia University, New York, produced in 1960 a picture-book bearing my title, which I did not have the opportunity of seeing until it came out in paperback in 1972. Joyce's first and most fulsome biographer, Herbert Gorman, finding no tenable connection between James Joyce's family and the Connemara homeland of the Joyces, dismissed the latter in disgust as 'the so-called Joyce Country'. Gorman could seldom be equalled in fatuous remarks, but in this instance a disgruntled Irish journalist who referred to 'this so-called twentieth century' was ahead of him. Gorman, however, scored again when he declared that Joyce's father always wore a monocle 'in one eye'. In fact, Simon Dedalus, Jack Joyce's surrogate, does not wear a monocle in the 'Cyclops' episode and even refers scornfully to 'flash toffs with a swank glass in their eye', but I think this is introduced deliberately to thicken the disguise of the narrator. Simon's remark is almost as good as Gorman's, having plural toffs wearing a singular glass (monocle) in their (*sic*) singular eye but this is at least partly in deference to the Homeric Polyphemus.

I do not complain about the pre-emption of my title: bread cast on the waters for more than a quarter of a century is very apt to be washed up into a transatlantic hamper, and during those years, while I wrote and lectured a good deal on Joyce, I did not have time for sustained work on the subject. In the four years 1969-1973, for example, I was engaged as *locum tenens* for H.C.E. himself in his corporate capacity as the personification of the City of Dublin, being City Commissioner performing the functions of the City Council while the members of the council were removed from office, acting in the same capacity as the three Commissioners, Murphy, Hernon and Dr Dwyer acted from 1924 to 1930—(see the section of Chapter 21, 'Permutations and Combinations', dealing with the Dublin Corporation).

One of my earliest chores in the Finance Section of the Department of Local Government was the reapportionment according to area valuation changes as between Dublin City and County, deaths of pensioners etc., of the annual liabilities of Dublin Corporation and Dublin County Council for the 'Collector General's Annuity', a term used for the total sum payable each year in respect of pensions of the surviving superannuated officers of the abolished Collector General's office. Jim Tully, stationery clerk to the Department, who brought me each day my quota of governmental publications and parliamentary papers, drew my attention to the fact that one of the pensioners for whose chargeability I was providing was John S. Joyce, 'the father of that fellow we were talking about lately'. Jack Joyce was pensioned off early on, in 1891 in fact, and did not hold his post until 1898 when the office of the Collector General was wound up, as I have seen stated in some commentaries. His accession to the post with the triumph of Parnell in 1880 and his purely coincidental loss of office in 1891 when Parnell was overthrown and died, became the basis of the family's veneration of the 'Lost Leader' and of James Joyce's psychological hang-up with his fall and his association of it with the symbolic 'Fall' theme of *Finnegans Wake*.

Tully knew the whole background of the Joyce menage. His father had been Collector of Customs in Galway, a post subsequently held by Michael Healy, uncle of Nora Barnacle. He knew her father, Tom Barnacle, a baker by trade:

A kind of invisible man. 'Gobra Goney' they used to call him because his wife, when they'd say how was it they never see him, would say in Irish or English, 'maise, bíonn sé ag obair i gcónaí' (sure he does be always working). Aye, night work at a thirsty trade; then off to Hosty's pub at the Bridge would open at any hour. Then home to sleep it off. And out again to do his stint the next night. Cock Colahan, you knew him, a medical professor in the College, Cock said 'Gobra Goney' was the Irish for 'Secret Drinker'.

Tully also knew Jack Joyce and met his son at least once before the incident related in my chapter 'To Slay his Da'. On that occasion Tully was introduced to James Joyce, as 'Mr Tully, a clerk in the custom house'. But the introduction occurred in the pub on Burgh Quay known as the Scotch House and Joyce was quick to rejoin 'a clerk out of the custom house'. Tully was not amused. Neither would he have been amused if he knew that Joyce was to lift his potato 'against the neuritis' and bestow it on Leopold Bloom.

While I did have a title in mind for a book on Joyce, I gave no thought to the writing of it, until some years ago at the conclusion of a lecture to a postgraduate class, the young university man who presided remarked, *à propos* of my identifying Shaun in *FW* with Mr de Valera, that he had always thought that this had been a joke on my part. I replied that I had propounded this thesis quite seriously and that it was accepted internationally—by writers such as Richard Ellman, Hugh Kenner, Richard Kain and Marvin Magalaner. I added that the only 'joke' which I had ever tried to perpetrate on the Joyce canon was a rejection of the findings in *The Quest for Corvo* on the ground that 'Corvo' was really James Joyce endeavouring to externalise the hidden part of his ego (his ambition to be a priest and to rise to eminence in the Church). My effort was defeated when Alec Newman, then editor of the *Irish Times*, telephoned me and asked me was I serious. I was obliged to admit that I was not. The idea was later developed in Flann O'Brien's *The Dalkey Archive*, where Joyce is depicted with an ambition to become Rector of Clongowes Wood College.

My article on the Shem-Shaun antithesis in *FW* was published in the *Irish Times* on 26 April, 1947. This was supplemented by my *Childe Horrid's Pillgrimace* in *Envoy* 5 (17) May 1951, where I supplied a series of quotations which I considered sufficient to identify the personality and career of Eamon de Valera. Hugh Kenner made these the subject of brief commentaries in *Dublin's Joyce* (1955) but he did not develop the subject. I was at that time offering these leads to anybody who cared to develop them, not having the leisure myself to deal with them in detail. Richard M. Kain, in *Joyce, the Man, the Work, the Reputation*, conceded the 'possibility that Joyce, unhappy and disappointed at his lack of Irish recognition, contrasts himself with the Shaun of Irish politics, Eamon de Valera, as Andrew Cass argued in the *Irish Times* of 26 April 1947'. All this shows why at this stage I have decided that my thesis needed to be re-stated and documented in depth as in the first three chapters of Part II of this work.

Incidentally, the first sentence in part IV of my *Envoy* article, 'It is indisputable that Shaun is Eamon de Valera', was interpolated without my authority by Brian Nolan *alias* Brian O Nualláin, Flann O'Brien, Myles na gCopaleen etc., the editor of that particular issue of *Envoy*. He apparently considered that I was unnecessarily cautious in my identification which he thought should be pronounced positively and unambiguously. The fact is, of course, that Shaun represents a number of other characters in varying contexts—Stanislaus Joyce, Wyndham Lewis, John Mac Cormack and possibly Joyce himself in schizophrenic intercourse with himself. Nolan did not appreciate that one cannot positively confine any character in *FW* to one specific personality seeing that it is postulated that 'that sword of certainty which would identifide the body never falls' (51.5,6). My request that the line should be omitted when the article was incorporated in *A Bash in the Tunnel* (ed. Ryan, 1970) was apparently overlooked.

Nolan also tells in his 'Editorial Note' to the same issue of *Envoy* a story about a friend of his (he meant me) who, sitting next at dinner to a 'well-known savant' (Dr Richard Best) reminded him that he was a character in one of Joyce's books and received in return 'a heated statement' lasting 'two hours' about his being a living man and not a character in fiction. All this was based on what Best told me, which I retailed to Nolan, about the attempt of BBC representatives to interview Best for their 1951 programme on Joyce and his response to their urging that it was incumbent on him to grant them an interview because he was 'a character in *Ulysses*'. Professor Richard Ellmann gives my version of this incident in his *James Joyce*, p. 374. Best also told me at the Royal Irish Academy dinner in question (cf. *Ulysses* 'K.M.R.I.A.' p. 147) that Joyce had sent him a presentation copy of *Ulysses*, but that he had never read it.

What exercised Nolan's mind in my account of Best was that, by importing real persons into *Ulysses*, Joyce made them 'legendary and fictional', a metabolism to which their living prototypes objected, whereas he, as Flann O'Brien, in his *At*

Swim-Two-Birds, had adopted a directly contrary technique: legendary and fictional characters were there recruited from Irish myth and legend and from the stock personnel of cheap fiction and, coming alive in their fictional author's 'creation', rebelled against him on the grounds of the unsavoury roles assigned to them in his story and the unsatisfactory conditions of their employment in the real life of modern Dublin.

Nolan had presented Joyce with a copy of his book which was published almost the same time as *Finnegans Wake* and Joyce was quite excited about it (*Letters*, III, 475) perhaps because both books by coincidence shared a common mythical hero (Finn McCool). But the only page marked by him (T.E. Connolly, *The Personal Library of James Joyce*, p. 29) was that (33) which contained the statement 'that a satisfactory novel should be a self-evident sham to which the reader could regulate at will the degree of his credulity.'

Shorter versions of Chapters 1 (Martellomache), 18 (The Trial of Festy King), and 20 (Bruinoboroff) have been published in *Ireland of the Welcomes*, July-August, 1972; *The Dublin Magazine*, Autumn 1973; and *Moderna sprak*, LXVII/3/1973, Göteborg, respectively, and a summary version of portions of Chapter 21 ('Permutations and Combinations') in the *James Joyce Quarterly*, Tulsa, Oklahoma, Spring 1974.

I wish to express my deep appreciation of the personal interest which Mr Gerard O'Flaherty took in having me write this book. Patiently, politely to the point of diffidence, but withal persistently, he was, as he expressed himself, 'the ghost of Roger Casement a-knocking at my door'.

My research and preparation were mainly conducted in my own library and with the use of unpublished material collected by myself over the years. I am however obliged in a special measure for the ready help vouchsafed at all times by Mr Dermot Foley, F.L.A.I., former Director of An Chomhairle Leabharlanna. His unique knowledge of the stony tablelands of the Burren was also of assistance in pinning Citizen Cusack back to the rock whence he was hewn. I thank Professor J.R. Timoney for the definition of NCR (*FW* 284), although, of course, he was able to give it off the cuff. Tomás O hAilín, M.A., was equally quick to identify Professor Atkinson as the source of Professor Mahaffy's quip on Irish literature which

John F. Taylor ascribed in 1900 to a professor in Ancient Egypt referring to Hebrew. Mr Joseph P. Walsh, former editor of the *Irish Press*, gave me the opportunity of using some lines about Dawson, 'Doughy Daw' of 'Aeolus', by referring me to the book of poems where it appears. Dr Denis Conniffe, Assistant Director of the Agricultural Institute, was good enough to supply me from his scientific journals with some references which were surprisingly relevant to certain aspects of my research. All the gentlemen mentioned in this paragraph share with me membership of a club loosely organised for social rather than academic purposes. It has been my good fortune that their specialities stood me in such good stead.

I am particularly indebted to Dr Evelyn Tully whose local knowledge brought me to the fountainhead of information in Bowling Green, Galway, to what would otherwise have been the ungetatable Willie Mulvey and the undiscoverable Gibraltar connection.

I must put on public record the thanks I have already expressed in private to my daughter Catriona (Mrs Proinsias Gallagher) who made legible my first rough (very rough) drafts and to my daughter-in-law, Maire, (Mrs Thomas C. Garvin) not only for producing the ultimate typescript to a standard that few could equal but also for improving the composition in various places where her 'good questions' made me alive to *lacunae* or whatnot.

PART I

An Empirical Inquest on Ulysses

Chapter 1
Martellomache

IN the year 1904 the course of James Joyce's life and writings
was determined. In June he met Nora Barnacle and in October
he took her with him to the Continent where he obtained teaching posts, first in Pola and then in Trieste. Meanwhile he
stayed for a short period in the Martello Tower at Sandycove
with Oliver Gogarty. His sojourn there has been surmised to
have lasted various periods from three weeks to the whole of
the early summer while he taught at the school in Vico Road.
It is now possible to determine the exact time and duration of
this sojourn, on which the opening episode of *Ulysses*—
'Telemachus'—is based. In the summer of 1904, Gogarty,
chronic medical student, apprentice poetaster and ribald jester,
was simultaneously preoccupied with the frenetic spell of
Swinburne's poetry and the acquisition of the Tower on lease
from the British War Office. In several letters to his Oxford
friend, G. K. A. Bell, (*Many Lines to Thee*, ed. James F. Carens,
Dolmen Press, 1971), he adjured him to contact Swinburne
despite the wiles of his curator, Watts Dunton, who was keeping him alive by holding him as a recluse in his house in Putney.
In the same correspondence he retailed the latest quips of his
friend, James Joyce, for whom he intended the Tower to be a
retreat where he might spend a year finishing his novel, *Stephen
Hero*, subsequently re-drafted as the more stylised *Portrait of
the Artist as a Young Man*, published in 1914. About half of
the first draft was published some three years after Joyce's
death under its original title.

'The Bard Joyce', Gogarty wrote to Bell (op. cit.), 'is to do
the housekeeping. He is to Watts Dunton me also.' These fanciful projects did not materialise. Gogarty signed the lease of the
Tower (countersigned by a British officer named Haines) and

went into occupation in August—unaccompanied by Joyce. On 27 August, he wrote to Bell that with him in the Tower was Samuel Chenevix Trench (an Anglo-Irish student from Balliol), also Starkey (the poet 'Seamas O'Sullivan'). He added tersely:

> I have broken with Joyce, his want of generosity became to me inexcusable, he lampooned AE, Yeats, Colum and others to whom he was indebted in many ways. A desert was revealed which I did not think existed amid the seeming luxuriance of his soul.

Joyce did, in fact acknowledge in *Ulysses* a loan from AE, George Russell, 'A.E.I.O.U.' (190) and, over the years, Yeats and Colum continued to befriend and assist him.

In the previous year, Joyce had reviewed unfavourably Lady Gregory's *Poets and Dreamers* in the *Daily Express*, a Dublin Tory newspaper. In the *Ulysses* National Library scene 'Mulligan' tells 'Stephen' that the paper's editor is sick 'after what you wrote about that old hake Gregory . . . She gets you a job on the paper and then you go and slate her drivel.' (216)

Now Joyce had done it again. His *Holy Office* had slated not only the writers mentioned by Gogarty but also Synge, W. K. Magee ('John Eglinton'), George Roberts (publishing manager of Maunsel & Co.) and Seamas O'Sullivan as members

> . . . *of that motley crew*
> *Those souls that hate the strength that mine has*
> *Steeled in the school of old Aquinas.*

Worse still, he held Gogarty himself up to public odium for the snob he was:

> *Or him whose conduct seems to own*
> *His preference for a man of ' tone '.*

The 'man of tone' was, of course, Chenevix Trench who had taken Joyce's place as Gogarty's companion in the Tower. These lines must therefore have been inserted in the *Holy Office* subsequent to that event.

Nevertheless, Joyce sought the shelter of the Tower on 9 September when he had apparently found residence with his father impossible and free lodgings were not to be had elsewhere. He stayed there for five or six nights in wet weather with, no doubt, various occasions of constraint arising. On 14 September, Joyce's brother, Stanislaus, noted in the *Diary*, 'At present he is staying on sufferance with Gogarty . . . (who) wants to put Jim out, but he is afraid that if Jim made a name some-day it would be remembered against him . . . Jim is determined that if Gogarty puts him out it will be done publicly.' On the same night (14 September), Trench shouted in his sleep about shooting a black panther and Gogarty discharged a pistol, not at Trench's nightmare, but at the pots and pans on the wall over Joyce's bed, bringing them rattling down on him. This was what Joyce was waiting for—any symbol of a notice to quit, not the Tower merely, but also Ireland, thus copper-fastening the myth that he had been ejected by the Irish people represented by his treacherous friends. He left dramatically, not waiting to pick up even his black 'Latin quarter hat'. Next day the prodigal wrote to Starkey, giving the address of his father's house in Cabra, stating that his trunk would be called for the following morning, asking him to pack his clothes, boots, hat, caps, etc., in it, also the MS. of his verses and adding in words that reveal a cold hatred: 'Also see that your host has not abstracted the twelfth chapter of my novel from my trunk.'

All this, of course, was histrionics to dramatise his decision to leave Ireland. His affair with the auburn-haired girl from Galway, Nora Barnacle, could not be comfortably pursued in the prevailing moral atmosphere of bourgeois Dublin. When he left the Tower, he went to stay at 103 North Strand Road, Fairview, the home of his uncle, William Murray, whose wife 'Aunt Josephine' was his only mature confidante and guide since the death of his mother. On the evening of that day, he met Nora and on the following day, (16 September), he wrote to her:

> When I was waiting for you last night . . . it seemed to me that I was a fighting a battle with every religious and social force in Ireland for you and that I had nothing to rely on but myself.

It would seem that Don Quixote's fray with the windmills was more real than Joyce's 'mortal strife' but, in any event, he over-came his fictitious foes, by a dagger of the mind, perhaps. Within a month, he and Nora were off 'out into Europe' on what Joyce was afterwards to call 'that wild-goup's chase across the kathartic ocean', (*FW* 185), to assemble at Trieste, Zurich and Paris, 'in silence, exile and cunning', the successive instalments of his *Ulysses* which would crucify Gogarty and the rest of his Dublin cronies on the cross of his cruel fiction.

The scene of the first episode of *Ulysses* is the Tower but the stay in it of Joyce's fictional surrogate, Stephen Dedalus, is antedated to a period ending on 16 June, to commemorate his first date with Miss Barnacle. It is the high noon of a glorious summer. The sea, the surrounding country and the mountains are awakening in the mild morning air. Every prospect pleases and only man is vile. The occupants of the Tower are Malachi Mulligan (Oliver Gogarty), Stephen Dedalus (James Joyce) and Haines, an English student from Oxford, i.e., Trench who is represented as an Englishman and given the name of the British officer who signed the lease of the Tower.

Stephen is cold towards Mulligan : the 'panther' incident is mentioned but not the pistol shots. Joyce is indebted to Oscar Wilde for the original of a number of the witticisms in this episode : 'the rage of Caliban at not seeing his face in a mirror'; Irish art, 'the cracked looking glass of a servant', so it may be well to recall from *The Green Carnation* that Wilde wrote to Vincent O'Sullivan : 'There is a dreadful youth waiting for me in Regent Street. He is pacing up and down before the door like a wonderful black panther'. 'Black Panther' was also the name of a racehorse. At length, Stephen reveals that his resentment stems from Mulligan's reference to his mother as 'beastly dead'. Mulligan tries to bluster his way out of this and says he had not meant to offend the memory of his mother. Stephen replies 'very coldly' :

—I am not thinking of the offence to my mother.
—Of what, then? Buck Mulligan asked.
—Of the offence to me, Stephen answered.
Buck Mulligan swung round on his heel.
—Oh, an impossible person! he exclaimed.
Oh, the supreme solipsist, might have been a more appropriate comment.

Going back to the facts of life and death, Joyce's mother died on 13 August, 1903, while the scene in the Tower occurred on 14 September, 1904. There is no evidence of any overt rift between Joyce and Gogarty in the intervening twelve months until Gogarty had had a look at *The Holy Office*, of which there is no mention in *Ulysses* nor, indeed, of any other cause of resentment against Joyce. Mulligan's alleged reference to his mother is linked in Stephen's soliloquies with his own remorse of conscience ('agenbite of inwit') at his having refused to kneel and pray at her death-bed, thereby importing into his projected abandonment of the Tower a factitious web of fundamental emotions, not based merely on remorse of conscience but extending to resentment of his dying mother's efforts to exercise a ghostly control over him, '. . . all the others praying on their knees, her hoarse loud breath rattling in horror. . . . Her eyes on me to strike me down.'

Again, at breakfast, as the old milkwoman measures out their morning quart, Mulligan, as betrayer, the woman (Ireland), her conqueror (England, represented by Haines) are all arrayed against Stephen in his purple patch of paranoia : 'They lowed about her whom they knew, dewsilky cattle. Silk of the kine and poor old woman, names given her in old times. A wandering crone, lowly form of an immortal serving her conqueror and her gay betrayer.' (20)

Stephen sat down to his meal on 'his upended valise'. This is the upgraded tin trunk which Joyce told Starkey would be called for at the Tower on 16 September. It was still a trunk on 1 April 1905, when Joyce wrote to his brother that he wished to sell it and buy a valise (*Letters* II). The trunk in the Tower posing as a valise in *Ulysses* is what Joyce would call an epiphany.

Leaving the Tower, Stephen locks the door and sees himself 'in cheap dusty mourning between their gay attires. . . .
He wants that key. It is mine, I paid the rent. Now I eat his salt bread. Give him the key too. . . . That was in his eyes.' In fact, of course, Gogarty was the lessee, paid the rent and was entitled to the key.

At the Forty Foot, Mulligan, preparatory to diving, flings his shirt on his suit and asks Stephen for the key 'to keep my chemise flat', also for twopence for a pint, pending Stephen's return from his school in Dalkey with his £3.12 wage out of which 'the bards must drink and junket'. Several commentators have failed to notice that Mulligan gets possession of the key at this point and suggest that he got it by a ruse at Westland Row railway station when Stephen was drunk, at the end of the 'Oxen of the Sun' chapter.

As he walks off, the episode ends with one word in Stephen's mind: Usurper. Much later in the day, in the 'Oxen of the Sun' episode, Stephen is still obsessed with his 'usurpation' —his 'eviction' by Mulligan and his replacement by Haines whose father, Mulligan said, 'made his tin by selling jalap to Zulus'.

> Bring a stranger within thy tower it will go hard but thou wilt have the secondbest bed. . . . Why hast thou done this abomination before me that thou didst spurn me for a merchant of jalaps.

All these 'usurpations' and appropriations are parallels to the extortions in the house of Odysseus by the suitors of Penelope which Telemachus, the Homeric equivalent of Stephen, must suffer until he gets his father back again. The analogy is contradicted by the facts, also recited in the text, which show that Stephen was living on Mulligan's charity and walking in his boots, 'borrowed brogues'. (*FW* 183)

In *Ulysses*, the conflict begun in the Tower, which I call 'Martellomache', will not be one of weapons but of 'wills gen wonts' (*FW* 4). Mulligan the medical, Stephen thinks, 'fears the lancet of my art as I fear that of his. The cold steel pen'. Joyce is here indebted to Frank Harris, who, in his book on Shakespeare, refers to the Earls of Essex and Southampton who could defend their parts in irregular love affairs with their swords, whereas Shakespeare's only 'weapon of offence was his pen'.

Brooding over his dead mother, while Mulligan first shaves and then goes downstairs, Stephen indulges in repetition of images, a practice characteristic of the whole book; he recalls on page 11 and again on page 16 the vision he had had of her, 'her wasted body within its loose brown graveclothes giving off an odour of wax and rosewood, her breath, that had bent upon him, mute, reproachful, a faint odour of wetted ashes'. The visions are hostile to him too: 'Her eyes on me to strike me down'. The scene is repeated in the climax of the book in 'Circe' (516-17).

In his father's house, Joyce had ceased to have a home. Towards the close of the first episode of *Ulysses* he has Stephen say, 'I will not sleep here tonight. Home also I cannot go.' From his lodgings in his aunt's house on the North Strand Road, he had opportunities of studying at number 164 the business of H. J. O'Neill's funeral establishment and the antics of Jim and John Ford, the eccentric twins, casual employees of Simon Kerrigan, O'Neill's manager, who were destined to be magnified into the Great Twin Brethren of *Finnegans Wake*, and who in fact are Joyce's own twins also, inasmuch as they were born in the same year as he was. They could never be restrained from singing 'The Croppy Boy', inaccurately quoted pieces of which are reproduced in the 'Sirens' episode. Joyce also sent, at Christmas 1934, an inaccurate and incomplete version of the song to his son Giorgio in the United States. One might conclude from this that he relied for the words on his memory of the twins' recital. Simon Kerrigan himself appears in *Ulysses* as 'Corny Kelleher'. He lived near his business establishment at number 170B and at number 159 lived F. Wetherup who gets a subheading of his own, WHAT WETHERUP SAID (128), in 'Aeolus'—'Get a grip of them by the stomach.' Wetherup was probably an authority on this mode of capturing sons-in-law and other dependents as he ran a business in the cattle trade from 113 Saville Place and Bloom would have known him from the period of his employment as Cuffe's sales clerk in the Dublin cattle market.

The memories culled from these last months of his life in Dublin were to be closely interwoven with the date of his first outing with Nora and the circumstances of her life. Walking to meet her, he would stride along the blank wall of Trinity College which faced the shops of Nassau Street 'luminous to larboard only like the lamps in Nassaustrass' (*FW* 178). Nearing the end of the wall he could descry the name of the first house in Leinster Street inscribed high up on its redbrick gable in large, white capital letters, FINN'S HOTEL. This was the hostelry entered in Thom's *Directory* as '1-2 Leinster Street: Private hotel and restaurant, M. and R. Ryan and 62 William Street, Limerick'. The weathering of seventy years has not yet eroded the sign but the trees in the adjoining grounds of the college are now high enough to obscure the sight of it in summer.

The name on the wall, inside which the loved one laboured as a chambermaid, would remain in Joyce's mind, to be identified with the heroic Finn Mac Cool and then with the hero of the Irish-American ballad 'Finnegan's Wake' and ultimately reappear in the title of his last work, with Finn lying latent in the landscape as the name lies leafhidden on the wall of 1 Leinster Street. His 'companion' however would vouchsafe no more recognition to its significance than she would to 16 June 1904 as the date of the action in *Ulysses*. But in Joyce's sense of personal destiny, these specific artistic signposts were ineluctable highlights of the literature that was to be.

Chapter 2

Japhet

WHEN Mulligan tells Haines that Stephen 'proves by algebra that Hamlet's grandson is Shakespeare's grandfather and that he himself is the ghost of his own father', he adds '—O, shade of Kinch the elder! Japhet in search of a father!'—exclamations which could be regarded as an epigraph for *Ulysses*.

Joyce always needed a father-figure, a protector or guardian, a *confidant*, preferably one who was prepared to listen to his monologues on art, literature and philosophy. In his adolescence and in Trieste up till 1914, he used his brother Stannie as his 'whetstone'. He was indeed more than a whetstone: his *obiter dicta* and his diaries often provided his brother with cornerstones for his early literary structures, titles for his books, material for short stories.

James came early to seek the company of John Francis Byrne, in Belvedere College and then in University College. Byrne was some years his senior, stronger physically and was soon disposed to treat Joyce with a protective paternalism and, above all, to be a silent audience for the younger lad's artistic pontifications. Byrne (*Silent Years*) describes young Joyce's ill-suppressed impatience as he waited for him to finish a game of chess on one of the chess tables provided in the DBC tearooms in Dame Street until John Howard Parnell would checkmate Byrne or vice versa, whereupon Joyce would hasten him out into the streets where he hoped to solve the problems of artistic creation by talking and walking.

To his brother Stannie, who objected to most of his university confreres, Joyce tended to write off Byrne as 'commonplace' and in *Stephen Hero* he condescendingly records, 'It was in favour of this young man that Stephen decided to break his commandment of reticence'. And long afterwards Stephen's reflection in

Scylla and Charybdis (*U* 185), 'My soul's youth I gave him, night by night', preserves with unabashed subjectivity his falsification of their relationship. The next paragraph is, 'Mulligan has my telegram.' One never knows how conscious Stephen may be of his own selfishness, but his commentary on Cranly suggests that Stephen should have addressed to himself the quotation from Meredith (199): *The sentimentalist is he who would enjoy without incurring the immense debtorship for a thing done.* Posing to Nora Barnacle as the master betrayed by his disciple, Joyce had written to her, 29 August 1904: 'I had a friend to whom I gave myself freely . . . He was Irish and he was false to me.' Byrne was silent not alone as recipient of Joyce's literary homilies; he was reticent also about himself. He gently deprecated Joyce's ignoring his mother's wish that he should make his Easter duty, without ever revealing to the budding young atheist that he himself had long before ceased to practise his religion. But he was not silent when Joyce visited Dublin in 1909 and Cosgrave tried to poison his mind against Nora: Byrne restored him to sanity by dismissing Cosgrave's account of her infidelities as a falsehood poured in the portals of Joyce's ear to unhinge his intellect. When Joyce said that he gave himself to Byrne freely, all he could mean was that he made free use of him as a sounding-board. Byrne (*Silent Years*) records his cousin Mary's dislike of Joyce: 'when he holds out his hand for you to shake, you feel nothing but five little cold raw sausages'.

Joyce's most intimate friend afterwards was Frank Budgen in Zurich, a man of independent mind but a good listener, as appears from his *James Joyce and the Making of 'Ulysses'* (1934) and *Myselves When Young* (1970). Joyce was having difficulties in finishing his book after he went back to Trieste from Zurich at the end of 1919 and then to Paris in 1920. He missed Budgen's passive assistance in his acts of creation and was constantly beseeching him to come to him, concealing his real need in whimsical exhortations.

Meanwhile, he had moved from the shelter of a father to a mother-figure. Miss Harriet Shaw Weaver's financial assistance, first by way of anonymous subventions and ultimately in the form of large capital endowments, left him free to concentrate on the completion of *Ulysses* (published with the benevolent aid of another woman, Sylvia Beach) and then to enter on the exploration of the sleeping mind and the Dark Night of the Soul.

During the gestation of *Ulysses*, 1914-1921, however, his surrogate, Stephen Dedalus, boarded out from *A Portrait of the Artist as a Young Man*, had to be depicted as Joyce histrionically conceived himself in 1904:

> *Unfellowed, friendless and alone,*
> *Indifferent as the herring-bone,*
> *Firm as the mountain ridges where*
> *I flash my antlers on the air.*

Joyce saw that Stephen needed to be complemented by another character in order to carry the diversified material in his book with which Stephen was not concerned, including the more mature mind of Joyce himself, now in his late thirties, while Stephen remains twenty-two. Thus Bloom is created at the age of thirty-eight and he and Stephen are rigged out to carry their own personalities through the epic events of one day as well as the symbolic *personae* of their counterparts in the *Odyssey*, Odysseus and Telemachus. Superimposed on these elaborate contrivances, the author proceeds to give his two surrogates the symbolic relationships of father and son, attempting at the same time to provide dramatic and theological bases for them from the ghost and the prince in *Hamlet* and from the heretical teachings of Sabellius.

The Homeric background of the Telemachiad is a parallel to Stephen's search. Telemachus finds Odysseus and Stephen ends up in the company of Bloom. They are kept apart until the closing chapters and their ultimate meeting is heralded by a violent atmospheric storm: 'A black crack of noise in the street here, alack, bawled, back. Loud on left Thor thundered, in anger awful the hammerhurler.' (392) Their coming together gives rise to even preternatural phenomena: the dead arise (Stephen's mother, Bloom's father, Shakespeare, Matthew Arnold and many others).

That more than a simple paternity adoption ceremony is being represented seems clear. Joyce is apparently engaged, with great mystery and under the guise of theological and heretical philosophising, in the task of forming a Trinity out of his own creations, Stephen and Bloom, and some other person or character, each of whom may, in the course of the novel, become fused with another, and all of whom are, in the ultimate, manifestations of the author. It is for this reason that there is an early reference (27) to 'the subtle African heresiarch who held that the Father was Himself His own Son'.

Stephen's lecture on *Hamlet* is also relevant to this theme. Joyce has him deliver his interpretation impromptu whereas, in fact, the Hamlet theme is a built-in set piece made up of material collected by Joyce from the writings of Frank Harris and others for lectures which he gave in Trieste in 1913. No doubt this material was rehashed for insertion in *Ulysses*, but the central thesis was probably left unchanged, viz., that Shakespeare identified himself not with Hamlet, but with the ghost of Hamlet's father. In talking around his subject, he has Stephen descant at length upon paternity as 'a mystical estate, an apostolic succession from only begetter to only begotten', but, as if becoming aware of his extravagances, he makes Stephen pull himself up— 'what the hell are you driving at?' and he makes him answer—'I know. Shut up. Blast you! I have my reasons.' It appears that Stephen is made to go through these schizoid paces to provide justification for Joyce's theogony.

Thus Joyce, managing director of his Trinity, plays with his consubstantial creations. Bloom tries to recall the name of 'that wise man what's his name with the burning glass'. Soon he remembers and exclaims, 'Archimedes. I have it! My memory's not so bad.' (375) Complacently triumphant at his feat of recollection, Bloom is unaware that Joyce has had him translate nicely *Eureka*! as 'I have it', the exclamation of Archimedes in his bath when another discovery swam into his ken.

Bloom, however, was intended to appear to be an original creation, standing on his own flat feet, and Joyce was most anxious that he should be accepted as such.

Bloom is, in fact, the *persona* of a modified Joyce from whose body, like Mr Duffy in *Dubliners*, Joyce lives at a little distance. He lacks his creator's learning and literary talents but he has qualities of prudence, temperance and stability which are not evident in Joyce himself. He is the person with the factual, realistic approach which Joyce did not have until he had recourse to Thom's Directory and his notes and press-cuttings.

He is differentiated from the author (and from Stephen) by his scientific, as compared with their artistic, temperaments. He is also remarkable for the amount of proverbial wisdom as well as the misinformation stored in his memory: *I.N.R.I.* stands for 'Iron Nails Ran In'. 'Eulogy in a country churchyard it ought to be that poem of whose is it Wordsworth or Thomas Campbell'. 'Eulogy' for 'Elegy' is surely Joyce's; the mistaken ascription of authorship is Bloom's.

Bloom looks across Davy Byrne's counter at the eatables: 'Sandwich? Ham and his descendants mustered and bred there.' Quite obviously it is Joyce, not Bloom, who is here misusing his sandwich of ham, mustard and bread.

Bloom muses in the Ormond, apparently thinking up a new way of making love: 'Ventriloquise. My lips closed. Think in my stom. What? Will? You? I. Want. You. To.' In this context, it is relevant to record that in addition to his other precocious accomplishments while a student at University College, Dublin, Joyce, has been reported by his classmates to have been quite a competent ventriloquist.

The new father that Joyce provides for his youthful *alter ego*, Stephen, is the exact opposite of his real father, Simon Dedalus. Bloom is a prudent man, addicted to mental arithmetic, particularly in regard to the cost of commodities and enterprises, reckoning up his outgoings, cash in hand, and possible incomings. He is a family man, concerned about the welfare of his wife and daughter and still given to doleful brooding over the loss of his long-dead only son. Racially a Jew and baptised first as a Protestant and then as a Catholic, he feels himself unfettered by any creed. Cosmopolitan in outlook, he seems antinational to the 'archons of Sinn Féin'. Sensual in his imagination he avoids the pitfalls of sexual involvement, confining his adventures to a surreptitious correspondence with Martha Clifford, whom he has never met, and to a titillating voyeur experience with Gerty McDowell (the Homeric Nausicaa) on Sandymount Strand. He has contributed generously (for a man of his means) to Paddy Dignam's bereaved widow and orphans, and has also made it his business to see that they get the deceased's insurance, evoking from John Wyse Nolan the almost unwilling tribute, *'I'll say there is much kindness in the Jew.'* He is also charitable in his concern for Mrs Purefoy who is having so difficult a delivery in Holles Street. He has views on nearly every material or scientific subject, including astronomy, so that 'Noman' of the *Cyclops* episode is obliged to say: 'I declare to my antimacassar if you took up a straw from the bloody floor and if you said to Bloom: *Look at, Bloom. Do you see that straw? That's a straw.* Declare to my aunt he'd talk about it for an hour so he would and talk steady.' (315)

A still higher and equally unexpected tribute is paid to Bloom in the 'Wandering Rocks' episode (234) by Lenehan who has been recalling to McCoy the delights of a jaunting car drive beside Mrs Bloom from Glencree across the Featherbed Mountain to Dublin 'at blue o'clock in the morning after the night before', with Bloom and Chris Callinan on the other side of the car, Bloom pointing out the stars and discussing astronomy:
'—He's a cultured allroundman, Bloom is, he said seriously. He's not one of your common or garden . . . you know . . . There's a touch of the artist about old Bloom.'

The closing remark meant, for Lenehan, that Bloom had something in him of the constructive imagination of an artist in the widest sense—an interesting talker, a writer manqué— but, for the author, James Joyce, it meant that Bloom as created by him was given some of his own personal and intellectual characteristics, for example, his sexuality and preoccupation with sexual symbols such as feminine lingerie, the cosmic and microscopic dimensions of his curiosity and his interest in and sympathy with all the vagaries and ills of humanity—the blind piano-tuner, the man in the macintosh, the long-suffering Mrs Purefoy and the intoxicated Stephen.

We have here, therefore, an abandonment by Joyce of the theory ascribed to his youthful prototype, Stephen, in *A Portrait of the Artist as a Young Man* about the necessity for the creative artist's not appearing in his work of art since he allows himself to be partially identified with Bloom as well as with Stephen who he insists is not himself but a portrait of what he was 'as a young man'.

Chapter 3

The Ashplant

STEPHEN'S ashplant, his constant 'familiar' (26), companion or attendant throughout the ulyssean day, is an item rich in symbolism of which the author was clearly cognisant.

An ashplant is a sapling growing separately from seed shed by the parent tree. It is not a limb of the parent tree. It is uprooted when grown to a size convenient for use as a walking-stick. The root may be trimmed and polished for use as a handle, or what Stephen ('Proteus') calls a 'hilt'. Seasoned in a chimney and with molten lead injected into the hollowed handle, it was a formidable weapon of offence, the loaded root being then the business end. It, and not the shillelagh, was the weapon commonly used in faction-fights on Irish fairgreens in past centuries. A gang with lead-lined ashplants up their sleeved waistcoats was a formidable force when primed with potheen. (Cf. *FW* 295 : I . . . curry nothung up my sleeve).

The ashplant which Joyce carried in the year before he left Dublin was probably, as will appear, a plant of the mountain ash, also called the quicken, quickbeam or rowan tree. It has two names in Irish, *caorthann* and *luis* and it was known as the Druids' tree. The Druids used it for divination and Stephen on Sandymount Strand called his plant 'my augur's rod' (53). It would help him to divine 'signatures of all things I am here to read'.

The letters in the Irish alphabet are named after trees. Joyce wrote, 1 January 1925, to Harriet Shaw Weaver : 'The Irish alphabet (ailm, beith, coll, dair, etc.) is all made up of the names of trees.' Unfortunately, the editor of *Letters* I, Stuart Gilbert, omitted the remainder of this reference. The letters were, in fact, anciently arranged in an order which suggest the succession of the months in a year. The first three letters as so arranged are B for January, L (luis) for February, and N for March. From these three letters the whole alphabet was called BLN which seems to be a stenographic rendering of the Irish word *bliain*, a year.

Whatever Joyce may have written in the unpublished part of his letter to Miss Weaver, he did have a list of the Irish and English names of the trees represented by the letters of the Irish alphabet and he used some of the English names as a runic script in *FW*, 361.7,8 :

Quicken, aspen; ash and yew
Willow, broom with oak for you.

The corresponding Irish words and the letters which they represent are luis (l), eabhadh (e), muin (n), iodha (i), sail (s), oir (o), and dair (d). In the order in which they are placed, these letters spell *len Isod* which might mean 'with Iseult'. Their interpretation in the present context is not important. They do however establish that Joyce made himself familiar with the possibility of using the names of trees representing Irish letters as codes or symbols and that he must accordingly have consciously carried his ashplant as a symbol of the letter L which in turn signified February, the month in which his birthday occurred, for him the most important day in the year, one to be scrupulously remembered by his family and friends and to be recognised by his publishers as the date with which they must synchronise the publication of his major works in 1922 and 1939.

The ashplant was also a symbol of more general aspects of what Joyce considered to be his destiny as a divinator, 'signatures of all things I am here to read' he exclaimed on Sandymount Strand, quoting the title of a seventeenth century theological work by a German cobbler named Jacob Boehme, and seeing himself as the predestined interpreter of all things on the daedal earth.

The Druids also used the rowan for putting down ghosts. In the 'Nighttown' episode of *Ulysses* when the ghost of Stephen's mother appears to him, he exclaims '*Nothung!*' (517) and the immediately following stage direction is : 'He lifts his ashplant high with both hands and smashes the chandelier.

Time's livid final flame leaps and, in the following darkness, ruin of all space, shattered glass and toppling masonry.'

'Nothung' is the sword of Siegfried in Wagner's *Der Ring Des Nibelungen*, which was originally drawn from the ashtree and named by Siegmund, father of Siegfried. In the 'Shem and Shaun' chapter, below, it will be shown that Shem (Dolph) equated his ashplant used as a school-room pointer with 'nothung' and related it to 'loosh', the rowan.

In the legendary days of King Cormac Mac Airt, a Munster druid named Mogh Ruith ('Magus Rotarum'), who had been a pupil of Simon Magus, came to a confrontation with Cormac's druid, Ciothruadh. The latter ordered every soldier in Cormac's army to hew him down a bough of the mountain rowan and then to make fires with the branches : if the smoke went southwards, they should charge; if northward, they must retreat with it.

Mogh Ruith, for his part, ordered each man to take merely a rowan faggot while their king should take a shoulder-bundle from a rowan tree growing on the side of the mountain which had three shelters, viz., first, from the March wind (N.E.), second, from the sea and third, from the conflagration winds. His magic produced a shower of blood on the northern enemy up as far as Tara to which Cormac retreated. Mogh Ruith also turned Cormac's three druids into stones.

Hoops and gads of the rowan tree were still fastened round the churn or churndash in the nineteenth century, to avert the spells of witches attempting to steal butter. In Wales the 'three rowan-rods growing out of the mouth of Einigan Gawr' had all manner of knowledge and sciences written on them.

In my opinion, Joyce acquired his ashplant during one of his visits to Mullingar (1900-1901), probably at Uisneach, south-west of Mullingar ('Now, springing quickenly from the mud-land Loosh . . .' *FW* 295), where the national May Day fires were kindled by the Druids against cattle-disease, and he gradually collected the folklore and legends which the Irish had woven about the tree. Around the same tree he wove his own webs (*FW* 500 et seq.), when he read a translation of the Norse Eddas in which it is said that the holiest stead of the Gods is at Yggdrasil's ash where they must hold their doom . . . of all trees the best and biggest, its boughs spread over the whole world: three roots of the tree hold it upstand wide apart.

Not only in his ashplant of augury but also in his writing before ever he left Dublin Joyce shows that the larger symbolisms of the future were already in his mind. In his paper, 'Drama and Life', he ended by bespeaking a realism in drama which would comprise the penetrating illumination of the imagination and be like the tree Yggdrasil 'whose roots are deep in earth but in whose upper branches the stars of heaven are glowing and astir'.

The rowan tree was regarded in ancient Ireland as a reliable protection against lightning—a magical lightning conductor, one might call it. If Joyce knew this (and he probably did), it would have been a sufficient reason for his carrying the rowan rod, as his notorious constitutional fear of lightning was so strong as to influence his selection of Vico's *Scienza Nova* as the basis of his philosophy of history. Vico considered religion to have been instilled in the savage mind by fear of thunder and lightning, the divine age thus created being succeeded by the heroic and civil epochs.

Richard Ellmann in his book, *James Joyce* (1959), considered that Joyce gave his *alter ego* in *Exiles* the name 'Richard Rowan' out of respect for the rebel leader Archibald Hamilton Rowan who had associations with Clongowes Wood where Joyce had been at school as a boy. The several strata of symbolism, in which Joyce's rowan sapling is found to have been rooted, must lead to a different conclusion—viz., that 'Rowan' in *Exiles* is derived from the rowan tree. Joyce was proceeding from the particular symbol of the ashplant to the general symbolism of the word 'Rowan' to include himself and his *de facto* wife, their lives and the literature which he was creating out of them.

Richard Rowan's wife, Bertha, also appears in *Ulysses* as one of the fashionable guests at the wedding of John Wyse Nolan of the Irish National Foresters with 'Miss Fir Conifer'. Her name is given as 'Mrs Rowan Greene' thereby suggesting an irregularity ('Gretna Green') in her own espousal, which seems to be confirmed by the reference in *FW* 212.10 to 'Grettna Greaney' and 533.19, 'Goosna Greene' which means Goose Green, a one-time open space in Clontarf, but this can also hide the identity of Miss Barnacle *alias* Greene, from Bowling

Green, Galway. The final, or as Joyce would suggest, the original, basis of this wordplay is contained in a letter from him to his brother Stanislaus after his registry office marriage with Nora on 4 July 1931: 'Having eloped with my present wife in 1904 she with my full connivance gave the name of Miss Gretta Greene which was good enough for il Cav. Fabbri who married us . . .'

This was mere familiar fooling with his brother, as the potentate 'Cav. Fabbri' whom he mentions is probably meant to connote marriage before a blacksmith—'who blocksmith her saft anvil?' (*FW* 197), while the name which he says Nora gave derives from Gretna Green in Scotland where runaway marriages were informally contracted.

Joyce however soon ceased to depend on ashplant or anvil as symbolic supports for the alleged nuptials of 1904. The matter was much more seriously and less dispassionately dealt with in a letter to Gorman of 6 June 1939, signed by Paul Léon, endeavouring to censor his biography of the Master. In the letter, reference is made to 'the question of his marriage in 1904 which subsequently and for testamentary reasons was supplemented by retroactive civil marriage according to English law in 1931'. This point, the letter goes on, 'is a very complicated legal problem which has already caused Mr Joyce heavy expenditure in the matter of legal opinions involving as it did the marriage laws of three different countries. It would be necessary to devote an entire chapter of your book to its elucidation and I doubt whether his solicitors in London would advise him to place the dossier concerning it at your disposal. For the purpose of your book, the only way now is to obliterate this passage and any subsequent reference of the same tenor, confining yourself to a formal statement.'

The passage which Gorman was obliged to 'obliterate' was a statement that Joyce could not live 'in sin' with Nora Barnacle in Dublin in 1904 and that for this and other reasons he had gone abroad in that year. The paragraph as revised, or rather curtailed, by Joyce's censorship reads: 'Besides his disgust with Ireland and his expectations of the larger world that lay beyond the waves of the English Channel there was a third element that was violently pushing him toward flight. It was Nora Barnacle, his present wife.'

The publishers who did not, and who after a decade, did, publish Joyce obviously were not the only censors : Gorman's book was described by Joyce as Gorman's *Martyrology* : it would seem that poor Gorman, and not the subject of his book, was the real martyr, doomed to the role of Bowdler rather than that of Boswell.

In addition to using a plant of the rowan (mountain ash) as his 'familiar' and as the symbol of his February-born self and adopting the tree as his name and that of his wife in his works, his preoccupation with it explains his otherwise inexplicable selection of the contents of B. Seebohm Rowntree's *Poverty, A Study of Town Life* to epitomise the horrors of slum life in Dublin (*FW* 534-5). The author's dull notes of his grim survey of living conditions in run-down urban areas in northern England are re-written by Joyce in a run-on summary in which the horrors lose nothing in their comic rendition : 'sharing closet which is profusely written over with eleven other subscribers . . . bangs kept woman's head against wall thereby disturbing neighbours . . . starving cat left in disgust' and (without adverting to the contradiction) 'copious holes emitting mice' (*FW* 544-5).

Mr James S. Atherton (*The Books at the Wake*) shows that Joyce went carefully through the whole of Rowntree's book and adds : 'Yet all this material is put into two short passages in the *Wake*. This is not Joyce's usual way of using a book . . .' It seems clear to me that Joyce's original urge to use the book at all stemmed from the fact that its author's name was Rowntree and therefore one to be associated with his own name and his own work where the symbolism of the rowan tree proliferated.

Chapter 4

To Slay His Da

SIMON DEDALUS, father in the flesh of Stephen, first appears in *Ulysses* in the 'Hades' episode where he shares a cab at Paddy Dignam's funeral with Martin Cunningham, Jack Power and Leopold Bloom. He is caustic about his son, Stephen, whom they pass in the street, about his son's associates, 'that Mulligan' and 'the Goulding faction' (i.e. the William Murray family), about the weather which he said was 'as uncertain as a child's bottom' and in O'Connell Street he curses the bent figure of Reuben Dodd: 'The Devil break the hasp of your back!' (95). They tell the story of Dodd's son having tried to drown himself in the Liffey and being fished out by a boatman to whom Reuben gave a florin for saving the boy's life. Mr Dedalus has been in the hands of Dodd the usurer and his dry comment on his gift of a florin is 'one and eightpence too much'. (96)

In Glasnevin, Mr Dedalus breaks down as he passes near his wife's grave: 'I'll soon be stretched beside her.' (106)

In the 'Wandering Rocks', Mr Dedalus encounters his daughter, Dilly, and after some pressure gives her a shilling out of the five shillings he has got for the sale of the curtains from his house. On her seeking more, he tells her that she is like the rest of them—'an insolent pack of little bitches since your poor mother died'. As Dilly persists, he says 'I'll leave you all where Jesus left the jews', but he gives her two more pennies—'Get a glass of milk for yourself and a bun or something. I'll be home shortly.' (237-8) Stephen next meets her, noting her 'high shoulders and shabby dress'. 'She is drowning. Agenbite. Save her. Agenbite. All against us. She will drown me with her . . .' (242) Like his mother's dying glance, the sight of his sister in flitters is a threat to the solipsist. He has more than three pounds in his pocket, much of which he will dissipate later in the day. But he does not offer her a shilling or even twopence.

In the Ormond hotel bar, Mr Dedalus obliges the company with a song, which is heard from the dining-room by Leopold Bloom, '*Martha* it is. Coincidence.' (273) Bloom was just about to write to Martha Clifford, which he does in the name of 'Henry Flower'. Simon Dedalus receives the plaudits of the people in the bar and Ben Dollard remarks: 'Seven days in jail, on bread and water. Then you'd sing, Simon, like a garden thrush.'

All in all, Simon Dedalus has been presented as one capable of being touched in more ways than one, an irascible and improvident character but sociable withal, who can captivate any company with his sweet tenor voice.

'Cyclops', which follows the 'Sirens' (Ormond Hotel) episode, is introduced by an unintroduced first person singular, known variously as The Narrator, Thersites or Noman (the latter two from the *Iliad* and the *Odyssey*, respectively):

> I was just passing the time of day with old Troy of the D.M.P. at the corner of Arbour Hill there and be damned but a bloody sweep came along and he near drove his gear into my eye. (290)

This sentence, like most of the narrative in the episode, is remarkable for the highly individualistic style of the speaker which (including the use of the adjective 'bloody') is maintained right through the chapter and also for the fact that it starts with the pronoun 'I' and ends with the noun 'eye', a technique also characteristic of the whole chapter, the undertones of which have reference to the blinding of Polyphemus by Odysseus. The anonymity of the speaker seems to have survived fifty years of exegesis. Stuart Gilbert, the earliest authoritative commentator, in *James Joyce's 'Ulysses'* (1930) states that 'the story is told by a simple and bibulous Dubliner, a nondescript, in the highly coloured idiom of the profane vulgar.' Dr Richard Ellmann, in his *Ulysses on the Liffey* (1972), cites Joyce's identification of the Narrator with Thersites in Shakespeare's *Troilus and Cressida*. He thinks that, because the Narrator describes himself as 'a collector of bad and doubtful debts', his occupation 'opens to him the worst secrets about everybody'. He thinks

that because he was 'passing the time of day with old Troy of
the D.M.P.', he is obsequious towards the 'Dublin Mounted
Police' (*recte* Dublin Metropolitan Police). But Troy as of the
time in question was not a D.M.P. man—he was 'old Troy *was*
in the force'—a Synge-like usage in the omission of the relative
pronoun 'who' after Troy's name, which is not out of keeping
with the Narrator's style of speaking.

When the Narrator says he is a collector of bad and doubtful
debts he is merely participating in the deflation which parallels
the gigantism of the episode. One cannot collect 'bad' debts
and the collection of 'doubtful' ones would be a dubious business. He was, in fact, a debt collector *simpliciter* and he introduced the epithets 'bad and doubtful' merely to emphasise the
lowness of his position as compared with the 'mighty' one
from which he had fallen. We find what his former occupation
was when he recalls his experience in it to denigrate Blazes
Boylan's father—'Dirty Dan the dodger's son off Island Bridge
that sold the same horses twice to the Government to fight the
Boers. Old whatwhat. I called about the poor and water rate,
Mr Boylan. You what? The water rate, Mr Boylan. You whatwhat?' (317-18).

The only character in *Ulysses* who could cite such an incident
as this was Simon Dedalus representing John Stanislaus Joyce, a
rate collector employed by the Collector General of Rates for
the rating authorities in Dublin City and County from 1880
to 1891, in which capacity he knew that the water rate, although
assessed separately, was collectible with the poor rate. Thus,
to get a full picture of the man whom Joyce deposed from
fatherhood in favour of Leopold Bloom we must integrate the
references in *Ulysses* to Mr Dedalus with those to Thersites or
Noah, the father of Japhet, who becomes Noahman or Noman,
Outis who bested Polyphemus and who, in *Ulysses*, has no
name because he is being replaced by Bloom. His ambivalent
attitude to his father is made explicit in *FW* 173, where Shem
(Joyce) is 'one moment tarabooming great blunderguns (poh!)
about his farfamed fine Poppamore, Mr Humhum, whom
history climate and entertainment made the first of his sept and
always up to debt, though Eavens ears ow many fines he faces,
and another moment visanversus cruaching three jeers (pah!)
for his rotten little ghost of a Pappybeg, Mr Himmyshimmy, a

blighty, a reeky, a lighty, a scrapy, a babbly, a ninny, dirty
seventh among thieves and always bottom sawyer'.

Afterwards, when Joyce wished to discount the importance of
Ulysses as compared with his *Work* then *In Progress*, he would
say that the former book was 'written' by his father. These
considerations will resolve some of the commentaries on the
difference between the paternal picture portrayed by Joyce in
his works and that presented by his brother Stanislaus in his
Dublin Diary and *My Brother's Keeper*. Harry Levin, in his
book on Joyce, concludes that 'To compare the genial warmth
of Simon Dedalus with Stanislaus's cold hatred toward their
father is to have the measure of James Joyce's sympathies'.
Stanislaus portrays his father as an alcoholic wag out of regular
employment from his early forties, changing house more and
more frequently to avoid liability for arrears of rent, the goods
and chattels borne from one lodging to another diminishing as
time went on, more and more items having been sold or pawned
beyond redemption. In *My Brother's Keeper* he remarks:

> It does not facilitate a boy's study to have a drunken man at
> the other side of the table asking him:
> —Are you going to win?
> —Well, I'll try.
> —That'll do. That's all I want. (Repeated about a dozen
> times).

In his *Diary* Stanislaus also tells of his father's constant threat
that he would break his wife's 'bloody heart', adding 'this was
exactly what he did. . . . He uses the threat to us now but adds,
"I'll break your stomach first though, ye buggers. You'll get the
effects of it later on. Wait till you're thirty and you'll see where
you'll be".'

By a passing reference in *My Brother's Keeper* (p. 180),
Stanislaus Joyce himself, apparently inadvertently, copperfastens
the identity of his father with the 'I' of 'Cyclops'—'My father,
Thersites-like, called me my brother's jackal.'

James has his surrogate, Stephen, picture a family meal in
the shell of his father's house emptied by improvidence and
extravagance, 'with his sister, Dilly, sitting by the ingle, her
hair hanging down, waiting for some weak Trinidad shell cocoa

that was in the sootcoated kettle to be done so that she and he could drink it with the oatmeal water for milk after the Friday herrings they had eaten at two a penny, with an egg apiece for Maggy, Boody and Katey, the cat meanwhile under the mangle devouring a mess of eggshells and charred fish heads and bones on a square of brown paper in accordance with the third precept of the church to fast and abstain on the days commanded'. (540)

Both James and Stanislaus were, however, preoccupied with more than mere paternal cruelty and mismanagement. In his *Diary* (p. 47), Stanislaus under date 13 August 1904, states that Jim 'boasts of his power to live and says, in his pseudomedical phraseology, that it comes from his highly specialised central nervous system. He talks much of the syphilitic contagion in Europe, is at present writing a series of studies in it in Dublin, tracing practically everything to it. The drift of his talk seems to be that the contagion is congenital and incurable and responsible for all manias, and being so, that it is useless to try to avoid it. He even seems to invite you to delight in the manias and to humour each to the top of its bent'. Stanislaus is half convinced : 'I see symptoms in every turn I take. It seems to me that *my* central nervous system is wretched . . .'

At the end of 'Telemachus' (56) Stephen ruminates in words, put down perhaps selfconsciously, that sound strangely different from his usual style of speech or soliloquy : 'My teeth are very bad, why, I wonder? Feel. That one is going too. Shells. Ought I go to a dentist, I wonder, with that money? That one. Toothless Kinch, the superman. Why is that, I wonder, or does it mean something perhaps?'

Stephen's meditations on his human condition recurred to me at the beginning of the year 1932 when Jim Tully came into my office bearing news of the death of Joyce's father. Well educated, unmarried and devoid of ambition for official advancement, he acted as his own porter in distributing official documents and press-cuttings. Although he was thirty-five years my elder, I was his senior in official grading and he entered my room his Gladstonian visage draped in an air of weighty import but when he found that I was alone his actor's mobile features relaxed. He wished me a happy New Year and wondered what kind of a New Year 'your man in Paris' was having. No return of the prodigal son for the funeral, but he sent an ivy wreath from himself and the family.

—'Twas on the evening papers yesterday, with Old Jack described 'late L.G.B.'

Jack Joyce of course was not an official of the British Local Government Board of which our Department was the successor but, Tully said, he liked to claim he was. Himself and the others in the Collector General's office preferred to be thought of as Civil Servants rather than as collecting agents for the Corporation and the authorities striking rates in county Dublin:

—That's why he liked to pal around with us from the Local Government Board. To be able to make out he had things from the horse's mouth, Sir Henry Robinson's Cadillac. If he were to be called 'late' anything, Tully continued, they should have put him down as 'late G.P.I.'

General paralysis of the insane? That certainly fitted in with some things I had read between the lines of his son's book. And a medical student who was in digs near the old man's lodgings said he knew what his ailment was before he knew anything about his son.

—Ah, but he was great crack in his time, Tully said. The expressions he used and his descriptions of people in all their shams and shames. And his stories, 'twas him could tell a story, only always 'twas himself was the hero of the tale. You had a right to come up with me to see him when I asked you: that was when he had the delusions of greatness and grandeur.

I reminded Tully that I had felt diffident about accepting his invitation, that it would be an intrusion on a stranger and that if I had gone I'd have wished to take notes which would have seemed an ungracious use of his hospitality . . .

—Not atall. Not atall. Delighted he'd be. He was well used to it anyhow. I can tell you now . . . but maybe I'd be interrupting you in your work?

—You've interrupted me already. You have succeeded as always in holding me by your glittering eye. But it's half past twelve: *datur hora quieti*; you can have the other half of the hour.

—Well, I left this place one evening and I walked up Eden Quay. I looked into Mooney's by the sea but there was no one there that I'd care to drink with. So I said to myself, I'll try the

Scotch House. On my way across O'Connell Bridge who did I see coming to meet me in a coachandpair only King Edward VII? So I doffed my bowler to pay my humble respects to His Majesty but damme if the bloody old showboy didn't pass on his way without as much as a royal greeting or even the apostolic benediction that he might have taken with him from Maynooth. Down with me into the Scotch and I joined Johnny Clarendon out of the office, with Ould Jack and Alf Bergan. There were plenty more coming and going and all the talk was about the political significance of the King's visit to Dublin and his call to Maynooth College and what not. After a while, Jack got up and went out. Not a word outa me until I got a few Taylors of malt within me and then I put on my declamatory tone, a solemn note of denunciation I used for my parody of Gibbon—the other act that used be in demand was the old woman's whine I put on for the Queen's Speech from the Throne when the situation in Ireland continued to cause her the gravest concern. I had a touch of neuritis in this left arm, a thing I blamed on the drink. If I was a T.T. then, like I am now, I wouldn't know what to blame it on. I carried a small potato in my pocket against the pain, a cure some old woman gave my sister. So I took out the potato, a poheen that had hardened as solid as a pebble, and I threw it up and caught it again whenever my oratory needed punctuation.

Tully paused and gave me a glance of clinical appraisal. He reminded me that he had prescribed the potato cure for my fibrositis contracted the previous year while rowing around Ireland's Eye in a heatwave. Did I carry it still? No, I said, I now had a chestnut in its place. Tully again glanced at me but I showed no sign of having intended a joke. Tully reverted to his narrative:

—Well, anyhow, I took out the potato and I started my speech something like this:

The King's visit to this distressful country is being canvassed as of this political significance or that other. The loyal heart rejoices at his sovereign's mere presence; the Nationalist sighs for Home Rule and wishfully thinks of the anthem being changed from *God Save the King* to *A Nation Once Again*. To historians and litterateurs of a coming age, however, it will redound to the discredit and obloquy of the royal visitor that he disregarded the clear true eye of natural-born genius when he met it in the street and returned to reimmerse himself in the dissipations of his seraglio and the seduction of the daughters of his nobility and gentry, leaving the noble-hearted James Henry Tully to nurse his mouldering talents in an obscure position in the Local Government Board.

With that, I hear somebody let a screech of laughter out of him and there is Jack's son, Jim, sitting in his father's place taking down my speech. So I frowned solemnly and said : 'At it again? What? Scribble, scribble, scribble. What? What?'

I resumed my oration, drawing down names of royal mistresses such as Lady Warwick and Mrs Langtry, the Jersey lily. I compared the era of British imperial decadence under his reigning majesty with the degenerate days of the Roman Empire where morals had attained such a pitch of depravity that it was related of the Empress Messalina that she preferred the titillating if attenuated attentions of an Egyptian eunuch to the ponderous pole of the Roman proconsul. Or words to that effect. You'll find my speech all spelt out now in your copy of the book you told me you got from Paris through the Free State diplomatic postbag, all dressed out in classical Latin that that rascal got some continental scholar to put on my well-balanced English prose.

I said that we could see that his authorship was put on record, but Tully disclaimed any wish to be quoted in connection with the book : he had had the good luck not to be included as a character in it as his friend Alf Bergan was.

I suggested that I could say that the Latin was Tully's and that people would think I meant Cicero. The proposed equivocation pleased him and he went on to recall how Jack Joyce returned to the company explaining that he had been delayed because his waterworks were out of order. The phrase caught my ear as being identical with Cissy's version of Bloom's reply to her enquiry as to what was the right time (359).

Meanwhile Tully proceeded with proficient mimicry to recount Jack Joyce's outburst on finding his son in his place :

—Can I not leave my seat for my statutory five minutes but you must take over on me? Drinking my drink, bad cess to you, and taking down what my friends are saying! Isn't it for that same Davy Byrne told me he had to put you out of his bar? I'm sorry, says he, that I had to show my door to a son of yours, but it's a thing I can't allow him or anybody else to come in here and copy down my customers' conversation, maybe to put them in some book he'd bring out in the time to come, holding them up to public odium and contempt.

Jim's face got a bit redder than usual but he bowed his father to his place and then, as he turned to go, he comes out with his mixture of Shakespeare and bog Latin:

—Bless me bottom, I am translated—into the Latin: *Jacobus fui, nunc Japhet filius Noahman, secundum Scripturas, patrem petens.* (Here Tully is responsible for the words; the erratic spelling of Noah represents my idea of Joyce's vague consciousness at the time of the mission which was later to be given to Stephen.)

Tully occupied the remainder of that *hora quieti* with his version of the affair in which Alf Bergan and he prevented Jack from boarding a Phibsborough tram, knowing that he lived in a room or two in a big rambling house in Dollymount, but not knowing that he had recently changed house to Cabra. His anecdote was practically identical with Alf Bergan's account of the incident which Professor Ellmann has published in *James Joyce*, pp. 109-10.

Tully's yarn and the medical student's testimony remained stored in the muniment room of my memory for thirty years until, in 1962, I had dinner with Tom Kiernan in the Cosmos in Washington. Kiernan was already preparing for President Kennedy's visit to Ireland in the following year: I spoke of the ocean, *thalassa*, a bowl of bitter waters (15)—tears poured out by Irish exiles—but it was of course, the Irish sea to which Stephen was referring and not the Atlantic Ocean, which Kennedy naturally considered the right route for an Irish exile, when he used the quotation in his speech to the members of the Dáil and Senate. From that we got on to Joyce and Kiernan took me back to the year in which I had left Tully for lunch: he was secretary to John Dulanty, the Free State High Commissioner in London at that time, and became friendly with the Joyces when they came there to get married 'for testamentary reasons'.

His jymes is out of job, would sit and write. He has lately committed one of the then commandments but she will now assist. (*FW* 181)

—He told me at that time, Kiernan said, that his father was bedridden in Dublin, near death in the last stages of G.P.I. But I don't want you to publish an article about this, that wouldn't do.

—Not, I said, until the time comes when it may *then* be told. But Joyce had already wiped his glosses with what he knew:

A baser meaning has been read into these characters the literal sense of which decency can safely scarcely hint. It has been blurtingly bruited by certain wisecrackers . . . that he suffered from a vile disease. (*FW* 33)

and

An infamous private ailment (vulgovarioveneral) had claimed endright, closed his vicious circle, snap. (*FW* 98)

Willie Fallon's 'no comment' seemed to be of eloquent relevance in this context: 'James Joyce was a model boy at Belvedere, prefect of the Sodality and regular going to Confession and receiving Holy Communion. I know what turned him against his father and against his religion. I've known it all these years and I told no one. I'm an old man now and I'll carry the secret with me to the grave.' This 'secret', which I was at pains to uncover in the foregoing pages, by putting together sundry pieces of circumstantial evidence, has since become no longer a subject for speculation, much less entombed in anyone's grave. In the *Irish Medical Times* of 9 May 1975, Dr F. R. Walsh of Kilkenny has published Jack Joyce's own statement to him in 1919-20 that he had had syphilis in his youth. But it remains of importance to keep on record that the fact was known to his contemporaries and that knowledge of it was the kinetic factor that drove two of his sons into exile.

After *Cyclops* there are no further personal appearances of Simon Dedalus except in Stephen's phantasies in 'Circe'. The first is on pp. 483-4:

FLORRY: (*To Stephen*) I'm sure you are a spoiled priest. Or a monk.

LYNCH: He is. A Cardinal's son.
STEPHEN: Cardinal sin. Monks of the screw.
(His eminence, Simon Stephen Cardinal Dedalus, Primate of all Ireland, appears in the doorway, dressed in red soutane, sandals and socks. Seven dwarf simian acolytes, also in red, cardinal sins, uphold his train . . . Round his neck hangs a rosary of corks ending on his breast in a corkscrew cross. . . .)
. . .
(A multitude of midges swarms over his robe. He scratches himself with crossed arms at his ribs, grimacing and exclaims) I'm suffering the agony of the damned. By the hoky fiddle, thanks be to Jesus those funny little chaps are not unanimous. If they were they'd walk me off the face of the bloody globe.

In this extract two suggestions are made by others to Stephen about himself, that he is a spoiled . . . monk and that he is a cardinal's son. In Stephen's mind these expand into the representation of his real father: as a cardinal, attended by seven simian acolytes, seven for the seven deadly sins and simian because the cardinal is a primate. The 'rosary of corks ending . . . in a corkscrew cross' symbolises the secondary role of the cardinal as Prior of the Monks of the Screw.

The Monks of the Screw was a social club founded by John Philpot Curran whose family house outside Rathfarnham, County Dublin, was known as The Priory. Here Curran entertained his convivial 'companions of St Patrick', re-naming them in a song 'The Monks of the Screw'.

Curran was a member of the Irish Parliament, a popular barrister and a prominent defence counsel in the trials of the United Irishmen. He often visited Sligo socially or professionally or in both capacities, and he was always entertained hospitably there by Bob Lyons, a rich attorney who lived at Mullaghmore, north of Sligo town, off the road to Bundoran.

When addressing a jury Curran made it his practice to concentrate on whatever juror seemed to him to look most hostile to his case. Once he had brought round the recalcitrant one to show signs of sympathy with his pleading, Curran felt convinced that he had the whole jury behind him. This procedure he called 'making the jury unanimous'.

On one occasion in winter weather, Curran's carriage got

stuck in a snowdrift at a place called Riverstown more than ten miles south of the town of Sligo and he was obliged to pig it for the night in the local shebeen. Next morning the land-lady expressed the hope that he had had a good night's rest.

—How could I rest, demanded Curran, with all the fleas in this damned village eating me alive, one regiment pulling me from another.

—I never knew there to be a flea in this house. Pulling you round, you say?

—Yes, pulling! By heavens, woman, if they were *unanimous* and all pulled the one way, they'd have pulled me out of bed entirely.

It is quite clear that Joyce had a truncated version of this tale. It is told in Sir Jonah Barrington's *Recollections* as having happened in Carlow but Barrington does not seem to have been aware of the undertones of Curran's law practice involved in his use of the word 'unanimous'. I cannot recall whether my version of the incident came to me from a book or from local tradition, but I am quite satisfied that it originated in County Sligo. I even have a few lines of a ballad commemorating Curran's curse on the occasion, which ends :

Bad luck to the night I met Riverstown fleas.

It is not clear why Joyce transforms the fleas into midges, save that he has the departing 'Cardinal Dedalus', once he has said his say, shrink to the midget dimensions of his simian acolytes. The seven deadly sins were indeed the proper and constant escort of Jack Joyce—pride, covetousness, lust, anger, gluttony, envy and sloth.

Later in the same episode, Simon intervenes twice, first with the familiar 'Ho boy! Are you going to win?' and a reference to the family coat of arms, 'An eagle gules volant in a field argent displayed' (510) and finally 'Think of your mother's people!' (515) which leads immediately to the climax of the book where—

Stephen's mother, emaciated, rises stark through the floor in leper grey with a wreath of faded orange blossoms and a torn bridal veil, her face worn and noseless, green with grave mould. Her hair is scant and lank. She fixes her bluecircled hollow eyesockets on Stephen and opens her toothless mouth uttering a silent word.

In the course of her transformation phantasy (495), 'Bello' uses to the enslaved and emasculated Bloom the words 'Die and be damned to you', which are words taken from Jack Joyce's intoxicated outburst to his dying wife :

—I'm finished, I can't do any more. If you can't get well, die. Die and be damned to you! (*MBK* 230)

Louis Gillet's account of Joyce's despair about the illness of his daughter Lucia relates to a later period but it refers back to the material of the present chapter :

De bonne heure, il dut reconnaître avec terreur chez sa fille des signes plus alarmants de déséquilibre nerveux. Comment une créature innocente, comment une beauté toute neuve et naïve apporte-t-elle a son insu, quelque part dans son corps, le germe qui la détruit?
Joyce ne buvait pas : je ne lui ai jamais vu boire autre chose que du tilleul ou, à table, un vin fort léger. Mais il avait derrière lui des siècles d'alcoolisme. Son père, le vieux drôle, lui avait laissé cet héritage. Joyce s'en accusait seul, se tenait seul pour responsable : c'était lui, encore une fois, non sa charmante femme, laquelle n'en pouvait mais, c'est lui qu'il estimait coupable. C'était sa faute : il était le père. Tout ce qui allait de travers, tout ce qui tournait mal pour ce fils et cette fille chéris, il en était la cause par tout ce que son génie contenait d'anormal. Cette pensée le crucifiait.

Gillet was mistaken in assuming that Joyce did not drink alcohol or that he was always temperate in his drinking. Joyce's own description of himself, 'a man of small virtue, inclined to alcoholism', was more accurate. Gillet must also have mis-understood the nature of the infection which Joyce said Lucia had inherited. He blamed himself for having transmitted to her the evil strain which unbalanced her reason but he implied that that strain had been transmitted to himself. By the time Lucia became seriously distraught Jack Joyce was dead and his son, in reaction, remembered his father only with affection and admiration.

In the years of the writing of *Ulysses*, however, he was obliged 'to slay his da' artistically in order to replace him with Leopold Bloom as the father of Stephen. This he does by portraying him as Noman in 'Cyclops' and by sending him offstage reduced to the size of a 'simian acolyte' in 'Circe'. This artistic parricide is but the literary reflection of the actual circumstances which obliged Joyce to leave Ireland in 1904. His father was the major factor in the milieu which he determined to abandon. He could expect no sustenance from him, no encouragement or support in his efforts to forge out a literary career—nothing but the famine and frustration in which Jack Joyce's useless life and blighted body was the centre of paralysis. His son was well aware of this and had taken the first steps in abandoning his father's house before ever Nora Barnacle crossed his path. She became what Gorman called another 'element that was violently pushing him toward flight'. This 'element' is not included in *Ulysses* and the parental imbroglio is overlaid with the mysteriously theological substitution of Leopold Bloom for Simon Dedalus as the consubstantial father. The quarrel with Mulligan is highlighted as an Ireland *versus* Stephen melodrama, in which the suffering artist is driven into exile.

In explaining to Arthur Power (*Conversations with James Joyce*) why it took him so long to produce *Ulysses*, the book of his maturity, Joyce said that Ulysses was always his hero even in his 'tormented youth'. But, he continued, it had taken him half a lifetime to reach the necessary equilibrium to express it, 'for my youth was exceptionally violent—painful and violent'.

In *Finnegans Wake* the sacrificial killing of the father figure, H.C.E., is periodically enacted and his wake repetitively celebrated, after the manner of the slaying of Osiris or of the seasonal gods in the *Golden Bough*. But in Joyce's own life the removal of the father was a real and terrible necessity—that, or the alternative which Joyce chose, removal from the father. That this was the impelling factor in Joyce's departure from Ireland may therefore be accepted but it should also be borne in mind, to discount all Joyce made of his exile afterwards, that temperamentally he would have been an exile anywhere, at home or abroad.

Chapter 5

Calypso

MOST commentators consider that the nymph of this episode representing the Homeric Calypso, the 'hidden one' (Greek, *Kalupto*, I hide) who detained Odysseus in her ocean cave, is represented by Molly Bloom concealed in her sheets. A substantial part of her is visible to Bloom when he brings her the morning post and, later, her breakfast tray, but this does not invalidate the case for her identity with the nymph, as Calypso was not hidden from her prisoner Odysseus. If, however, Molly were the nymph, then in view of her subsequent parts in the story, with Boylan in the afternoon and as the medium of the interior monologue that night, she would become an ephemeral creature whose lifespan was limited to this 16 June 1904, a mayfly appearing as a nymph in the morning, a green drake with Boylan and a spent gnat at the end of the day. This is contradicted by her memories which flood the monologue, going back over thirty years in Dublin and Gibraltar. But is the date 16 June, or is it 14 September, the actual date on which Joyce left the Tower? Even if it is the latter, Molly is still ruled out as the hidden nymph, for which she could have qualified up to her birthday on 8 September, as the constellation Virgo is (or was) occluded from 15 August to 8 September.

We must therefore consider alternative candidates: '*The Bath of the Nymph* over the bed. Given away with the Easter number of *Photo Bits*: Splendid masterpiece in art colours.' (67) Then there is 'the nextdoor girl' at Dlugacz's counter where Bloom waits to buy his morning kidney (61), whom Bloom has often watched whacking a carpet on the clothes-line. 'She does whack it, by George. The way her crooked skirt swings at each whack.' There is their daughter, Milly, a nymph just turned fifteen, now apprenticed to the photo business in Mullingar and writing to say a scrap picnic is planned at Lough

Owel on Monday. The mayfly could still be rising by 20 June, since it has never recognised Lord Chesterfield's statutory excision of eleven days from the Old Style calendar in 1752. Finally, there is Martha Clifford, a rather faded nymph perhaps, but the most profoundly hidden of all for, though Bloom corresponds with her under the *alias* 'Henry Flower', he has never agreed to meet her and probably never will. Martha, however, is not introduced into the story until her letter is presented in the next episode and is therefore scarcely qualified as the nymph of this one.

The nymph who appears in 'Circe', where everybody appears in his true, too true, colours, is she who adorns the wall of the Blooms' nuptial chamber in the splendid masterpiece, the 'Bath of the Nymph', and she may therefore be taken to be equated to the Calypso of this episode.

As regards Bloom's visit to Dlugacz's shop, Professor W. Y. Tindall, in *A Reader's Guide to FW* (p. 6), observes that 'making a pork butcher of Moses Dlugacz, one of Joyce's students at Trieste and an ordained rabbi, must be accounted a private joke—a gargoyle on the fabric of analogies and reciprocal correspondences.'

It is true that Dlugacz did hold a certificate permitting him to act as a rabbi, but it is also true that he was a porkbutcher by trade—in Trieste, not in Dublin. Mr Hyman Levy, principal of a girls' school in Haifa, was on sabbatical leave in Dublin in 1967, and as reported in the *Evening Herald* of 1 March 1967, displayed a photograph of Dlugacz with members of his family and of his rabbi's certificate. Mr Levy also had a copy of the circular advertising the model farm at Kinnereth on the lakeshore of Tiberias which inspired in Bloom some nostalgic thoughts of the east, the promised land, concluding apathetically, 'A dead sea in a dead land, grey and old.'

The episode closes with one of those excrementitious exercises betraying that 'cloacal obsession' of Joyce's which H. G. Wells had perspicaciously diagnosed as early as 1917 when he read *A Portrait of the Artist as a Young Man*:

He kicked open the crazy door of the jakes. . . . Asquat on the cuckstool he folded out his paper turning its pages over on his bared knees. (70)

Unnecessary description of necessary act? And yet there may be a purpose in it all. Sir John Harington (1561-1612) had published in 1596 'A new Discourse of a stale Subject, called the Metamorphosis of Ajax'. (He had invented a kind of water-closet for his house at Kelston, near Bath, and he described himself in the act of using this novel contrivance as 'Ulysses on Ajax'.) In Homer's account of the visit of Odysseus to Hades, Ajax refuses to speak to him. Here perhaps Joyce has his own Ulysses get his own back on Ajax. Joyce was aware of Harington's cloacal work. In *FW* there are references (266) to 'Harington's invention' and (447) 'the sludge of King Haarington at its height'.

In the plan of *Ulysses* and its Homeric correspondences given by Joyce to Stuart Gilbert for his book, *James Joyce's 'Ulysses'* (1930), the Art designated as appropriate to the Calypso episode is Economics. Gilbert saw this 'Art' exemplified only in the daily ration of cream taken for the exclusive use of Mrs Bloom, 'The custom of the house, its *economics*.' This would be a very limited application of the art of the episode which, in fact, includes also Bloom's speculations on how grocers' curates in Dublin amass the money which enables them to buy out their bosses. 'Coming up redheaded curates from the county Leitrim, rinsing empties and old man in the cellar. . . . Off the drunks perhaps. . . . A bob here and there, dribs and drabs. On the wholesale orders perhaps. Doing a double shuffle with the town travellers. Square it with the boss and we'll split the job, see.' (60) (Incidentally, Gilbert's definition of 'old man' as 'the drink a customer leaves in his glass' is not correct : 'Old man' is the wastage of liquor and froth in pouring draught stout.) There is also the economics of Agendath Netaim, planter's company : 'To purchase vast sandy tracts from Turkish government and plant with eucalyptus trees.' (I had been under the impression that Lord Tennyson was the sole proprietor of 'sandy tracts' overlooked from Locksley Hall.) These trees are 'excellent for shade'. (So they should be, *eu kalupto*, I shade well . . .) 'Your name entered for life as owner in the book of the union. Can pay ten down and the balance in yearly instalments.' Mr Bloom's considered decision is : 'Nothing doing. Still an idea behind it.'

'Economics' might therefore be accepted as the 'Art' of the

episode. The strange thing, however, is that Joyce had already given Carlo Linati a *schema* of his book, in which the 'Art' appropriate to *Calypso* is given as 'Mythology'. The whole Homeric background in all the episodes is, of course, mythological, and it is not clear why *Calypso* should be singled out as being particularly based on myth. There is one new myth introduced where Molly has 'Metempsychosis' transmigrated into 'methimpikehoses' and the possibility of another in the scene where Ulysses sits on Ajax, but all in all Joyce leaves the question of the two 'Arts' in the air.

Another enigma is 'whatdoyoucallhim out of. . . . His back is like that Norwegian captain's' (63). Both the unknown passerby and his likeness, the Norwegian captain, are left in the air. But we meet the captain elsewhere—*FW* 309-31—where the dense writing is based on a story which Joyce's father was wont to tell about a Norwegian seacaptain who bespoke a suit of clothes from a Dublin tailor named Kerse. When the captain complained that the suit did not fit him the tailor retorted that it was he who did not fit the suit—on account of the hump on his back. Writing to Alf Bergan, 25 May 1937, Joyce mentions his version of the tale published in *Transition* the previous February and remarks that if his dead father could get a copy in the shades his comment would be, 'Well, he can't tell that story as I used to and that's one sure five!'

Chapter 6

The Flower in Bloom

THE 'Lotus-Eaters' episode could well be a further chapter in the 'paralysis' of which Joyce deemed Dublin to be the centre. Nothing keeps on happening. Odysseus made himself superior to the charms of the root which threatened to make his crewmen prisoners and so Bloom must show some signs of activity. He obtains a letter from Martha Clifford addressed to him *poste restante* in Westland Row post office under his *alias* 'Henry Flower' but this is part of a purely negative game, holding lechery on the long finger of correspondence. He gives Bantam Lyons a tip that the Ascot Gold Cup will be won by Throwaway but he does this unwittingly and even when it involves him in a row in *Cyclops* he is still unaware of the cause of it. Still less is he aware that 'Throwaway' also symbolises the Homeric Trojan Horse.

The 'scene' of the episode is 'The Bath' but Bloom does not have his turkish bath until the episode has ended. It ends with Bloom's vision of himself in the bath 'naked, in a womb of warmth, oiled by scented melting soap, softly laved'. This version is Narcissistic and 'Narcissism' is the 'Technic' of the episode.

Here, as always, Joyce is writing a section of his life and simultaneously living a chapter of his book. It is proposed here to disentangle this phase of his life and his literature and to indicate the embellishments which he added to the facts of life when he portrayed them in fiction.

* * *

The back windows of Zurich's Universitatstrasse 29, where Joyce went to live late in October 1918, overlook some of the back windows of Culmannstrasse, through one of which he first saw Marthe Fleischmann, as he told his artist friend, Frank Budgen, 'in a small but well-lit room in the act of pulling a chain' (*Myselves When Young*). Yet he affected great astonishment when he met her in the street. This was due, he explained afterwards, to her extraordinary resemblance to the girl on Dollymount Strand sixteen years before, the sight of whom confirmed him in his intention to devote his life to the art of literature. It was certainly extraordinary if they bore any resemblance to each other. The wading bird-like girl had long slender legs, 'her bosom was as a bird's' and she had long fair hair. The Zurich woman was dark and Jewish-looking and was what ex-mariner Budgen called 'high up in the fo'c'sle and fairly broad in the beam'. She walked with a limp. Perhaps Joyce was telling fairy-tales to himself as well as to Martha. He told her that he was thirty-five (he was thirty-seven), the age at which Dante was entering the Dark Night of the Soul and at which Shakespeare was enchanted by the Dark Lady of the Sonnets. He gave her copies of some of his books and wrote her grandiose loveletters in his best French. The affair was platonic and came to an end soon after he brought her to Budgen's studio for a short tripartite talk in the light of a seven-branched Jewish candlestick lit to celebrate his thirty-seventh birthday and the feast of the day, Candlemas.

Like all other human material he encountered, Marthe was grist to Joyce's literary mill, in this case to the grinding out of *Ulysses*. Her limp was transferred to Gerty McDowell on Sandymount strand and her Christian name was given to Martha Clifford, the *poste restante* correspondent of Leopold Bloom.

In Joyce's letters to Marthe he altered his handwriting by substituting the Greek for the Roman 'ee' (Ellmann, p. 463). He has Bloom take the same puerile precaution in the Ormond Hotel when he writes to Miss Martha Clifford 'c/o P.O. Dolphin's barn lane, Dublin', encloses P.O. for a small sum and subscribes himself 'Henry Flower'.

While, therefore, 'Martha' comes from *eine platonische Liebe* in Zurich, there is no indication as to the origin of 'Clifford' nor of the *alias* for Bloom which Martha called 'the beautiful name you have'. The quest brings us back from Zurich to Dublin where, on the eve of the twentieth century, Joyce, aged eighteen, was already emulating that active collector-general, the magpie, in picking up anything that might suit his book. The 'Painful Case' of Henry Flower is given here as it was described in newspaper reports of coroners' and police courts' proceedings. Although set out in the bare, bald reportage in which it originally appeared, it could well be the first draft of a sixteenth story in *Dubliners*. It will be observed that there was a flower, a dahlia or an aster, involved in the case as well as the man, Henry Flower, a coincidence that is echoed by the 'yellow flower with flattened petals' which Martha enclosed in her letter to 'Henry Flower'.

* * *

Early on the morning of 23 August 1900, the body of a sturdy-looking woman about thirty years of age was found in two to three feet of water in the River Dodder, between Londonbridge Road and Herbert Park. The body was unclothed to the waist. The torn remains of a flower, a dahlia or aster, were found on the bank, a flower which it was afterwards testified deceased had been wearing on the night of her death.

Three members of the Dublin Metropolitan Police, Division E, were sent to the scene from the Londonbridge Road station. They were Sergeant John Hanily and Constables Flower and Toal. While the body was being escorted to the Londonbridge Road Morgue, Flower uncovered the face and said something to himself between his teeth.

At the inquest no evidence of identification was forthcoming and the verdict was 'death from drowning'. The woman's remains were interred in Glasnevin Cemetery.

Then Margaret Clowry, formerly a parlourmaid in Carisbrook House, but at this stage out of work, reported to Constable Toal that a friend of hers, Bridget Gannon, was missing since the night of 22 August. A second inquest was convened, at which Clowry swore that Gannon was a parlourmaid at 124 Lower Baggot Street. They had both been similarly engaged in another place. On an evening some time before 22 August, Gannon had called on her in her lodgings and about nine o'clock they walked down Northumberland Road from Haddington Road. They met two police officers, constables Thomas Dockery and Henry Flower. Dockery had known witness for many years but had 'cooled off' of late and now walked past. Flower, however, halted, though it appears that he had not known them before. When he did so Dockery joined them and they walked as far as Baggot Street, witness with Dockery, and Flower escorting Bridget Gannon. At the intersection of Baggot Street and Fitzwilliam Street she and Dockery left the other pair together at the corner.

On 22 August she and Gannon went out and met Flower at the same corner. In Baggot Street deceased bought plums and Flower who was in plain clothes had a drink in Davy's public house. The three walked together as far as Carisbrooke House, which, on a broad hint from Flower, witness entered to pick up some property of hers left there since she had been previously in it.

The case was adjourned for a week and on resumption Mr T. Harrington, M.P., appeared for Flower. Harrington at this time was nearly fifty years of age and had been elected a member of Parliament for County Westmeath in 1883, a circumstance which may explain the job of revising voters' lists in that county having been given to Joyce senior in 1900. He was counsel for Parnell in the 1888 Commission of Inquiry into the *Times* allegations in 'Parnellism and Crime'. He was Lord Mayor of Dublin in the three years 1901-4, and wrote a 'reference' or testimonial for James Joyce before he went to Paris in November 1902, in which he stated that he had known him since childhood and was also well acquainted with his family. In the 'Circe' episode he is referred to as 'late thrice Lord Mayor of Dublin' (455).

Harrington proceeded to question the procedure under which a second inquest was being held, the matter at issue being already *res judicata* by virtue of the finding at the first inquest.

On 5 September, Mr Justice Barton made a conditional order quashing the first verdict and on 7 September made the order absolute. (In 'Scylla and Charybdis' Judge Barton will be found cited as a searcher for clues to prove that Shakespeare was an Irishman [198].)

The second inquest was then resumed and Patrick Gannon identified as his sister the remains of deceased which had been exhumed. Henry Flower denied having been with, or having ever known, deceased. Constable Thomas Dockery of the

D.M.P. Station, Irishtown, deposed that he and Flower met the deceased and Margaret Clowry and were in their company on an occasion prior to 22 August. Medical evidence by Doctors E. J. McWeeney, O'Donoghue and Synnot was to the effect that there was no attempt at violation and no sign of violence. There was no sign that intoxication or drugs had affected the deceased.

On 11 September Flower was arrested. On 14 September a further sensation was created by the announcement that Sergeant Hanily had committed suicide by cutting his throat. Hanily, a kindly man, had become upset by the events involving his station. Flower was eventually returned for trial, having made five appearances in the police court.

On 16 October a commission for the City and County of Dublin was opened by Mr Justice Gibson. Sir Joseph Downes, City High Sheriff, and the High Sheriff for the County, Major Cusack, occupied seats on the Bench. When Flower appeared in the dock it was observed that he looked troubled and worn and considerably thinner than before his committal. The Judge advised the Grand Jury that it was their function to decide whether to return a true bill on which the prisoner would have to stand trial before a petty jury, or, alternatively not to return such a bill.

The Grand Jury returned a 'No Bill' verdict. The prisoner was discharged and is said to have disappeared from the Dublin scene promptly and permanently.

* * *

About forty years afterwards a priest was ministering to a dying woman in a tenement house in Gardiner Street. Acting on his advice, the old woman asked that a solicitor be brought to draft a dying declaration which she was prepared to sign. A solicitor was fetched and took down the dying woman's statement which she endorsed by her signature. The statement was to the effect that she was Margaret Clowry and that she met Bridget Gannon after Flower had left her and quarrelled with her about the money which she had. She pushed her in the river and when she was dead she purloined her cash. The solicitor who took down the dying woman's statutory declaration was John Cusack, a son of Michael Cusack, 'the Citizen' of *Ulysses*. Henry Flower was never traced and his 'beautiful name' was never publicly cleared of suspicion. The money which Margaret Clowry wrenched from Bridget Gannon's lifeless bosom is the other side of the 'small gold coin' that shone in the palm of the gallant Corley.

It will now be evident that the misfortunate constable of the E division was the Henry Flower whose name Joyce borrowed as a pen-name for Leopold Bloom and that those who praised him for his creative imagination in inventing the name should instead have applauded either his memory, his notes or his press-cuttings. Professor Ellmann (*James Joyce*, p. 166) relates that Joyce sent Nora Barnacle a pair of gloves on 21 July 1904, and signed himself 'Aujey'—'a partial anagram of his initials which suggests the mind that conceived of Henry Flower as Bloom's clandestine *nom de plume*.' But 'Aw Jay' was not primarily Joyce's invention any more than was 'Henry Flower' his conception : it was a watered down invocation of the Holy Name signifying a protest, an expletive such as might be used by a girl in real or pretended expostulation at liberties being taken by her escort. The expression may be seen in Mulligan's parlance on page 18 of *Ulysses*, 'O, jay, there's no milk.' As regards 'Martha Clifford', Joyce had to choose 'Martha' to accord with the name of his own Dark Lady of Zurich, but in doing so he also seems to have retained traces of the name of the second woman in the Flower case, Mar(garet) Cl(owry).

The appearance in real life of Michael Cusack's son to witness the declaration clearing the character of the real personage whose name was the *alias* of Leopold Bloom, Michael Cusack's fictional adversary in Barney Kiernan's, is a denouement which might seem extravagant even to Joyce's association mania.

Henry Flower, *nominis umbra*, remains in the uneasy custody of Bloom's hatband until, in Nighttown, he acquires a separate if shadowy identity when his card falls out of the hat and he is immediately accused : 'Henry Flower. No fixed abode. Unlawfully watching and besetting.' (441) He appears in the ensuing phantasy (480), impersonating the tenor, Mario, prince of Candai, touching the strings of his guitar and singing, 'There is a flower that bloometh.' Later (491), he is 'Henry Fleury of Gordon Bennet fame', one of the potential violators of Mrs Miriam Dandrade.

Once one is apprised of his actual identity one feels that he carries that identity with him into his fictitious role as the *alias* of Bloom in Joyce's novel, retaining at the same time a strange affinity with the much blamed Bloom who is banished by the xenophobes from Barney Kiernan's and well-nigh immolated in 'Circe'. One feels also that the sense of this affinity resided in the mind of the author although he refrained from disclosing the factual basis of it.

Flower and Bloom jointly prefigure the culprit/scapegoat, H.C.E., in *Finnegans Wake* and all his trials and errors.

The evidence about the finding of Bridget Gannon's body is sketched in 'Hades' (102): 'Her clothing consisted of. How she met her death. . . . The body to be exhumed.'

C

Chapter 7

Hades

MARTIN Cunningham, Jack Power, Simon Dedalus and Leopold Bloom occupy the same funeral carriage from the Star of the Sea Church to Glasnevin Cemetery. 'Martin Cunningham' is a named borrowed from Nora Barnacle's memories of her youth in Galway. His family were connected with the Bodkins, one of whom, Michael, is the original of 'Michael Fury' in 'The Dead', the last story in *Dubliners*. 'Martin Cunningham' in 'Hades' is Joyce's name for Matthew Kane who was drowned in Dublin Bay on 10 July 1904. He is the corpse expected in 'Telemachus' to be 'swept up that way when the tide comes in about one. It's nine days today'. (27) That would make the date 18 July. In fact Kane's funeral took place on 13 July. But even if we antedate this event in the book to 16 June, Martin Cunningham is both a corpse in the sea and a living passenger in the cab with Jack Power attending Paddy Dignam's funeral. They have already appeared together in *Dubliners* ('Grace'), visiting Mr Kernan after his accidental fall down the basement stairs of a pub. Martin Cunningham, a character in the book, and Matthew F. Kane, the real person on whom he is based, friend of Joyce's father, appear on the same page (625), as Bloom sees Stephen off: 'Martin Cunningham (in bed)' and Matthew F. Kane, 'defunct . . . (accidental drowning, Dublin Bay)'. In *FW* 387 and 393, it is Cunningham who is 'the official out of the castle on pension, when he was completely drowned off Erin's Isles'. The persons and characters are confused and the deceased Dignam may really represent the drowned Kane so that it might be said that in this episode Martin Cunningham is attending his own funeral.

Matthew Kane held a post as chief clerk in the Crown Solicitor's office from which he had apparently retired by 1904, and Stanislaus Joyce, who called him 'the Green Street Shakespeare', regretted his death because 'this throws Pappie more on me' (*Diary*, 43). Evidently Kane had become a fairly constant companion of Jack Joyce. Another friend was Charley Chance on whom both Bloom and C. P. McCoy are partially modelled. Bloom will give the reporter at the funeral the name of C. P. McCoy who is unable to attend because 'there's a drowning case at Sandycove may turn up and then the coroner and myself would have to go down if the body is found'. (77) '—Charley, Hynes said, writing. I know. He was on the *Freeman* once.' (113)

Simon Dedalus and Leopold Bloom sit in the cab side by side—two of Stephen's four fathers, the others being Daedalus and Odysseus. As the carriage passes up D'Olier Street, the occupants are saluted from the door of the Red Bank restaurant by Blazes Boylan 'airing his quiff' as he flashes the white disc of his straw hat.

> Mr Bloom reviewed the nails of his left hand, then those of his right hand. The nails, yes. Is there anything more in him that they she sees? Fascination. Worst man in Dublin. . . . They sometimes feel what a person is. Instinct. But a type like that. My nails. I am just looking at them: well pared. (94)

Boylan is to bring the programme of their concert tour to Molly at four o'clock. She will be singing 'La ci darem' with J. C. Doyle and 'Love's Old Sweet Song'. The implications will be exercising Bloom's mind throughout the day but here, the first time 'the worst man in Dublin' is epiphanised as a character, he maintains an impassive face. His nails. He is just looking at them: well pared.

It is inconceivable that Joyce wrote these words without adverting to his *Portrait* postulate that the artist must remain 'above his handiwork, invisible, refined out of existence, indifferent, paring his fingernails'. The scenario for Boylan's act of adultery is being prepared in Bloom's mind, here in D'Olier Street and later whenever the self-doomed cuckold catches sight of his rival in the streets and in the Ormond Hotel. Even when he leaves to keep his assignation Bloom's imagination follows the jaunting-car to 7 Eccles Street. In his phantasy in 'Circe' the scene is depicted in the lewdest and most vivacious terms, Bloom himself acting as a compliant lackey in his own betrayal.

In all this Bloom is 'the artist' to whom, under Joyce, we are exclusively indebted for information. My interpretation of Lenehan's remark (quoted at the end of Chapter 2 above) about there being 'a touch of the artist about old Bloom' may now be extended by reference to other characteristics peculiar to the author which he lends, first to Richard Rowan in *Exiles* and here to Bloom. In *Exiles*, written immediately before Joyce concentrated on the composition and compilation of *Ulysses*, the author's surrogate, Richard Rowan, speaking to Robert Hand, says

> . . . in the very core of my ignoble heart I longed to be betrayed by you and by her—in the dark, in the night—secretly, meanly and craftily. By you, my best friend, and by her. I longed for that passionately and ignobly, to be dishonoured for ever in love and in lust . . . to be for ever a shameful creature and to build up my soul again out of the ruins of its shame.

Bloom is thus meditating treason against himself, through the medium of his wife, sitting remote in the cab or immobile in the Ormond dining-room, his nails well pared. It is the same 'artistic' act of creation as that which kept Gabriel Conroy awake in the Gresham Hotel as he pondered in 'The Dead' over his posthumous betrayal by Sonny Furey (based on Joyce's own thoughts about Sonny Bodkin). Bloom is subjecting himself to the masochistic ordeal of imagining Boylan's projected betrayal. This affair in *Ulysses* is therefore a continuation in a cruder form of the theme of *Exiles*, which Joyce in his notes to that play described as 'a rough and tumble between the Marquis de Sade and Freiherr v. Sacher Masoch', and which is itself a sophisticated elaboration of the theme of 'The Dead' in *Dubliners*.

Meanwhile the progress of the funeral procession was marked by the statues of dead men motionless in their own Hades in the approach to O'Connell Bridge and in O'Connell Street—William Smith O'Brien, Daniel O'Connell ('the hugecloaked Liberator's form') 'Gray's statue', 'Nelson's Pillar' and 'Foundation stone for Parnell'. Conversation in the cab is preoccupied with death, murder, suicide (actual or attempted), Martin Cunningham tactfully diverting Mr Power from further discussion of self-slaughter knowing that Bloom's father had taken his own life in the Queen's Hotel, Ennis. Bloom's own thoughts run on the same lines : his father's death, hospice for the dying, dead meat trade, municipal funeral trams. . . .

Their carriage was stopped by the passage of a drove of cattle and sheep 'for Liverpool probably' which prompts Bloom to remark : 'I can't make out why the corporation doesn't run a tramline from the parkgate to the quays. All those animals could be taken in trucks down to the boats.' (99-100) Later in the day Father Conmee, walking along the North Circular Road wondered 'that there was not a tramline in such an important thoroughfare.'

This thoroughfare may be discerned dimly in *FW* 284, amidst a reference to some of the illuminated capital letters of the TUNC page of the Book of Kells. The letters NCCR from the words *Tunc crucifixerant* are used to make an enlarged capital C out of the two c's and to produce with the preceding and succeeding N and R the letters NCR, being the characters of an algebraic symbol in Combinations, where N represents the number of objects under consideration, C the combinations and R the number of groups which can be selected from N—possibly a source of worry in schooldays which may naturally recur to the sleeping mind of the adult. But the fact that the letters may stand for 'North Circular Road' is not overlooked, for the reference to these letters in footnote 5 runs 'A gee is just a jay on the jaunts cowsway.' This should not be interpreted as 'Giants' Causeway'—it means that the traffic problem of cattle 'on the hoof' being driven along the North Circular Road from the cattle market to an abbatoir or to the quays has again occurred to Joyce. Whatever may be their immediate destination, a local slaughterhouse or exportation to England, their ultimate destiny ('jaunts cowsway') is identical : they will be butchers' meat, cut into joints.

In the mortuary chapel in Glasnevin Cemetery, Bloom is the objective, non-christian observer who is made to see the forms of the funeral service without any ostensible appreciation of their religious significance : 'brass bucket with something in it'; 'something' is explained by 'the priest took a stick with a knob at the end of it out of the boy's bucket and shook it over the coffin'. A deadpan recital of events seen but not understood. Joyce's alternatives to this way of describing the service would have been to reproduce the whole service in Latin with appropriate variations or to substitute an exaggerated, mock-heroic service on the lines of the blessing of Barney Kiernan's premises in 'Cyclops'. Instead, he uses Bloom to lend objectivity to his own memories of scenes at his brother's and his mother's funerals.

Bloom's platitudinous meditations proceed: 'Once you are dead you are dead. That last day idea. Knocking them all up out of their graves. Come forth, Lazarus! And he came fifth and lost the job.'

That corn was neither fresh nor green even in 1904.

John O'Connell's story of the drunks looking for the grave of a friend of theirs whose funeral they had got too drunk to attend. Meanwhile the widow had had a statue of our Saviour erected. Flann O'Brien (Myles na gCopaleen) had made this story his own, with improvements. One of the drunks was an introvert with downcast eyes: he spotted the inscription: *Sacred to the memory of Terence Mulcahy.* The other kept his head up and saw the face of the statue. '*Not a bloody bit like the man*, says he, *That's not Mulcahy*, says he, *whoever done it.*' (109)

By this time, Bloom's mind and imagination are crawling with maggots, decomposing corpses, charnelhouses. Joyce himself lends a hand weakly with *de mortuis nil nisi prius*. Joe Hynes is taking the names for the *Evening Telegraph* which will give Bloom as 'L. Boom' and the mysterious figure in the brown macintosh as 'M'Intosh'. Bloom has already displayed interest in this person: 'Now who is that lanky-looking galoot over there in the macintosh? Now who is he I'd like to know? Now, I'd give a trifle to know who he is.' (111)

When he wishes to correct Hynes who has scribbled 'M'Intosh', he finds that the stranger has gone. 'Where has he disappeared to? Not a sign. Well, of all the.' (114)

The man in the brown macintosh should not in fact have had his name or his macintosh inscribed amongst the list of mourners at Paddy Dignam's funeral. James Joyce, one of the reporters of the exciting scenes in Barney Kiernan's in the 'Cyclops' episode, reveals that 'The man in the brown macintosh loves a lady who is dead.' (332) He appears again in person at the end of 'Oxen of the Sun', a hungry man, 'Walking Mackintosh of lonely canyon' 'once a prosperous cit' (424). He also probably is the 'dark mercurialized face' which is seen in 'Circe' (441).

It only remained for Bloom to get snubbed by John Henry Menton when he drew his attention to a dinge in his hat. But Menton is Ajax in the Odyssey and Bloom has already had his own back on him. 'Yes, Menton. Got his rag out that evening on the bowling green because I sailed inside him. Pure fluke of mine: the bias. Why he took such a rooted dislike of me,' Bloom recalls, unaware that Joyce is having him render an alternative meaning of the word 'bias'.

The corresponding hostility of Ajax to Ulysses in Hades had been occasioned by the award to Ulysses of the arms of Achilles. The bowling game in Terenure which Bloom recalls may have been intended as an echo of Pope's lines in his *Essay on Criticism*:

When Ajax strives some rock's vast weight to throw,
The line too labours and the words move slow.

Another encounter, just before he experienced the rebuff from Menton, left a more lasting impression on Bloom's mind:

An obese rat toddled along the side of the crypt, moving the pebbles. An old stager: great grandfather: he knows the ropes. The grey alive crushed itself in under the plinth, wriggled itself in under it. Good hidingplace for treasure. . . .
Tail gone now.
One of those chaps would make short work of a fellow. Pick the bones clean no matter who it was. Ordinary meat for them. A corpse is meat gone bad. (116)

Shortly afterwards, in the *Evening Telegraph* offices, Bloom catching sight of Hynes thinks, 'account of the funeral probably'. And hearing the printing machines he thinks of 'the remains of the late Mr Patrick Dignam'—'fermenting. Working away, tearing away. And that old grey rat tearing to get in' (120). One would imagine it to be rather premature on the rat's part to try to tear its way into a freshly interred coffin. The rat he had seen had in fact been on its way into the recesses of the crypt of one Robert Emery, but he becomes the symbol of death that dogs Bloom's footsteps as far as the abode of 'Circe' where there is a vision of Paddy Dignam followed by 'an obese grandfather rat on fungus turtle paws under a grey carapace' (453).

Joyce has lent Bloom his sense of horror and revulsion at the appearance of a rat. He has had Stephen, feverish in the Clongowes infirmary, feel the prefect's cold damp hand on his warm damp forehead 'the way a rat felt, slimy and damp and cold . . . Sleek slimy coats, little little feet tucked up to jump, black slimy eyes to look out of'.

Stephen's father renews the rodent image during the row at the Christmas dinner-table associating it with the 'betrayal' of Parnell. 'When he was down they turned on him to betray him and rend him like rats in a sewer.'

The rats pursued Joyce into exile and were much in evidence in 1921 when the proofs of *Ulysses* were being revised for publication of the book in 1922. One summer's evening, while he was having a glass of wine in the Brasserie Lutétia, his companion, Robert McAlmon, directed his attention to a rat coming down the stairs. Joyce cried out, 'That's bad luck!' and fainted. It was the prelude to an attack of iritis which laid him up for five weeks. Then, at the end of August, he wrote to McAlmon, whom he had seen off from the Gare Du Nord, that on his way home from the station 'a filthy rat ran by me'. A subsequent collapse at a theatre was, he thought, the result of this apparition.

Chapter 8

Bladderbags

THE 'Organ' of this episode is 'Lungs', the 'Art' is 'Rhetoric' and the 'Technic' is 'Enthymemic'. The material is divided into sections each with its caption like a newspaper headline or sub-heading. The 'Rhetoric' is rendered by reading or reciting examples of what Mr Bloom calls 'high falutin stuff'. Dan Dawson ('Doughy Daw'), whose flowery speech is being read by Ned Lambert and hooted by his audience, Bloom mentally terms a 'Bladderbags'. This equates Dawson and the other rhetoricians quoted to the bags in which Aeolus kept the winds imprisoned to facilitate the return of Odysseus to Ithaca. When his men released them his fleet was wrecked in chaotic tempests. 'Bladder' is probably intended also to include 'Blather', rubbish, and 'Blatherskite', one who babbles rubbish. The episode is written under the inspiration of the action of its 'Organ', the Lungs—respiration. The trams move in to Nelson Pillar and move out again. Doors open and shut. Breezes blow in and out through the newspaper office which is the scene of the episode. The printing office itself is a constant noisy process of inflation and deflation, 'the obedient reels feeding in huge webs of paper. Clank it. Clank it. Miles of it unreeled'. . . . 'Sllt. The nethermost deck of the first machine jogged forwards its flyboard with sllt the first batch of quirefolded papers'.

The device of presenting the episode in headlined sections, the headlines themselves evolving from the prim propriety of Victorian captions to the 'humorous' or scare headlines of modern journalism, has discomfited some commentators. 'Their authorship', remarks Professor Ellmann (*Ulysses on the Liffey*, 1972), 'is unclear . . . By whomever composed, the headlines serve as a warning that the view of reality so far presented may not suffice indefinitely, that the world may move less reliably in later chapters than it has so far.'

This and similar commentary on the later chapters suggest that Professor Ellmann does not appreciate that James Joyce, when writing *Ulysses*, no longer adhered to the postulate put into the mouth of Stephen Dedalus in *A Portrait of the Artist as a Young Man*, that the artist should remain 'within or behind or beyond or above his handiwork, invisible, refined out of existence, indifferent, paring his fingernails'. Even in this wording, one of the locations permitted for the artist is *within* his handiwork. In *Ulysses*, more particularly in this and the subsequent chapters, he is within his handiwork which is beginning to run away with him; he is even in its margins, galley-slaving at his galleyproofs to give them further baroque embroidery including those captions, none of which had been there at the first printing. He is playing with the characters and, by the manipulation of his successive styles, with the reader. The ideal reader is expected masochistically to enjoy their literary sadism.

The first 'bladderbag' to be unloosed, Dawson, whom Professor MacHugh calls 'Doughy Daw' and Bloom surmises to have been 'in the bakery line', was Charles Dawson, member of Parliament for County Carlow and Lord Mayor of Dublin in 1882 and 1883. He was a baker by trade, with his chief business establishment in St Stephen's Street, Dublin. On vacating the Mansion House in Dawson Street at the end of his term of office as Lord Mayor, one John Christopher Fitz-Achary addressed the following lines to him ('written on New Year's Day, 1884'):

> Tho' Dawson now in Dawson Street
>   No more as Lord controls
> Yet in St Stephen's him we'll greet
>   As *Master of the Rolls!*
> (*The Bridal of Drimna and Other Poems*. Dublin: James Duffy & Sons, 1884.)

Dawson was a spry little toff easily intoxicated by his own eloquence. His son, Willie, was the birdlike 'Avis' of *St Stephen's*, who described Joyce's paper on Mangan as the best that had ever been delivered before the Literary and Historical Society.

More important is the speech attributed to John Francis

Taylor (1850-1902), in support of a paper advocating the revival of the Irish language, which Joyce has Professor Mac Hugh (Hugo MacNeill) recite in 'Aeolus' as an example of public oratory. The speech, Joyce has MacHugh say, was delivered at the Trinity College Historical Society. In fact it was delivered at the inaugural meeting of the Law Students' Debating Society in the King's Inns on 24 October 1901. One version of it was given by the late District Justice Michael Lennon in an article in the *Irish Independent* in the early 1950s as taken from, I think, a report in the same newspaper in October 1901 and it ran as follows :

> Suppose a great message, ethical or poetical, was to be given to the human race again, in what language was it likely to come to them? Was it likely to come in a language encrusted with materialism or in the simple language of the poor?
>
> The greatest message that had ever been given to man, and upon which the Christian religion had been founded, was not given in the imperial language of Rome or the intellectual language of Greece or even in the stately literary language of the Temple. It was given in the rustic dialect of a far-off corner out of which no good thing could come and it was to the Jews a stumbling-block and to the Greeks foolishness.
>
> I believe from the experience of history that the message would be more likely given in a language which had kept itself pure and spotless from contact with the world.

Another version stated to have been copied from *The Freeman's Journal* of 25 October 1901 was given by Lennon to Professor Ellmann (*James Joyce*, p. 95). This displays a series of verbal alterations from, while preserving the sense of, that given above, and contains a further paragraph in which the speaker says he could understand an intellectual Egyptian speaking to Moses and saying . . . 'I have no patience with you talking about your history and literature. Why, I asked one of the learned professors of your literature the other day what it was like, and he told me it was made up of superstitions and indecency.'

Taylor's reference to the position of the Jews in Egypt was clearly an *obiter dictum* intended as an acid aside on evidence given by Professor J. P. Mahaffy in 1900 before a Commission on Intermediate Education in which he said that he had been advised by an expert whose name he was not at liberty to disclose (actually Atkinson, a professor of Languages in Trinity College) that it was 'impossible to find a text in Irish which was not either religious or silly or indecent'. This statement was challenged by Dr Douglas Hyde and the controversy was given considerable publicity.

In his re-writing of Taylor's speech Joyce sidesteps the principal analogy, that with the Christian evangel with which he has a love-hate relationship. He pitches instead on what was a casual reference to Egypt and the Jews, ignoring Taylor's purpose in referring to Hebrew literature, and building the whole case for Irish revival on 'the Language of the Outlaw' having become the medium through which He whom Joyce vaguely calls 'the Eternal' delivered the Decalogue to Moses.

The speech which Joyce has Professor MacHugh recite as that of John F. Taylor differs as to the main theme and completely in style from either that quoted by me above or that given by Ellmann. It is, in fact, a piece of oratory composed by James Joyce himself, which he makes Professor MacHugh claim to be extempore, and one of two selected as examples of his best prose for phonographic record, the other being the closing passages of 'Anna Livia Plurabelle'. He has his surrogate, Stephen, apostrophise himself as MacHugh begins to speak: 'Noble words coming. Look out. Could you try your hand at it yourself?' Here are Joyce's 'noble words' (142-4):

> *Mr Chairman, ladies and gentlemen, great was my admiration in listening to the remarks addressed to the youth of Ireland a moment since by my learned friend. It seemed to me that I had been transported into a country far away from this country, into an age remote from this age, that I stood in ancient Egypt and that I was listening to the speech of some highpriest of that land addressed to the youthful Moses.*
>
> *And it seemed to me that I heard the voice of that Egyptian highpriest raised in a tone of like haughtiness and like pride. I heard his words and their meaning was revealed to me.*
>
> *Why will you Jews not accept our culture, our religion, and our language? You are a tribe of nomad herdsmen; we*

are a mighty people. You have no cities nor no wealth; our cities are hives of humanity and our galleys, trireme and quadreme laden with all manner of merchandise furrow the waters of the known globe. You have emerged from primitive conditions; we have a literature and a priesthood, an age-long history, and a polity.

You pray to a local and obscure idol; our temples, majestic and mysterious, are the abodes of Isis and Osiris, of Horus and Ammon-Ra. Yours is serfdom, awe, and humbleness; ours thunder and the seas. Israel is weak and few are her children; Egypt is an host and terrible are her arms. Vagrants and day labourers are you called; the world trembles at our name.

But, ladies and gentleman, had the youthful Moses listened to and accepted that view of life, had he bowed his head, and bowed his will, and bowed his spirit before that arrogant admonition, he would never have brought the chosen people out of their house of bondage, nor followed the pillar of the cloud by day. He would never have spoken with the Eternal amid lightnings on Sinaï's mountaintop, nor ever have come down with the light of inspiration shining in his countenance and bearing in his arms the tables of the law graven in the language of the outlaw.

The foregoing is what Mr Crofton of the 'Ivy Day' story in *Dubliners* might well have called 'a very fine piece of writing'. But it is also mere rhetoric.

'Enthymeme', the 'Technic' of *Aeolus*, is a rhetorical term for an argument consisting of only two propositions, an antecedent and a consequent. It is a syllogism in which the major proposition is suppressed. MacHugh before reciting the speech, had already given an example of such defective reasoning: 'That he had prepared his speech I do not believe for there was not even one shorthandwriter in the hall.' MacHugh (or Joyce) also fails to explain how the 'noble words' remained in the reciter's memory. That there were at least two notetakers in the hall is suggested by the *variae lectiones* of the speech, given in the *Freeman* and the *Independent*.

Bloom has earlier in this episode, meditating on his dead father, reading backwards from his hagadah book, forestalled

O'Molloy's commentary with the words 'O dear! All that long business about that brought us out of the land of Egypt and into the house of bondage' (124).

The analogy with the prospects for the Irish language revival is not expressed and Bloom's comments suggest that, even if it were included, it would betide only failure.

O'Molloy has already contributed an example of forensic eloquence attributed to Seymour Bushe, descriptive of Michelangelo's Moses—

that stone effigy in frozen music, horned and terrible, of the human form divine, that eternal symbol of wisdom and prophecy which, if aught that the imagination or the hand of sculpture has wrought in marble of soultransfigured and of soultransfiguring deserves to live, deserves to live. (141)

Bloom thinks of O'Molloy: 'Cleverest fellow at the junior bar he used to be. Decline poor chap. That hectic flush spells finis for a man. Touch and go with him. What's in the wind, I wonder. Money worry.' (126)

Money worry it was. O'Molloy had come in hoping to get a loan from the editor, Myles Crawford, but he failed to 'raise the wind'. 'Gambling . . . reaping the whirlwind . . . wellread fellow.'

O'Molloy lights a cigarette (132), flings it away (139), takes out his cigarette case again (140), intones the words about the Moses of Michelangelo, and has his second cigarette lit (140). The organ of inhalation and exhalation is being exercised.

'J. J. O'Molloy,' his symptoms of phthisis, his declining legal practice, his cigarettes and his quest for loans are a partial disguise for the person on whom he is based, an acquaintance of Joyce's in 1904, J. J. O'Neill, who at that time worked in the National Library under librarian Lyster but who subsequently became librarian of University College, Dublin, on the death in 1917 of D. J. O'Donoghue, the latter being the first appointee after the creation of the National University of Ireland and its federated University Colleges. Joyce was in Ireland at the time (1909) and was also interested in the librarian job. He wrote to Stanislaus on 3 November informing him of O'Donoghue's appointment.

O'Neill was tall and thin, palefaced, with a slight flush on each cheek, but he is not known to have been tubercular. He was a chronic cigarette smoker.

C. P. Curran (*James Joyce Remembered*, 1968) published a note from O'Neill of his meeting Joyce with Seán T. O'Kelly (formerly an assistant in the National Library, ultimately President of Ireland) at a lecture given by John Kells Ingram in Capel Street Library in 1904. After the lecture Joyce, O'Kelly and O'Neill walked away together and O'Neill showed Joyce Sir Samuel Ferguson's house in North Great George's Street and Parnell's house in Temple Street. Joyce appeared much interested and spoke for a considerable time about Ferguson and Parnell.

Parnell is a regular inmate of Joyce's books, an obsession, a source of controversy and a symbol of Irish betrayal. To Ferguson's *Burial of King Cormac* Joyce owed what little he knew about Cormac Mac Airt and he took all he wanted from his *Mesgedra* to adorn the poetic landscape of youthful Anna Livia :

> When glades were green where Dublin stands today
> And limpid Liffey fresh from wood and wold,
> Bridgeless and fordless, in the lonely Bay,
> Sank to her rest on sands of stainless gold.

Stephen's ostensible mission to the *Evening Telegraph* office on this June day shortly after noon was to get Crawford to publish Mr Deasy's letter advocating 'Koch's preparation' as an alternative to the slaughter of cattle then in progress to counter an outbreak of foot and mouth disease. Had Deasy's suggestion been adopted we should now have this disease endemic in Ireland as it is in those continental countries where the authorities are content to leave it dormant by inoculating the herds.

Crawford asks Stephen to write for his paper 'something with a bite in it. You can do it . . . Put us all into it'.

This is the invitation which supplements what Stephen (or Joyce) regarded as Mulligan's (Gogarty's) eviction. He is cast out from Ireland, from Paradise—Milton's Park (*FW* 96)—and he is asked to write.

Write he will—but not for the *Evening Telegraph*.

In Trieste, in September 1905, he prays to some vague deity

to give him 'a pen and an ink-bottle and some peace of mind' . . . 'and if I don't sharpen that little pen and dip it into fermented ink and write tiny little sentences about the people who betrayed me, send me to hell' (*Letters* II, 110).

Meanwhile his contribution to the 'rhetoric' of 'Aeolus' is a piece of naturalism about two old girls who climbed Nelson Pillar. Professor MacHugh finds an antithesis in the balanced account and also applauds a reference to the 'onehandled adulterer'; 'Finished?' Myles Crawford said in the tone of Aeolus when he ceased to succour Odysseus.

Joyce's actual experience of the *Evening Telegraph* and *Freeman's Journal* offices occurred in 1909. During his first visit to Dublin in that year he attended the Abbey Theatre *premiere* of Shaw's *The Shewing Up of Blanco Posnet* when it had been banned in England by the Lord Chamberlain, whose powers in this respect did not extend to Ireland. This circumstance lent the presentation international attention and Joyce was admitted on his card as a journalist purporting to represent *Il Piccolo de la Sera* of Trieste. In this guise he made himself known to Piaras Beaslaí, then drama critic of the *Evening Telegraph*, who invited him to call at the newspaper office next day. Beaslaí describes the aftermath:

> He stayed a long time and out of that and subsequent visits he derived the material for a large portion of 'Ulysses' [*recte, Aeolus*] . . . [in which] Stephen Dedalus (Joyce himself) plays a leading part in the conversation but in reality he was very quiet and reserved. . . . He was never aggressive or dogmatic in stating his views but always courteous and considerate.

Beaslaí went on to say that, long afterwards, he was greatly surprised 'to learn that Joyce, who had introduced himself to us all as a journalist was never one, but a teacher in the Berlitz School of Languages at Trieste and that he was never on the staff of the *Piccolo de la Sera* though he had contributed some articles to it.'

Joyce's *Piccolo* card also procured him a free return ticket to Galway and a first-class pass to London on his way back to Trieste.

There are two references in this episode which seem to be

divorced from its 'Art' of 'Rhetoric'. Each of them is brief yet dignified with a separate caption. 'His grace phoned down twice this morning' is headed THE CROZIER AND THE PEN, and 'Where's the archbishop's letter' has the caption NOTED CHURCHMAN AN OCCASIONAL CONTRIBUTOR. Professor Ellmann (*James Joyce* 297) ascribes these to a 'feud' between Dr Walsh and Thomas Sexton of the *Freeman's Journal* but I believe them to be based on the maledictive virtuosity of a piece of invective attributed to the editor when, on a complaint from His Grace that a letter of his had been drastically curtailed, he was informed by his sub-editors that they were obliged to cut out portions of it to fit it in between reports of political oratory on the Parnellite controversy. The editor's philippic concluded with the observation that they might as well be cutting the testamur off a Papal Bull as cutting chunks out of the archbishop's letter. (I myself have taken the liberty of editing the editor by replacing a vernacular noun in the dual number by the correct designation of the appendix of a papal edict.)

Chapter 9

Lestrygonians

THE name given to this episode is that of the cannibals who descended on some of the ships of the Odyssean fleet and captured and ate their crews. The 'Organ' is 'Esophagus' and the symbol 'Constables' (the squad of D.M.P. men debouching after lunch from the College Street police station, 'foodheated faces, sweating helmets' [162]). The episode is mainly concerned with food, drink, hunger, thirst. In the course of Bloom's walk from O'Connell Street to Duke Street all occasions conspire to concentrate on and to multiply lists of culinary items. Some examples of these are given here to warn the reader that he may expect to be fed up: girl selling scoopfuls of cream to a christian brother for a school treat; 'warm sweet fumes of Graham Lemon's' (lozenges and comfit manufacturer) (150); Y.M.C.A. young man distributing 'Blood of the Lamb' throwaways; memory of Molly's craving for Malaga raisins; Stephen's sister, Dilly, waiting outside the auction rooms, underfed, potatoes and marge (151); won't get much from the clergy who tell the people to increase and multiply. 'Bring your own bread and butter'—i.e.

> Bring your own bread and butter
> Bring your own tea and sugar,
> But you'll come to the wedding, won't you come?

(Cf. *FW* 24: 'Have you whines for my wedding, did you bring bride and bedding' etc.)

Smoke from a brewery barge with export stout, 'Rats get in too. Drink till they puke again like christians.'

The *Elijah* 'Blood of the Lamb' throwaway Bloom flung to the seagulls. No bid. No symbolism either, on Bloom's part—its course downstream is marked at intervals with the aid of a stopwatch by the author, Mr Joyce, to assist the observation of co-existing time-space phenomena. Bloom expended a penny on two Banbury cakes for the gulls which pounced on their prey like the Lestrygonians on the Homeric mariners. He crosses O'Connell bridge and in a short intermission from eatables he meditates about the Liffey. 'It's always flowing in a stream, never the same, which in the stream of life we trace. Because life is a stream.' (153) The original lines from which Bloom's quotation is reconstructed are in the ballad 'In Happy Moments Day by Day' in the opera *Maritana*:

> Some thoughts none other can replace
> Remembrance will recall
> Which in the flight of years we trace
> Is dearer than them all.

This is scarcely a misquote that can be attributed to Bloom. 'Stream of life' seems to have been a carefully considered substitute for 'flight of years', with its reversed assonance. This, with the next thought, 'Because life is a stream,' seems to be a subconscious intimation that in another decade *Abha Life*, the river Liffey, would be the central character in another volume, under the name of Anna Livia Plurabelle.

But back to our muttons: 'Remember when we got home raking up the fire and frying up those pieces of lap of mutton for her supper with the Chutney sauce she liked. And the mulled rum,' (Capital C for Chutney, lower case for christian.)

Remembrance won't recall any more for the moment. Here is Mrs Breen to tell him of her mad husband, 'a caution to rattlesnakes', who has had a bad turn with the new moon and wakened her up in the night to tell her that the ace of spades was walking up the stairs. This morning he got a postcard bearing the inscription 'U. P.: up' (157). 'And now he's going round to Mr Menton's office to take an action for ten thousand pounds, he says.'

Mr Bloom, who has been inhaling the noonreek of hot mock-turtle vapour from Harrison's in Westmoreland Street, bids her 'watch him' as another lunatic passes, staring through a heavy stringed glass. 'From his arm a folded dustcoat, a stick and an umbrella dangled to his stride . . . His name is Cashel Boyle O'Connor Fitzmaurice Tisdall Farrell,' Bloom tells her, but Mrs Breen should herself have recognised this familiar apparition known to everybody as 'Endymion'. Bloom passes on, having learnt that (158) Mrs Purefoy is now three days in Holles Street hospital, her baby not yet born. The news will lead to a shift of scene later in the day.

'He crossed under Tommy Moore's roguish finger. They did right to put him up over a urinal: meeting of the waters' (162). 'Joyce', said Jim Tully, 'has that book of his crammed with stale chestnuts we fell out of our cradles laughing at before he ever saw the light.'

'Michaelmas goose . . . good lump of thyme seasoning . . . Pyramids in sand. Built on bread and onions. Slaves. Chinese wall. Babylon . . . Provost's house. The reverend Dr. Salmon: tinned salmon. Well tinned in there.' Some of this reverie seems intended to be associated with the 'Art' (Architecture) designated for the episode, but its inclusion with the liberal stuffing provided for the organ (Esophagus) seems artistically maladjusted. It is, however, relevant where related to malnutrition and slavery or, as expressed in *FW* 71, 'faminebuilt walls'.

The stream of thought is interrupted by the sight of John Howard Parnell: 'Look at the woebegone walk of him. Eaten a bad egg. Poached eyes on ghost'. Bloom surmises that the dead Chief's brother will drop into the D.B.C. for his coffee and play chess there, because Joyce had often seen him there, while he waited for him and John F. Byrne to finish their game of chess. All the Parnells, Bloom muses, were 'a bit touched. Mad Fanny and his other sister Mrs Dickinson driving about with scarlet harness. Bolt upright like surgeon M'Ardle' (165).

The simile in the last sentence does not refer to surgeon M'Ardle's posture in a carriage. He was, Jim Tully said, 'a damn good surgeon but a notorious womanizer. Made buckets of money but lost a lot in the crim. con. actions the husbands brought against him. What he made with his knife he lost with his fork. "Did you sleep with the lady?" "Not a wink." '

The lady was a Mrs Bishop who, when retiring, obliged M'Ardle by leaving her bedroom blind undrawn to enable him to exercise episcopal functions with his binoculars from Merrion Square south to Merrion Square north, the poles of their respective residences.

George Russell (AE) passed with a listening woman. 'That

might be Lizzie Twigg' who might in reality be Susan Mitchell (165). 'Coming from the vegetarian . . . Don't eat a beefsteak. If you do the eyes of that cow will pursue you through all eternity.'

Bloom looks in at the Burton (The Bailey): 'men . . . swilling, wolfing gobfuls of sloppy food' . . . 'Table talk. I munched hum un thu Unchester Bunk un Munchday. Ha? Did you, faith?' (169)

Still thinking of food and communal kitchens of the future, he makes his way to Davy Byrne's where he has a glass of burgundy and a Gorgonzola cheese sandwich (171).

Davy Byrne is asked for a tip for the Gold Cup race.

—I wouldn't do anything at all in that line, Davy Byrne said, and, leaning heavily on an Anglo-Irish idiom, 'It ruined many a man the same horses.' (173) This famous sentence with the comma carefully omitted after the word 'man' and the subject noun placed at the end is based on an Irish grammatical construction which would be more accurately rendered: 'It's many a man they ruined the same horses.'

Bloom left Davy Byrne's and reached the gate of the National Museum just in time to miss Blazes Boylan for the second time. 'Straw hat in sunlight. Tan shoes. Turnedup trousers. It is. It is.'

Joyce's imagination, when not preoccupied with ladies' lingerie, tended towards delectable visions of food. The account of the dinner party in Ushers Island ('The Dead' in *Dubliners*) proceeds from 'a fat brown goose', 'a great ham . . . peppered over with crust crumbs' and 'a round of spiced beef' to 'jelly, red and yellow', 'blancmange and red jam', 'bunches of purple raisins and peeled almonds', Smyrna figs, 'custard topped with grated nutmeg, chocolates, sweets, celery stalks, oranges and American apples,' delicacies here somewhat deflavoured by my omission of the adjectival adornments in which they are lovingly dressed in the original. Elaborate as the description is, it amounts, in effect, merely to an itemised menu: as early as 1907 Joyce had fixed on this 'listing' process as an easy means of 'filling in', a technique which was later to dominate the structure of his major works (Cf. *FW* 405-7).

On the want of food Joyce could be equally eloquent. To his mother he wrote from Paris in March 1903, a month before he received a telegram 'mother dying come home father': 'my next meal . . . will be at 11 a.m. tomorrow (Monday): my last meal was 7 p.m. last (Saturday) night. . . . Two meals in sixty hours is not bad, I think. As my lenten regulations have made me somewhat weak I shall go up to my room and sit there till it is time to go to bed.'

In Rome in 1906, Joyce feasted and fasted alternately, 'blowing' the money when it was received and then badgering Stanislaus in Trieste for supplementary subsidies. 'I have eaten nothing today except a soup to economise.' Then the feast: 'Here is the full and exact list of what we ate yesterday:

10.30 a.m.	Ham, bread and butter, coffee.
1.30 p.m.	Soup, roast lamb and potatoes, bread and wine.
4.00 p.m.	Beef-stew, bread and wine.
6.00 p.m.	Roast veal, bread, gorgonzola cheese and wine.
8.30 p.m.	Roast veal, bread and grapes and vermouth.
9.30 p.m.	Veal cutlets, bread, salad, grapes and wine.'

Joyce passes on his own and Nora's gluttony to Molly Bloom: 'I wished I could have picked every morsel of that chicken out of my fingers it was so tasty and browned and as tender as anything only for I didn't want to eat everything on my plate.' (671)

The predilection of Joyce and his menage for expensive food became noteworthy, once his financial prospects improved with the publication of *Ulysses*. On 9 March 1922, Ernest Hemingway wrote to Sherwood Anderson:

Joyce has a most goddamn wonderful book. It'll probably reach you in time. Meantime the report is that he and all his family are starving but you can find the whole celtic crew of them every night in Michaud's where Binney and I can only afford to go about once a week. . . . The damned Irish, they have to moan about something or other, but you never heard of an Irishman starving.

If Hemingway had read Joyce's 'goddamn wonderful book' with attention he could have observed that the Citizen (328) told how 'the Sassenach tried to starve the nation at home while the land was full of crops that the British hyenas bought and sold in Rio de Janeiro. Ay, they drove out the peasants in hordes. Twenty thousand of them died in the coffinships.'

Even in contemporary Ireland families could also be left starving. While Dilly Dedalus waited outside the auction-rooms, her sister Katey, home from a futile visit to the pawn-shop, went to the range and peered with squinting eyes.

> —What's in the pot? she asked.
> —Shirts, Maggy said.
> Boody cried angrily :
> —Crickey, is there nothing for us to eat?
> Katey, lifting the kettlelid in a pad of her stained skirt, asked :
> —And what's in this?
> A heavy fume gushed in answer.
> —Peasoup, Maggy said.
> —Where did you get it? Katey asked.
> —Sister Mary Patrick, Maggy said. (225-6)

Here the Dedalus family exhibit frustration and rage at their lot whereas a few years earlier, in *A Portrait*, Stephen depicts sympathetically their quiet resignation and retreat into the consolation of music :

> . . . only the last of the second watered tea remained in the bottoms of the small glassjars and jampots which did service for teacups. Discarded crusts and lumps of sugared bread turned brown by the tea which had been poured over them lay scattered on the table.
> . . . began to sing the air *Oft in the Stilly Night*. . . . They would sing so for hours, melody after melody, glee after glee, till the last pale light died down on the horizon, till the first dark nightclouds came forth and night fell. . . . He was listening with pain of spirit to the overtone of weariness behind their frail fresh innocent voices.

Chapter 10

Iago Joyce

HERE the 'Art' is 'Literature' and the organ is 'Brain', so that one might look forward to another 'very fine piece of writing' and also some high thinking. But first 'composition of place', as St Ignatius Loyola enjoins. Joyce has Stephen early on (188) make his composition of time and place for Shakespeare, 'this hour of a day in mid-June . . . The flag is up on the playhouse by the bankside'. We must make the composition of time and place for Joyce in his writing of the episode.

It is the drear December of 1918, with social unrest in Zurich following on revolution in Germany, aftermath of the war just concluded. The great influenza epidemic is only now beginning to subside. Joyce is emotionally disturbed by the tantalising glimpses he has had from the back window of his apartment of his Dark Lady through a small back window of an apartment in a street abutting on Universitatstrasse. His mind is also on Shakespeare who was spurned by his Dark Lady (202). He writes in *Bahnhofstrasse*:

> *Ah star of evil! star of pain!*
> *Highhearted youth comes not again.*

On his interpretation of Hamlet he adjures his surrogate: 'Local colour. Work in all you know.'

All Joyce knows has been long agathering. He has read, and is working in for all they are worth, Brandes's *William Shakespeare: A Critical Study; The Man Shakespeare and his Tragic Life-Story* by Frank Harris and Lee's *A Life of William Shakespeare*. He breaks the Unity of Time to have John Eglinton quote Herr Bleibtreu's ascription of Shakespeare's plays to the Earl of Rutland (213-14) although this was not published until 1907. Judge Barton (198) and Professor

Dowden (204), both of Dublin, are invoked, as is quondam Dubliner, G.B.S. (196). We do not know how many of these writers and how much of their material were used by Joyce in his 1913 lectures on *Hamlet* in Trieste but the fact is that Stephen's allocution on the subject, purporting to be delivered impromptu in the National Library in 1904, was being mulled over by Joyce before and in 1913 and afterwards up till it was written as part of *Ulysses* in 1918 with the scene set in another (this time a fictitious) composition of time and place; it is a time between two and three o'clock of an afternoon in mid-June, 1904. The place is the director's office in the National Library, a room behind the public counter with complete privacy from the common readers in the Reading Room outside. Inside are Dr T. W. Lyster, director of the Library, and his assistants, Dr Richard A. Best (distinguished Celtic scholar and, sub-sequently, Lyster's next successor but one as director), W. K. Magee (who wrote literary essays under the name 'John Eglinton') and Stephen and another visitor, George Russell (AE). Lyster is urbanely interested in young Stephen's thesis, Magee is argumentative in favour of Plato as against Socrates, Best supplies Stephen with pabulum from Mallarmé and crumbs of polite exegetic encouragement, but he also agrees tacitly with Russell who tush-tushes Stephen's Hamlet-Shakespeare reconstruction. Russell must be laid low, in common with his colleagues in the Dublin Lodge of the Theosophical Society with their bibles, *Isis Unveiled*, by Madame H. P. Blavatsky, and A. P. Sinnett's *Esoteric Buddhism*. This is no trouble to young Stephen, aged twenty-two, who, like James Branch Cabell's Jurgen, is endowed with the mature mind of his thirty-seven-year-old begetter and the secondhand material on Shakespeare and Elizabethan London which he had filched from other writers. Stephen evades the whirlpool of Russell's platonic mysticism by meditating but not speaking in criticism of Blake's followers and of their creeds. His 'dagger definitions' are mere daggers of the mind. But in a few years Joyce will not hesitate to adopt these discredited oriental theosophies as a scaffolding for *Finnegans Wake*. Meanwhile he feels free to use Shakespearean language to decry his taste for an overloaded stage of corpses. Twisting the reference in *Hamlet* to 'sledded Polacks on the ice', he has Stephen say that 'not for nothing was he (Shakespeare) a butcher's son wielding the sledded poleaxe'. Joyce knew quite well that the reference was to Polish soldiers ice-borne on sleds or sleighs, but he could not resist the temptation to sneer at Shakespeare's origins and to inject another problem passage into his own text.

The interpretation of *Hamlet* which Stephen essays to prove is that Shakespeare, by taking the part of the ghost in his play, is 'speaking his words to his own son's name (had Hamnet Shakespeare lived he would have been Prince Hamlet's twin) : . . . I am the murdered father : your mother is the guilty queen, Ann Shakespeare, born Hathaway'.

Into the effort at this demonstration we need not enter. What is interesting is the revelation of Joyce's firm conviction that what Shakespeare wrote was based on his own personal experience, that he is the youth seduced by an older woman (goddess) in *Venus and Adonis*, that the villains in his historical plays who bear the names of his brothers are chosen for the very reason that 'the theme of the false or the usurping or the adulterous brother or all three in one is to Shakespeare, what the poor is not, always with him'. This is an indirect revelation of the solipsistic mind of James Joyce himself. Best has quoted, in support of Stephen, Mallarmé's poem about Hamlet : '*il se promène, lisant au livre de lui-même.*' Of Ann Hathaway John Eglinton remarked (190) :

—The world believes that Shakespeare made a mistake and got out of it as quickly and as best as he could.

—Bosh! Stephen said rudely, A man of genius makes no mistakes. His errors are volitional and are the portals of discovery . . .

—A shrew, John Eglinton said shrewdly, is not a useful portal of discovery . . .

On 12 July 1905, and before the birth of their son, Joyce wrote to his brother Stannie about Nora's illness and unhappiness in Trieste : 'One of the English teachers said that she was not worthy of me and I am sure this would be many people's verdict but it requires such a hell of a lot of self-stultification to enter into the mood which produces such a verdict that I am afraid I am not equal to the task.' (*Letters*, II) Here we have the obverse of the coin bearing the image and inscription of the egoistic artist whose errors are all volitional: to accept any other verdict would be 'self-stultification'.

Under the guise of its relevancy to a point in his discussion of the Shakespearean plays, Joyce has Stephen pontificate emphatically on the essential subjectivity of the artist (196): 'His own image to a man with that queer thing genius is the standard of all experience, material and moral.' In other words the artist is, like God, an *aseitas*, existing out of himself and this is the theme that informed Joyce's social and moral ethos as well as his artistic conscience.

The same, presumably, applies to the personalities created by a man of genius, a father, and a son consubstantial with him, between whom 'a certain analogy there somehow was, as if both their minds were travelling, so to speak, in the one train of thought' (577). Stephen muses about Shakespeare's exile from Stratford in London (202): 'In a rosery of Fetter Lane of Gerard, herbalist, he walks, greyedauburn.'

Later in the day, between four and five o'clock in the *Sirens* episode, Bloom, having addressed an envelope to Martha Clifford, says to himself:

'Music hath charms Shakespeare said. . . . To be or not to be.' Shakespeare did not in fact say that about music but Stephen's image of him percolates to Bloom by some process of delayed telepathy in the next paragraph which runs in part: 'In Gerard's rosery of Fetter lane he walks, greyedauburn.' (279)

There seems to be no rational explanation of this echo of Stephen's thought being interpolated into Bloom's meditation, except of course on the intervention of the writer, which some commentators would consider to be an absurd supposition. Such a convergence and merger of characters and their thoughts are usually reserved for *Circe* where no rationale is required.

There follows (207) Stephen's speech on fatherhood and the incertitude of paternity, in which he apparently dismisses the madonna as part of a possible trinity. This would seem to rule out a trinity in *Ulysses* consisting of Bloom, Stephen and Molly, as some writers have suggested. Molly's birthday is 8 September, the same as that of the Virgin Mary and not that of Nora Barnacle, which was said to be 25 March, the day of the Annunciation, but in fact was 28 March 1884.

Judge Eglinton summed up.

—The truth is midway, he affirmed. He is the ghost and the prince. He is all in all.

—He is, Stephen said [thereby abandoning his thesis]. The boy of act one is the mature man of act five. All in all. In *Cymbeline*, in *Othello* he is bawd and cuckold. He acts and is acted on. Lover of an ideal or perversion, like José he kills the real Carmen. His unremitting intellect is the hornmad Iago ceaselessly willing that the moor in him shall suffer. (212)

This, in the context of the preceding generalisations about 'the artist', means that Joyce, writing the book of himself, is Iago whose 'unremitting intellect' wills that the Bloom in him shall suffer or, to put it more accurately than is expressed in Joyce's oblique words, he is Iago whose unremitting masochism obliges his intellect to will that the Bloom in him shall suffer. The weapon with which Iago Joyce metes out his sadistic punishment to his masochistic self, Bloom, is Blazes Boylan, another extension of Joyce's personality. His name approximates in assonance more closely to 'James Joyce' than does either of the fictitious names in which he presents himself in 'The Dead' (Gabriel Conroy) and in *Exiles* (Richard Rowan). It shares with the latter the alliteration of the initials as in Joyce's own name. In giving 'Hugh' as Boylan's real name, Joyce is probably telling himself that it is 'You', that is, himself subjected to what he calls (594) 'the phenomenon of ebullition'.

In a contemptuous reference to the Theosophical Trinity, Stephen quotes its three names, 'Formless Spiritual Father, Word and Holy Breath'. (185) In *Ulysses* these would be represented by Bloom (Father), Stephen (Logos) and Boylan (Holy Breath). Bloom (71) has recalled Molly's remarking of Boylan : 'I noticed he had a good smell off his breath dancing.' This remark was obviously recollected for a purpose.

Joyce would not in 1918 be averse to his being identified with him whom Bloom stigmatised as 'the worst man in Dublin'. In Zurich at that time he himself was called 'Herr Satan'. If his relations with Marthe Fleischmann did not go beyond the Platonic stage, the flesh was willing but the will was weak. His intentions, at least, were bad, but he was nervous and cautious. Bloom was in his personality as well as Boylan. For Joyce, as well as for his creation, Bloom, Boylan is the 'assumed dongiovannism' which Joyce attributes to Shakespeare (196).

Photographs of Joyce in 1918-19 show him more or less as he pictures Boylan, 'a young gentleman stylishly dressed in an indigoblue serge suit . . . and wearing a straw hat very dressy' (278), although nowadays we should not expect that outfit to end up in 'smart tan shoes' (263). We do not have to look for an act of adultery on Joyce's part to parallel Boylan's affair with Molly Bloom. This, as reflected in her soliloquy in 'Penelope' and as projected in Bloom's hallucinatory phantasmagoria in 'Circe', is in keeping with what is known of the sex relationships between Joyce and Nora in the early years of their cohabitation. These are revealed to some extent in the letters which he wrote to her during his two visits to Dublin in 1909, some of which are published in *Letters II*, but those of them with evidence of perverted marital practices are still withheld from publication in Cornell. At times he thinks of her poetically, spiritually—'Her soul! Her name! Her eyes! They seem to me like strange beautiful blue flowers growing in some tangled, rain-drenched hedge. And I have felt her soul tremble beside mine, and have spoken her name softly to the night, and have wept to see the beauty of the world passing like a dream behind her eyes.' This was written on 19 November 1909, putting her in the third person when he was uncertain of her response. He repeats the sentiment on 2 December and adds: '*But*, side by side and inside this spiritual love I have for you there is also a wild beast-like craving for every inch of your body, for every secret and shameful part of it, for every odour and act of it'. Another time he feels helpless and needs her maternal succour. 'Shelter me, dear, from harm! I am too childish and impulsive to live alone'. The sex act he called 'a brief madness' . . . 'I know I lose my reason for the time it lasts'.

The correspondence discloses Joyce both as a satyr qualified to act the part of Boylan and also fit to double for the uxorious, henpecked Bloom.

In 'Circe' (508), Bloom immediately after witnessing ('his eyes wildly dilated') Molly and Boylan *in flagrante delicto*, 'Stephen and Bloom gaze in the mirror'. The stage direction runs : *The face of William Shakespeare, beardless, appears there, rigid in facial paralysis crowned by the reflection of the reindeer antlered hatrack in the hall.* Shakespeare speaks *in dignified ventriloquy.* 'Iagogogo.' The beardless Shakespeare here is Bloom and Stephen with Shakespeare's Iago borrowed to act the part of Boylan and thus complete the Trinity. Joyce himself is the 'all in all'. Frank Harris's book *Shakespeare the Man* purported to find evidences of Shakespeare's personality in the characters of Romeo, Macbeth and, more particularly, Hamlet but they all added up to something more like Harris than Shakespeare. Joyce, who had read Harris, achieves a more complex epiphany by projecting his own three personae in a composite picture on the melted down imago of Shakespeare.

Ten years after the 1909 correspondence, about the time when Joyce was writing this episode ('Scylla and Charybdis'), Nora tearfully confided to Frank Budgen (*Myselves when Young*) that Jim wanted her to 'go with other men so that he would have something to write about'.

In between these dates Joyce constructed that enigmatic triangle, *Exiles,* on the complex psychological and sexual relations between two friends and the wife of one of them. The themes are friendship, love and loyalty or infidelity, but the husband is responsible for his wife's infidelity, if any infidelity occurred. The incertitude on which the play ends feeds the masochistic preoccupations of the husband, Richard Rowan. *Exiles* is thus a stepping stone between Joyce's monogamy and his mental and literary experiments in other relationships. In his later years he had lost both his physical and metaphysical interests in such things : mention of 'love' left him inclined to vomit.

In Saint-Gerard-le-Puy in 1940, while the Joyces awaited permission to remove to Switzerland, they went to tea with another refugee, Mrs Elliott, to whom Nora said, 'There sits a a man who has not spoken one word to me all day.' 'What is there to talk about when you have been married thirty years?' was Joyce's comment. 'You can at least say "Good morning",' Mrs Elliott suggested, to which his only reply was a grunt.

Chapter 11

The Cyclops

PROFESSOR Levin, in his *James Joyce*, says tautologically that Joyce's 'ubiquitous ear is everywhere, and his mimicry is everybody. He is a hard-bitten hanger-on at Barney Kiernan's, gossiping of Bloom's discomfiture. He is a sentimental lady novelist, gushing over Gerty MacDowell.' While it is conceded that, by and large, Levin is correct (his thesis here is part of the present writer's understanding of the book), the first example he offers must be rejected: the 'hard-bitten hanger-on', as has been shown earlier, is Simon Dedalus hanging on anonymously as 'Noman', waiting, as he says the citizen was waiting, 'for what the sky would drop in the way of a drink'. And Simon Dedalus and his narrative in this episode are merely an edited version of one of Jack Joyce's maudlin accounts of his adventures and observations retailed on his return home, which his son James encouraged and his younger son, Stanislaus, as far as possible avoided. The writers who regard the 'I' of this episode as an impersonal mouthpiece for the author ('The anonymity . . . imposes a kind of featurelessness on the language—lively and picturesque enough, but unindividual and uninventive'— *Joysprick*, Anthony Burgess) are wide of the mark. Once the narrator is recognised as Jack Joyce his personality can be at once identified with that of Simon Dedalus in *A Portrait* and in 'Hades', 'Aeolus', 'The Wandering Rocks', 'Sirens', and here in 'The Cyclops'—where, however, he exhibits a new dimension. He lives up fully to the description of him given by C. P. Curran in *James Joyce Remembered*:

He was a man of unparalleled vituperative power, a virtuoso in speech with unique control of the vernacular, his language often coarse and blasphemous to a degree of which, in the

long run, he could hardly himself have been conscious. . . .
A notable singer with a wide knowledge of Italian opera . . .
[his] stories would be of a perfectly drawing-room character
till suddenly, as if taken unawares, he would slip into the
coarse vein and another side of his nature and vocabulary
would be revealed.

This account is perfectly in keeping with the different aspects
of the personality of Simon Dedalus successively revealed in
the cab and in the cemetery in 'Hades', in the newspaper audience dismissing 'Doughy Daw's' fustian with a smelly execra-
tion, in dealing with his daughter Dilly at the auctioneering
rooms where he has procured five shillings for the household
curtains of which he gives her one shilling and two pence, and
in his 'rendition' (as Kernan would call it) of 'Martha' in the
Ormond Hotel. In Barney Kiernan's, the other side of his nature
and vocabulary is revealed with the sanguinary adjective in
evidence to such an extent that it alone should identify the Jack
Joyce known to Dublin people in the streets and pubs from
1880 to 1930 and familiar in Dublin folklore for the last forty
years.

So of course Bob Doran starts doing the bloody fool with
him :
—Give us the paw! the paw, doggy!
Arrah! bloody end to the paw he'd paw and Alf trying
to keep him from tumbling off the bloody stool atop of the
bloody old dog . . .
And the citizen and Bloom having an argument about the
point, the brothers Sheares and Wolfe Tone beyond on
Arbour Hill and Robert Emmet and die for your country,
the Tommy Moore touch about Sara Curran and she's far
from the land. And Bloom, of course, with his knockmedown
cigar putting on swank with his lardy face. Phenomenon!
The fat heap he married is a nice old phenomenon with a
back on her like a ballalley. (303-4)

The foregoing is a mild version of the language of Jack
Joyce of whom his son wrote on 17 January 1932, a few weeks
after his death :

I was very fond of him always, being a sinner myself, and even liked his faults; Hundreds of pages and scores of characters in my books came from him. His dry (or rather wet) wit and his expression of face convulsed me often with laughter. When he got the copy of *Tales Told* etc (so they write me) he looked a long time at Brancusi's Portrait of [me] (a cartoon in the form of a spiral convolution) and finally remarked: Jim has changed more than I thought.

The execution scene (304-8) is a comically heartless extravaganza in which an old score is paid off, reducing Rumbold from the status of British ambassador to that of the public hangman. Still more improbably the British officer in charge is given a 'limey' accent. Of everything in the 'Cyclops' narrative that is not taken from Jack Joyce, Joyce *fils* is the onelie begetter. Professor Ellmann would have us believe that there is another unintroduced contributor, Dr Pangloss, who is responsible for the high falutin parody and pastiche interpolations and the almost interminable lists. He is followed in this by Mr Anthony Burgess (*Joysprick*) already quoted as believing that these techniques involved the elimination of the artist as bespoken in *A Portrait*.

Taking the first of these lists, the images of Irish heroes and heroines engraven on the seastones hanging from the hero's girdle (295): these include Brian of Kincora, the Ardri Malachi and Art MacMurragh, all of whom are featured in *Finnegans Wake*; Soggarth Eoghan O'Growney whose *Simple Lessons in Irish* was Joyce's textbook at college; Dante Alighieri whose works Joyce used and quoted all his mature life; Patrick W. Shakespeare from 'Scylla and Charybdis' where it is pointed out that Hamlet swore by St Patrick; Dick Turpin, the ballad on whom suggested the title, *Sephen Hero*; the Colleen Bawn from the play of that name by Dion Boucicault and also the title of a song from *The Lily of Killarney* with both of which Joyce was preoccupied in his work; and others of greater significance in his writing which need no annotation: Dark Rosaleen (Mangan), Tristan and Isolde and Marshall MacMahon, whose part in *Finnegans Wake* will be dealt with in *Bruinoboroff*, below.

Another 'list' (330) adorns the handkerchief which the citizen

D

takes out to swab himself dry, having 'spat a Red bank oyster out of him right in the corner'. This is the facecloth 'attributed to Solomon of Droma and Manus Tomaltach og MacDonogh, authors of the Book of Ballymote', in the cornerpieces of which 'one can distinctly discern each of the four evangelists in turn presenting to each of the four masters his evangelical symbol, a bogoak sceptre, a North American puma (a far nobler king of beasts than the British article, be it said in passing), a Kerry calf and a golden eagle from Carrantuohill.' These are Joyce's versions of the symbols of the four Evangelists, viz. Matthew, an angel or winged man carrying a lance; Mark, a lion (often winged); Luke, an ox (often winged); John, a flying eagle. They are no parody or pastiche; it is Joyce's own material from the Book of Kells which became an integral part of the structure and symbolism in *FW*, where, however, evangelists and masters are, like everything else, inextricably intermingled, with the four provinces, four winds and four waves of Ireland also mixed in for good measure.

The fact is that Joyce is not alone responsible for the set pieces, parodies and juvenile mockery (such as the presentation of a delegation of cotton magnates 'to His Majesty the Alaki of Abeakuta by Gold Stick in Waiting, Lord Walkup on Eggs'), but he also interferes with the virile, racy vernacular of the customers, as purveyed by his father or by Michael Cusack.

—And our eyes are on Europe, says the citizen. We had our trade with Spain and the French and with the Flemings before those mongrels were pupped, Spanish ale in Galway, the winebark on the winedark waterway. (326)

This could well represent the genuine forthright utterance of the citizen, Michael Cusack, propagandist for Gaelic athletics and Ireland's glorious past—all except the last clause which is an obvious purple patch added by the editor, Joyce *fils*, from his fund of Homeric clichés and which Cusack was incapable of concocting in his own vernacular. Joyce was, in fact, so pleased with the phrase that he echoed it in a description of H.C.E., 'the megalomagellan of our Winevatswaterway' (*FW* 512).

The citizen passes from Irish ships of old to current training practices in the British Navy at Portsmouth—'the crew of tars

and officers and rearadmirals drawn up in cocked hats and the
parson with his protestant bible to witness punishment and a
young lad brought out, howling for his ma, and they tie him
down on the buttend of a gun', a practice called

> caning on the breech.
> And says John Wyse:
> —'Tis a custom more honoured in the breach than in the
> observance. (327)

Joyce had obtained details of this practice from Frank Budgen
in Zurich. Budgen had explained that the punishment was
administered with the youth's feet strapped to the gun carriage
with his arms pulled forward 'so that he half bestrode the
breech of the gun and presented a taut backside to the cane'
(*Myselves when Young*). Budgen's description is not adequately
reproduced in the text where the version given is ascribed to
'Disgusted One' who had sent his revelations to the newspaper.
The citizen is introduced when Joe Hynes and 'I' enter Barney
Kiernan's (293):

> —There he is, says I, in his gloryhole, with his cruiskeen
> lawn and his load of papers, working for the cause.

These are the papers which the structure of the episode
provides as cues for introducing a subject and for changing to
an alternative topic. (Alf Bergan is also available to initiate
the conversation about hanging by handing round letters from
hangmen offering the High Sheriff their services *in the above-
mentioned painful case*.)
The 'skit' on the visit of the Zulu chief (332) is inaccurately
referred to the *United Irishman*. It is introduced by the citizen
with reference to the newspapers which he is supposed to have
before him, but which are really based on Joyce's press extracts.
J. J. O'Molloy gives the citizen the opportunity of introducing a name unknown to the generality of Irish for a decade after
1904:

> —. . . Did you read that report by a man what's this his
> name is?
> —Casement, says the citizen. He's an Irishman.

Again Martin Cunningham, with his simple toast, 'God bless

all here is my prayer' (336) has his prayer answered in over
two pages of lists of 'mitred abbots and priors and guardians
and monks and priors' with their 'acolytes, thurifers, boat-
bearers, readers, ostiarii, deacons and subdeacons,' all assembled
to bless Barney Kiernan's.

Reverting to the Citizen's insanitary expectoration (330)
when 'he spat a Red Bank oyster out of him right in the corner',
this was his wordless commentary on Bloom's claim that Ireland
was his nation, that he was born here, in Ireland. The Citizen's
handkerchief, as has been shown, proceeds to exhibit symbols
of the historic Irish past of which Bloom, despite his claim to
Irish nationality, might be presumed to be ignorant. The spit
was in itself pantomimic commentary in this context. The
Citizen, Michael Cusack, was born at Poulaphouca in the
parish of Carron in the stony district of county Clare called
The Burren which abuts on the Atlantic Ocean on the southern
shore of Galway Bay. Bernard Shaw sets the scene of Part IV
of *Back to Methuselah*, 'The Tragedy of an Elderly Gentleman', at this place: 'Burrin [sic] pier on the south slope of
Galway Bay in Ireland, a region of stone-capped hills and
granite fields'. Here, less than ten miles from Cusack's birthplace, about a mile from New Quay which Shaw calls Burrin pier,
in an inlet named Carranroo Bay, was the oysterbed then owned
by the proprietors of the Red Bank restaurant in D'Olier Street,
Dublin, 'red bank' being their English translation of the Irish
'Carranroo' which they used both for the name of their establishment and its oysters.

Joyce's friendship with George Clancy ('Maurice Davin' of
the *Portrait*) gave him the opportunity of meeting the Citizen
and learning of his origins and the origin of Red Bank oysters
'in the Baronry of Burren in the County of Clare' as Cusack
was accustomed to declaim. No doubt he also heard Cusack
frequently call down the curse of the good God on the Sassenach
but one may quite confidently credit the Artist and not the
Citizen with the pejorative revision of the epithet 'good' to
'goodfornothing' (323).

Chapter 12

The Encyclopaedist

WHEN Joyce wrote to Carlo Linati on 21 September 1920, sending him a *schema* of *Ulysses*, he gave him also an outline of his epic concluding, 'It is also a sort of encyclopaedia.' He was still adding to the text a year afterwards. On 3 September 1921, he told Robert McAlmon : 'I have now written in a great lot of balderdash all over the damn book.' This was in keeping with Crawford's advice, 'Put us all into it, damn its soul. Father Son and Holy Ghost and Jakes M'Carthy.' (136)

Some of the 'balderdash' has already been touched on in the 'Cyclops' chapter : the list of Irish heroes and heroines of antiquity (295), the execution scene (304-9), the embroidered cornerpieces on the citizen's handkerchief and 'the scenes depicted on the emunctory field' (330), and the ecclesiastical response to the call for a blessing on Barney Kiernan's premises with its lists of saints and martyrs, virgins and confessors who joined the local clergy in praying for the benediction.

The 'Oxen of the Sun' episode with its pastiche of successive English literary styles over nine centuries has had interpolated in it two pages (397-8) on 'An Irish bull in an English china-shop' which treats with vulgar and juvenile extravagance of Pope Adrian's Bull *Laudabiliter* and the Lord Harry (Henry II) who in the course of the essay becomes Henry VIII. It will be shown in Part II, Chapter 19, 'Popes and Paschs', how this theme is treated in a much more scholarly—if denser—manner in *FW*. In the same episode the sight of a red triangle on the label of a bottle of Bass gives Bloom a vision of Agendath Netaim about which he had read that morning but which has now become the haunt of a zodiacal multitude of ghostly beasts, elk and yak, the bulls of Bashan and Babylon, mammoth and mastodon, all trooping to the Dead Sea, while over them blazes Alpha, a ruby and triangled sign upon the forehead of Taurus

(411). Bloom, of course, was incapable of conjuring up those cosmic scenes or of finding language to give them expression, although it is his correspondent or his daughter, 'Martha thou lost one, Millicent, the young, the dear, the radiant' (or one or other of them) who appears 'coifed with a veil of what do you call it gossamer' which creates the symbol of Alpha. Joyce has, in fact, borrowed Bloom to become the medium of another 'fine piece of writing'.

When charges are coming fast against him in *Circe* (452), Bloom mutters some exculpatory expressions about 'Girl in the monkeyhouse'—this is delved up from Joyce's notes about the arrest in November 1906 of Caruso, the Italian tenor, for indecent behaviour towards a young lady in the New York Zoo.

The illiterate Irish phrase, *sgenl inn ban bata coisde gan capall* in the Circe episode (464), has been the subject of several interpretations and the wording was correctly revised by Vivian Mercier for Weldon Thornton (*Allusions in 'Ulysses'*), as *sgéul i mbarr bata, cóiste gan capall*, but without interpreting its real import. There are two items in the phrase, here divided by a comma. The first, 'news on top of a pole', refers to the electric telegraph; the second 'a coach without a horse' connotes an automobile. Both are, and have been for more than a century, ascribed to Irish saints, vaticinators or other prognosticators, who lived centuries before telegraphy, steam or electrical traction or internal combustion engines were invented, but who were held to have had the power to dip into the future and see the wonders that would be.

Like 'take off that white hat' in *Finnegans Wake*, Parnell's silk hat is one of Bloom's recurrent memories in 'Eumaeus': 'He saw him once on the auspicious occasion when they broke up the type in the *Insuppressible* or was it *United Ireland*, a privilege he keenly appreciated, and, in point of fact, handed him his silk hat when it was knocked off and he said *Thank you*' (570). This recollection is repeated at twice the length in the passage (575) beginning 'His hat (Parnell's) was inadvertently knocked off and, as a matter of strict history, Bloom was the man who picked it up . . .' and this time he is rewarded with 'Thank you, sir'.

This is one of Joyce's apocrypha: Parnell's hat could not have been restored by Bloom in the street because he was in the office of the *United Ireland* paper at the time and it had been knocked off inside. Parnell had dismissed the editor, Matthew McDonnell Bodkin, who on William O'Brien's cabled instructions, had brought the paper over to the side of the anti-Parnellites. Bodkin refused to accept dismissal from Parnell who ordered that Mr John Clancy, the sub-sheriff, be called. Clancy who was a Parnellite partisan arrived with an excited mob and threatened to throw Bodkin downstairs. Bodkin accepted the inevitable and left. Sub-sheriff John Clancy of this incident is 'Long John Fanning' in *Ulysses* (*Recollections of an Irish Judge* by M. McDonnell Bodkin and *Life of Charles Stewart Parnell* by R. Barry O'Brien, Chapter XXIV).

In *Ithaca*, 'Bloom assented covertly to Stephen's rectification of the anachronism involved in assigning the date of the conversion of the Irish nation to christianity from druidism by Patrick, son of Potitus, son of Odysseus, sent by pope Celestine in the year 432 in the reign of Leary to the year 260 or there-abouts in the reign of Cormac Mac Airt († 266 A.D) suffocated by imperfect deglutition of aliment at Sletty and interred at Rossnaree' (587). King Cormac had been in Bloom's mind earlier in 'Lestrygonians' with relevant reference to refection, the primary theme of that episode: 'That last pagan king of Ireland Cormac in the schoolpoem choked himself at Sletty southward of the Boyne. Wonder what he was eating. Something galoptious. Saint Patrick converted him to Christianity. Couldn't swallow it all however.' (169) Bloom's version is, as usual, inaccurate, mixing up King Cormac with Leary who was the reigning High King at St Patrick's advent. Leary, in fact, refused to be converted by the saint.

But it seems clear that neither Stephen nor Bloom nor their author, Joyce, knew much more about Cormac's alleged conversion to a belief in Christ and his death by druidical maledictions than what is related in Sir Samuel Ferguson's poem 'The Burial of King Cormac'—the 'schoolpoem' referred to by Bloom:

> Till, where at meat the monarch sate,
> Amid the revel and the wine,
> He choked upon the food he ate
> At Sletty, southward of the Boyne.

The legend was that the Druids, incensed by Cormac's defection, sent a *Siabhradh*, a demon of metamorphosis in the shape of a salmon, into the Boyne where it allowed itself to be caught so that Cormac would be choked by one of its bones.

This 'King', according to *Ogygia*, a book written in Latin by Roderic O'Flaherty (1630-1718), translated into English by the Rev. James Hely, A.B., and published in Dublin, 1793, 'Cormac the son of Artur the Melancholy, after the battle of Crinna, ascends the throne, (A.D 254). He was called Cormac Ó Cuinn as being the grandson of Conn of the Hundred Battles, and Cormac Chorainn, as being born in Corann, at Athcormaic, near the mountain Céis' (in county Sligo).

Of Cormac's birth the old men related long ago what had been handed down to them in the lore of their forefathers for two millenia without any written records or glosses polluting the well of racial memory. Their tradition is as follows:

His father was Art Aonar, Art the Lonely One [cf. 'Art-alone', *FW* 418 and 'arth the onely', *Scribbledehobble*, 23], because he was carried off by the fairies and kept apart from his young wife and his people. So the wife was to give birth to Cormac and for fear that Mac Con (the man who took the throne after Art disappeared) for fear that he'd do away with herself and her child, she set out on her way to Bally-golan of Fenagh where her father, O'Dolan Donn, was the chieftain of Céis Chorainn. She was nearly there when her pains came on her but she wouldn't deliver the child until a certain star, that should be a token of his birth and his fortune, would be shining in the sky just above her. So she sat under a mountain ash at the foot of Céis and held on until the star was up and when the child was born she fainted away. But a well sprung up forby them and washed the babe where he lay on the grass and then didn't two wolves come down from the caves in the cliff-face of Céis and carry the child off to their den. He was reared there for two years until the wolves were seen helping him to walk, holding a stick in their mouths and getting him to hold on to the stick while he tried out his steps.

Cormac was rescued and in due course became king at Tara and we have an account of his appearance:

Flowing and slightly curling was his golden hair. A red buckler, with stars and animals of gold and fastenings of silver upon him. A crimson cloak in wide descending folds around him, fastened at his neck with precious stones. A rich torque of gold around his neck. A white shirt with a full collar and intertwined with red-gold thread upon him. A girdle of gold inlaid with precious stones was around him. Two wonderful shoes of gold with golden loops upon his feet. Two spears with golden sockets in his hands with many rivets of red bronze. And he was himself besides symmetrical and beautiful of form without blemish or reproach.

The circumstances of Cormac's birth, heralded by a stellar phenomenon, his father invisible, his being taken away from his mother, his fosterage with wolves and his mature epiphany, beautiful and unblemished, are all manifestations of a god, not of a king who could be a *materies Christiani* likely to convert the Irish from paganism, as is suggested in Stephen's prochronistic rectification of what he considered an anachronism. When Christianity did come to Ireland, Cormac was demythologised and enthroned as an all-wise ruler and potential Christian in a golden age just beyond the fringe of history.

Cormac, as well as his contemporary, Finn Mac Cool, are featured in *Finnegans Wake*, Finn as the aged lover of Cormac's young daughter, Grainne, when he was already father of the poet Ossian, and grandfather of Oscar. The situation is summed up in *FW* 68, where a dish is said to be served by 'our own little Graunya of the chilired cheeks . . . to the greatsire of Oscar, that son of a Coole'.

What did Bloom do at the range?
He removed the saucepan to the left hob, rose and carried the iron kettle to the sink in order to tap the current by turning the faucet to let it flow.
Did it flow? (591)

Yes—from a large storage reservoir, near Roundwood, in the county Wicklow which covers an area of 410 acres and can hold 2,400,000,000 gallons of water, equal to seven months' supply. Attached are filter beds through which all the water is passed before being admitted into mains; the water is conveyed through a tunnel nearly eight miles long to Callowhill and thence through an iron pipe, thirty-three inches in diameter, to Stillorgan, a distance of about twenty-two miles. This (Stillorgan) reservoir contains 84,000,000 gallons and the level is 200 feet above the quays in Dublin.

The foregoing paragraph is not the reply given in *Ulysses* to the question, 'Did it flow?' It is an abbreviated extract from 'Dublin Annals' in Thom's *Official Directory*, under the year 1868 when the Vartry Waterworks scheme was completed. Reference to the reply in *Ulysses* (591) will indicate that Joyce's wording is substantially the same as that quoted here, but it is followed by an account of the prohibition of the use of municipal water 'for purposes other than those of consumption' (*sic*) meaning probably domestic consumption in a period of water scarcity due to drought. Reference is also made to a dispute with the South Dublin Guardians, i.e., the Poor Law Guardians of the South Dublin Union, who had been 'convicted' of a wastage of 20,000 gallons per night. This suggests that Joyce, although he undoubtedly had a copy of Thom's *Directory*, was using an account of the water wastage which the Law Agent, Ignatius John Rice, had sent to the newspapers prefaced by the usual description of the waterworks system, a set piece which was never altered from 1868 to 1930.

A brilliant piece of writing on water, its universality, constancy in seeking its own level etc. is followed by a reference to hot water and the advantages which attended shaving by night. This proved too much for the encyclopaedist's gravity so that he was forced wearily to let the subject trickle away in rhyming prose droplets. Hydraulics are followed by what a builder would call 'dry filling'; itemised expenditure during Bloomsday, long lists of the contents of dresser shelves and drawers; the manipulation of the mathematical relationship between Bloom's and Stephen's ages based on an impossible premise which results in the date of Bloom's birth being pushed back to the year 81,396 B.C. (600).

The tip on the Gold Cup race which Bloom had unconsciously given Bantam Lyons when he told him that he was about to 'throw away' the *Freeman's Journal* is adverted to in an amusing parody of the rhetorical piece in 'Aeolus' about Moses on

Mount Sinai, in which Bloom is said to have thereupon 'proceeded towards the oriental edifice of the Turkish and Warm Baths, 11 Leinster Street, with the light of inspiration shining in his countenance and bearing in his arms the secret of the race, graven in the language of prediction'. (596)

When, finally, Stephen got up to leave (we thought he would never go) and Bloom saw him out 'from obscurity by a passage from the rere of the house into the penumbra of the garden' they were confronted by 'the heaventree of stars hung with humid nightblue fruit'. (619) This purple line leads to astronomic and cosmic infinities of space and time in which the 'years of allotted human life formed a parenthesis of infinitesimal brevity'. It is a relief to get back from Sir Robert Ball's Outer Space to a listing of the books in two bookshelves in the front room hallfloor of 7 Eccles Street and, thirty pages later, to get Bloom to bed. And so to our contemporary astronomy which features red shifts, black holes and cosmic distances of 80,000 million light years.

The Wandering Rocks episode (218-254) is an encyclopaedia of Dublin topographical nomenclature which it is not proposed to analyse here. There is, however, one item amongst the record of salutations to Lord Dudley which requires notice: 'From its sluice in Wood quay wall under Tom Devan's office Poddle river hung out in fealty a tongue of liquid sewage.' (251-2).

At the request of my friend, Professor Clive Hart, I had a check made on the location at which the River Poddle enters the River Liffey and I ascertained that the Corporation records indicate that the entry point is at Wellington Quay and that there is no evidence that it ever entered the Liffey elsewhere.

However, it seems also to enter *Finnegans Wake* (181) where Shem is said to have been 'ordered off the gorgeous premises in most cases on account of his smell which all cookmaids eminently objected to as resembling the bombinubble puzzo that welled out of the pozzo'.

The 'Ithaca' episode has been included in this chapter as coming within the encyclopaedic range of the dry and wet filling which enhances the range and swells the volume of *Ulysses*. But it also serves another purpose. It is the necessary supplement to Joyce's presentation in previous chapters of his characters in action. The supposedly invisible author is intended to be allowing the characters themselves to reveal their personalities. Joyce indeed fell down initially in this effort: the first paragraph of 'Calypso' is too obviously an introductory intervention of the author describing Mr Bloom's gastronomic leanings towards 'the inner organs of beasts and fowls'.

'Ithaca' is intended to be a substitute for all such interventions, for all the direct narration of fictional characters' origins, ages, appearances, weight, domestic conditions, past history, present position and future prospects. The perusal of information on all these and other matters affecting the principal *dramatis personae* in the narrative is the price the reader has to pay for meeting Stephen and Bloom without detailed introduction in previous chapters and for the deferred pleasure of listening in to Molly Bloom in the next and concluding episode.

The technique of 'Ithaca' is essentially that of the bureaucrat who gets personnel information compiled in common form but Joyce, typically, uses, not the *curriculum vitae* or other method prescribed nowadays for collecting and assorting standard information, but a form of Socratic dialogue combined with a medieval catechetical, inquisitorial procedure, liberally extended to subserve the encyclopaedic objectives of the episode as a whole. What it all amounts to is that some industrious glossator has here the material (supplemented by the information which may be gleaned from Molly's *obiter dicta* in 'Penelope') which would enable him painstakingly to re-write *Ulysses* as a more or less conventional novel, from the point of view of narrative technique. The present writer hastily declines in anticipation any invitation to attempt such a reconstruction, but the potentiality of the undertaking makes it evident that Joyce's cold steel pen was engaged, through the writing of *Ulysses*, on the careful redistribution of material in seemingly chaotic form which had been previously assembled in meticulously ordered working notes.

AE was quite right when he observed in 1902 that young Joyce did not have sufficient chaos in him.

Joyce's encyclopaedic approach was, by this stage of the composition of *U*, coming near the *schema* of *FW*. There is a logical progression in his mind from his name endorsed on a schoolbook as of Clongowes Wood, Sallins, Co. Kildare, Ireland . . . the Universe, to the artistic representation of all human history as a universalisation of the solipsistic projection of the imago of James Joyce.

Chapter 13

Penelope

IN Joyce's letter of 9 October 1906, to his brother Stannie (from which I have already quoted his list of the Gargantuan meals that they had had the day before), Nora interrupted the flow of his subsequent discourse on cooking to write:

> Dear Stannie:
> I hope you are very well I am sure you would be glad to see Georgie now he is well able to run about he is able to say a lot has a good appetite he has eight teeth and also sings when we ask him where is Stannie he beats his chest and says non c'e piu
>
> Nora

When Joyce resumed his letter he wrote:

> You will see from this interpolated letter the gigantic strides which Nora has made towards culture and emancipation. . . . Do you notice how women when they write disregard stops and capital letters?

It will be noticed how Joyce writes 'women' instead of 'this particular woman' and proceeds therefrom to a fallacious generalisation about women's way of writing. This was the basis for his committing Molly Bloom's long soliloquy to writing with no punctuation marks and no apostrophes. In most appropriate cases, however, such as personal names, placenames and book titles, he conceded the use of initial capitals.

This source of his inspiration for the use of 'run-on' writing Joyce did not, of course, divulge to Valery Larbaud, Carlo Linati or any of those friends and admirers of *Ulysses* who assisted in bringing the book to the notice of the continental and cosmopolitan avant garde of 1922. The absence of punctuation was allowed to be tacitly accepted as being, in itself, an intrinsic part of the structure of the 'interior monologue' and proof of its constituting a dimension of a woman's ruminating mind newly plumbed and expounded in appropriate prose. Joyce acknowledged that the form of the *monologue intérieur* had been already used by Edouard Dujardin in *Les Lauriers sont coupés* without, of course, comparing the content of that almost forgotten book with the special mixture provided in 'Penelope', which is mainly a rehash of the events and personalities in the previous chapters served up in well-seasoned, pungent prose with the stops pulled out. Bloom himself is, as might be expected, dealt with at length: he keeps popping up at various stages of the chapter in the lights (mainly hostile) in which he presents himself to his wife's memory and finally in the acceptable light to which she responds 'yes'. Other characters also come in for attention. Pages 694-5, for example, review the background of Josie and Denis Breen, Paddy Dignam and his widow, Tom Kernan 'that drunken little barrelly man that bit his tongue off falling down the mens WC drunk in some place or other' (in 'Grace' in *Dubliners*, in fact), Martin Cunningham and the two Dedaluses and Fanny McCoy's husband, the Glencree dinner and 'Ben Dollard base barreltone'.

One of the more erotic portions of the episode is really a narration by recall of an episode otherwise omitted (save in 'Circe'—the 'Love's Old Sweet Song' rendition by Molly and Boylan during the previous afternoon in 7 Eccles Street.

Nora Barnacle is Joyce's model for Molly Bloom; he is at pains to conceal her origin by various forms of superficial artifice: Nora is a blonde, Molly has raven tresses; Molly (Madame Marion Tweedy) is a prima donna while singing is not listed as one of Nora's accomplishments. (Nora disclaimed identity with Molly on the ground that she was 'not that fat'), Nora is a native of Galway while Molly hails from far-off Gibraltar.

On the first page of 'Penelope' (659) one finds Molly postulating, 'if it was a thing I was sick', a turn of speech which she never picked up in Gibraltar. It is a literal translation of a form of conditional clause in Irish, '*Dá mba rud é go raibh . . .*' with which Nora would have been perfectly familiar in Galway.

There is at least one memory which Nora and Molly have

in common, that of a brief, lighthearted love affair with a man called Mulvey. Nora knew him in Galway where he lived on a northern outskirt of the town, called Bohermore. Willie Mulvey was a Protestant and Nora's uncle, Tommy Healy, who wished to stop her from walking out at night with any boy, was doubly intent on preventing such intimacy with a non-Catholic. In order to meet Mulvey *sub rosa*, Nora put on an alibi act based on the Abbey Church in Francis Street and her pal, Mary Holleran, with whom she purported to go to evening devotions. They both walked to the church from which Nora made her escape in the direction of Bohermore. At about 10 o'clock she picked up Mary at the church and they made their way home to Bowling Green together, as if they had not parted throughout the evening.

Tommy Healy was tall and sturdy, 'with a lame step in him' and he patrolled the Galway streets walking alone with the aid of a blackthorn stick, whistling between his teeth an air the Irish words of which Stephen was to write (608) somewhat incorrectly for Bloom as an example of the 'ancient Irish language':

> Siubhal, siubhal, siubhal a rún,
> Siubhal go socair agus siubhal go ciúin,
>   My love my pearl,
>   My own dear girl,
> My mountain maid arise.

Joyce learned from Nora in Pola how the affair had developed to a climax and he passed the intelligence to his brother, Stannie, in Dublin on 3 November 1904:

> She was opposed at home and this made her persist. Her uncle got on the track. Every night he would be home before her. 'Well, my girl, out again with your Protestant.' Forbade her to go any more. She went. When she came home uncle was there before her. Her mother was ordered out of the room (Papa of course was away) and uncle proceeded to thrash her with a big walkingstick. She fell on the floor fainting and clinging about his knees. At this time she was nineteen! Pretty little story, eh?

Uncle Tommy's puritanical, penal blackthorn drove Nora to

a job as chambermaid in Finn's Hotel in Dublin, thence to un-canonical cohabitation with an infidel in Pola, Trieste, Zurich and Paris. Meanwhile Willie Mulvey joined the British army. He served for many years in Gibraltar. He was invalided home with a stiff leg and he died in St Brigid's Terrace, Prospect Hill, Galway, when still fairly young.

The fact that Mulvey soldiered in Gibraltar subsequent to his parades of the purlieus of Bohermore with Nora must have suggested to Joyce that he locate Molly's birthplace and youth-ful memories in Calpé's lofty mount and have Mulvey meet her there and give her her first kiss under the Moorish wall : 'Molly darling he called me what was his name Jack Joe Harry Mulvey was it.' Slight memories, but as her thoughts swirl on to her final 'yes' to Bloom, 'he' includes Mulvey and also Boylan with Bloom winning at the end by a short head.

It is not clear when, in the course of the composition of *Ulysses*, Joyce decided on the inclusion of the Gibraltar back-ground, but the last chapter, 'Penelope', was in fact the last portion of the book which he wrote and he was still collecting local colour for Molly's memories as late as August 1921, although the completed book was due to be published in February 1922. On 16 August 1921, he wrote to Frank Budgen for a book entitled *Sieges of Gibraltar* and for Conan Doyle's *South African War*, the latter being required to fill in Molly's recollections of her father's reminiscences of the Boer War. He had already got from Budgen extracts from a Gibraltar guide-book. As late as 6 November 1921, he asked Budgen to send him 'any book on fortune telling by cards'. This enabled Joyce to have Molly recall her laying out the deck the previous morning, which gave her a hindsight of 'a young stranger neither dark nor fair' (696).

It would seem from this that all Molly Bloom's Gibraltar background as sketched in the last chapter of *Ulysses* is mere ersatz material pilfered from guide-books and histories, in sub-stitution for Nora Barnacle's Galway background which would have been too personal, less exotic and equally irrelevant to the central Dublin scene.

Discarding those portions of Molly Bloom's soliloquy which the author used as footnotes on other characters and events in the preceding chapters, and her sudden passion for flowers, forest trees and pastoral scenes (which is used to have her symbolise Gea, the Earth, Tellus, *ut periti dicunt*), Molly's remaining characteristics may be equated to the personality of Nora Barnacle : she is lazy, sensual, neurotic, sullen, with a narrow-minded selfcomplacency which leaves her assured that she herself knows best, so that unfamiliar attitudes and motivations are dismissed as irrelevant or even idiotic. Her literacy extends only to an ability to read 'smutty' books, the longer words in them remaining misunderstood and mispronounced. ('Aristotle', in an illustrated volume of gynaecological, gestatory and parturitional curiosities wrongly attributed to the allwisest Stagyrite, she recalls as 'Aristocrat'). The style of the monologue is, perhaps, somewhat superior to Nora's way of talking, necessarily so since it has to be all-inclusive as the epilogue to the book. Her remark about a book in *Calypso* is more in keeping with Nora's style : 'it must have fell down'.

Finally, she is a shrew, as John Eglinton shrewdly remarked about Ann Hathaway in 'Scylla and Charybdis'. 'What a time you were' is her thanks to Leopold when he brings her breakfast tray to her bedside. Joyce, in his letters to Nora from Dublin in 1909, repeatedly and humbly besought her not to be so rude to him on his return to Trieste as she had been in the past. Her beautiful auburn hair, too, would look better if she took the cinders out of it. He frankly appealed also to her avarice and love of finery : money and silks and satins and furs would be hers when he came into his kingdom.

James Branch Cabell's Jurgen's favourite opening ploy in his affairs with women was, 'My wife does not understand me.' James Joyce had perhaps more reason to voice this complaint in his life with Nora, than have most men in real life, whatever about adulterous adventurers in the land of Cockaigne or the Garden between Dawn and Sunrise. He did admit, however, that in the realm of his art, which to him was almost his whole existence, she took no interest whatever. Throughout their thirty-seven years together she had not even a clue as to his aims or his achievement. After the passing of about half that period she was prepared to accept that he was (almost) the greatest writer in the world : there remained, as an active competitor, only 'that Shakespeare', a London writer whom he had still to surpass.

Some of the material for this chapter I owe to a denizen of Bowling Green, Galway, where the Barnacle family lived. I am indebted to Dr E. Tully, a relative of my old friend, Jim Tully, for gaining me access to this source. I now reproduce this material in a form which might be entitled 'Monologue in a Bowling Green Interior' but it is, in fact, a copy of my notes of the replies which I received to a number of questions which are not material to the content of the answers.

The Healys lived in Patrick's Avenue, off Eyre Square. Michael was tall and thin, kinda queer in himself, would hardly speak to you. He was listing recruits for the army after 1916 and the Sinn Fein fellows would shout after him, how many took the shilling from you today?
Ah, then aren't you the villain, Michael Hale?
Ah, then aren't you the villain?
For to give the Saxon shillin'
To do England's dirty killin', Michael Hale?
After that he got a big job in the Custom House and he had a great pension when he retired. Very pious, in and out of some church or other every hour in the day. Wasn't he got dead in the Abbey over there, in the heel of the hunt?
Michael's brother, Tommy, was big and tall, he had a lame step in him and walked with a blackthorn stick and, like his brother, he always walked alone, whistling between his teeth, 'shooal, shooal, shooal, aroon'.
Their sister, Mrs Barnacle, had a tough life of it from the day she married that Tom Barnacle, a man from God knows where. A dipso. They lived here in Bowling Green. He worked in Griffin's bakery with Johnny Kilkelly. Who, Peggy? There was a Peggy, but she never went to Dublin. (cf. MARTHA: (*Sobbing behind her veil*) . . . my real name is Peggy Griffin—'Circe', 442). Night work Barnacle had in the bakery. Then off with him to Hosty's at the bridge for his skinful. They had one son and five daughters and they're all dead now. Michael Healy must have helped to rear them. He never got married. Mrs Barnacle used to do his washing for him. Nora lived with her grandmother and she worked in the Presentation Convent, a portress she was. She was only fifteen or sixteen when she met Michael Bodkin and he

died not long after, you can see his tomb in Rahoon. It says
he died in February, 1900, aged 20. He'd be an uncle of
Miss Bodkin that married Jack Cunningham a relation of
Martin Cunningham and he'd be the same to Dr Bodkin
that died in London a while back (1958). Willie Mulvey was
from up in Bohermore. He joined the British Army and he
was out foreign. He was a long time in Gibraltar. He came
back home with a stiff leg and he lived then in St Brigid's
Terrace, Prospect Hill. He wasn't too old when he died.

With this romance with Sonny Bodkin and then her affair
with Mulvey, Nora Barnacle had to leave Galway or her
uncle Tommy would kill her. She came home after a few
months and away with her again and then she wasn't seen or
heard from for seven years. But a coupla years before that
there appeared this young man, James Joyce. He stayed with
Michael Healy in Domnick Street and he was in here a few
times, talking to Mrs Barnacle. *Shames Showe* we started
calling him and 'The Man with the X-ray Eyes'. He had
blue eyes and he'd stare at you as much as to say, 'what are
you looking at? Have I anything on me belonging to you?'

Says Mrs Barnacle at the door, 'my son-in-law is inside,
Mr James Joyce', and her daughter, Dilly, in the door with
her, so we didn't see him that day, but, come on, says I,
there was no use talking, whatever we said would be turned
the wrong way. She'd snap the knuckles of her right hand
into the palm of her left, as much as to say if anyone laughs
I'll let them have it. What harm but I was tempted to say,
is that the James Joyce was run outa Dublin?

Then, maybe ten years or more after that, Nora herself
came home and her son and daughter with her, a wedding
ring on her finger and all. She lodged in Casey's in Nuns
Island. What troubles? There were no troubles that time,
no Civil War. Well the Free State army were in Renmore
and the IRA were in the Great Southern Hotel and they'd
have the odd shot at each other and no harm done. If they
claim they were shot at, it is all my eye. It was a good bit
later in the year the right Troubles came with trains raided
and Jack Lohan shot and Liam Mellows and all the rest. But
whether they were in dread of their lives or not, they hooked
it out of Galway fairly smart.

I'd say 'twas another ten years and then the cat was outa the bag. The news of their marriage in London was in the *Sunday Dispatch*. There was an awful to-do. You could hear Mrs Barnacle roaring a mile away. But they had to put up with it. The report was they got married only when they had to—for making a will. That was 25 years and more after they went away together.

Kathleen, well Kathleen Barnacle was a head case like the rest of them. She was to marry this fellow, I forget his name, but he thought they'd get a lot of money out of her uncle Michael, but didn't it turn out her so-called intended was married already. Chris Holleran, a brother of Mrs Mary Morris from here in Bowling Green, was to be best man. Then she had to carry on with her paper-packing for Tom Cork in the *Connacht Tribune* and take to the drink when her nerves would be at her. She'd send for Dr Tom Powell from San Antonio Terrace in Salthill, him that was a member of the Dail. I knocked at the door. 'Come in. It's only Dr Powell.' Dr Powell gave a wry smile. He took himself more seriously than that. 'What do you think is wrong with her?' says he. I gave one look and turned on my heel out the door again. Drunk she was. But at her best she was lovely-looking. She musta been near fifty when she married Johnny Griffin, one of a family of French-polishers in Whitehall, a different family from the bakery Griffins. And as far as I ever heard, they had stormy weather, here and in England too. She died of leukaemia over there.

She went to Professor O Briain in University Road, before she got married to get advice on the value of Jim's books (Jim is what she called him), and she came back in one of her tantrums, what kind of a professor is he, says she, working at books every day in the week, and he says he can't tell what prices these books of Jim's should go. That was the time she was getting married, when she thought Jim's books oughta make up her dowry.

The foregoing 'Monologue' would suggest that one of Nora Barnacle's maternal uncles was a religious maniac and the other probably a puritanical sadist. That her father was a drunkard was already well known.

There is no doubt that the Michael Bodkin referred to in the 'Monologue', who died (or was buried) on 13 February 1900, aged twenty, and whose name is inscribed on the tomb in Rahoon cemetery above Shantalla, now a northern suburb of Galway, was the Michael Bodkin on whom was based the character called Michael Fury in 'The Dead'. Joyce had already encountered so many difficulties with publishers to whom he had submitted the other stories in *Dubliners* that he obviously was playing the 'lapwing' to divert attention from the real identity of Nora's 'dark lover' whom, later on, he exhumed from Oughterard and re-interred in his proper grave when he had Nora lament him in *Rain on Rahoon*.

The name of Dilly, Nora Barnacle's sister, referred to in the 'monologue', is borrowed by Joyce in *Ulysses* and given to Stephen's sister who meets both Stephen and her father in the course of Bloomsday's 'Wandering Rocks'.

As to whether Nora shared her sister Kathleen's condition of being a 'head case', commentators on the Joyce ménage have generally been either tacit or tactful. Budgen, however, tells how, when he renewed acquaintance with the Joyces after their move to Paris and was seeing Joyce home after a late night, 'out of a suddenly opened topstorey window appeared a pinkish splodge, a woman's face, and out of it winged words spoken in a magnificent Irish brogue descended on me . . . what I thought I could do in Zurich I was not going to do in Paris. That, and more to the same effect.' (*Myselves When Young*) Frank Budgen, by the way, was inclined to acquit Molly Bloom (or Nora Barnacle) of responsibility for the meditations (including the morose delectations) of the 'Penelope' episode on the ground that 'Molly Bloom is the creation of a man'. This is, of course, true. It was the creation of James Joyce but so also in a sense was Nora Barnacle, as Robert tells Richard of Bertha in *Exiles*: 'You have made her all that she is.' Joyce may therefore have considered himself justified in making his trainee regurgitate in her soliloquy the language he had taught her in the style to which he had made her accustomed.

A hothead, perhaps, if not a head case. Austin Clarke was the only acquaintance of the Joyces whom I remember to have denied Nora's good looks. Sir Harold Nicolson in 1931 saw in her 'the remains of beauty'. Everybody said she had beautiful auburn hair but, to judge from her photographs, her features seem, to say the least, to have been ordinary. Thomas Wolfe was then a keen student of *Ulysses* while preparing to write his own *Look Homeward Angel*. On seeing Joyce and his family in the course of a bus tour in September 1926 to the scene of the battle of Waterloo, he remarked that Nora 'had the appearance of a thousand middle-class French women I've known— a vulgar, rather loose mouth, not very intelligent looking'.

The name of Martin Cunningham mentioned in passing in the 'Monologue' will be recalled as having been given by Joyce to a character in *Ulysses* who shares the same cab as Bloom, Simon Dedalus and Jack Power at Paddy Dignam's funeral and who shows up afterwards in Barney Kiernan's.

It would not be just to close this chapter without a tribute to Nora's loyalty and devotion over the vicissitudes of long years and in circumstances where a less steadfast character might well have abandoned such a thankless task. She was the only person who could and did provide the stabilising influence which, to some extent, could contain Joyce's mercurial temper and irregular ways. As well as being his emotional refuge, what he learned of her own emotions, particularly incidents in her life before he met her, contributed important artistic material for his work. She drew his soul to the West, to Rahoon, where her dead lover lay; he transmuted her into the young Molly Bloom in Gibraltar to receive the embraces of Willie Mulvey there; her memories of her father and of her grandmother's place in Mayo of the Saxons are recalled in the trial of Festy King and the same landscape is recalled (*FW* 479) 'at my grandmother's place . . . my little grey home in the west, in or about Mayo when the long dog gave tongue and they coursing the marches and they straining at the leash'.

Chapter 14
Cacata Carta

ON 31 August 1909 Joyce wrote from Dublin to Nora in Trieste, 'Every coarse word in speech offends me now for I feel that it would offend you. When I was courting you . . . it was the same.' (*Letters*, II, 242) On his second visit to Dublin in the same year, he wrote, 3 December, 'I thought of the letters I wrote you last night and the night before. They must have read awful in the cold light of day. Perhaps their coarseness has disgusted you. . . . As you know, dearest, I never use obscene phrases in speaking. You have never heard me, have you, utter an unfit word before others. When men tell in my presence here filthy or lecherous stories I hardly smile.' (ibid. 270) To Damaso Alonso, who was translating *A Portrait* into Spanish, Joyce wrote on 31 October 1925 the following circumlocutory explanation of a use of the word 'sugar' : 'A euphemism used by Cranley [*sic*] in as much as it begins with the same letter for [*sic*] a product of the body the monosyllabic term for which in English is sometimes used as an exclamation and sometimes as descriptive of a person whom one does not like. In the French language it is associated with Marshal Cambronne, and the French (the females at least) sometimes use a similar euphemism employing the word miel instead of the word used by the military commander' (*Letters*, III, 129-30). The latter word, said to have been Cambronne's reply when called on to surrender at the battle of Waterloo, is 'merde'. The alternative reply attributed to him on that occasion and more appropriate to a *miles gloriosus* was, 'Le Garde meurt, mais ne se rend pas.' Joyce obviously opted for the pun on 'meurt'.

From his 1909 declarations to Nora and his 1925 evasion of the use of a simple but unsavoury tetragrammaton for Alonso's information, one may conclude that Joyce reserved filthy and lecherous words as tools of his art, to be used otherwise only as an incentive to telepathic intercourse with Nora. The letters on the latter intimacies, heretofore denied *verbatim* reproduction by their Cornell custodians, are described in some detail in Darcy O'Brien's *The Conscience of Joyce.*

Even in an artistic context he sometimes displays unexpected restraint. The words 'of a' followed by the English equivalent of 'merde' should have been inserted after the word 'shot' in the last words of the *Cyclops* episode, 'like a shot off a shovel'. They are needed to complete a simile intended to signify swift motion as well as to reinforce the alliteration of the clause. The shovel in question would be the implement used by a sanitary services employee of the Dublin Corporation in Joyce's youth when the domestic privies, euphemistically termed 'dry closets', had to be cleaned. It was a malodorous job which even a lazy workman might be expected to perform speedily. The act involved, however, is an antithesis of Bloom's ascent to glory 'at an angle of forty-five degrees over Donohue's in Little Green Street', and thereby suggests that his was but a mock-heroic apotheosis.

Joyce liked to leave something to be read between, or added to, his lines. Stanislaus mentions (*MBK*) how, on his return from Paris at Christmas 1902, his brother sang French songs in the Sheehys' house, *Cadet Rousselle* and *Viens, poupoule*, 'and amused himself by omitting perfectly innocent lines and humming and nodding significantly to the company instead in order to see them smile their cultured smiles, shocked but complacent, as who would say, "We too have been in Arcadia".'

A similar *suggestio falsi* is probably intended in 'Telemachus' (19) where Mulligan is described as growling 'in a hoarsened rasping voice':

—For old Mary Ann
She doesn't care a damn,
But, hising up her petticoats . . .

In their book on song in Joyce's work, Mr M. J. C. Hodgart and Miss Mabel Worthington hazard a guess that the Mary Ann in question was 'Mick McGilligan's daughter, Mary Ann', but 'old Mary Ann' belonged to an older generation. I have never seen any query or speculation as to the content of the missing line which is required to complete the rhyme and lend it reason. Readers of *Ulysses* over the last fifty years have been left to use their Arcadian imaginations on the question,

> What is she doing, this old Mary Ann,
> Down in the field by the river?

The answer is purer and simpler than a satyr's mind would suggest. Out of the exuberance of her bladder and her carefree innocence, old Mary Ann has disdained to Q for a P and the missing line runs:

> Is pissing like a man.

Joyce said to Jacques Benoîst-Méchin in October 1921, 'I've put in so many enigmas and puzzles that it will keep the professors busy for centuries arguing over what I meant, and that's the only way of insuring one's immortality'. He might have added that the enigmas and puzzles are supplemented by omissions and suppressions which also thicken the 'sombrer opacities of the gloom' (*FW* 473) through the tenebrae of which the professors are put to peer and ponder.

When *Ulysses* was published in 1922 it was hailed by the post-war literary and social rebels as their text-book for emancipation. They were mistaken. Bourgeois Joyce was not a protagonist of any school of literature or morals. He was simply writing 'the book of himself', giving expression to his cloacal obsession and externalising his erotic preoccupations. The realistic but sympathetic treatment of Bloom attracted and has continued to attract a growing number of Jewish adherents, some of whom, with guarded acclaim, endeavoured to maintain an ambivalent attitude. In 1923 Con Leventhal, quondam lecturer in Trinity College, Dublin, wrote under the name 'Laurence K. Emery': 'I say this, however, that only an artist could handle his material as Mr Joyce has done. In other hands there would really be a grave risk of a descent into the morbid and the pornographic'. Leventhal was, of course, young at the time, but even so it was rather fatuous on his part to suggest the possibility 'in other hands' of a descent into two characteristics already manifestly inherent in Joyce's 'material' as presented.

A more exalted personage in the same institution, Provost

Mahaffy, was more forthright : 'But for the Jesuits, Joyce today would be one of the cornerboys spitting into the Liffey over Carlisle Bridge'. The remark was probably intended to belittle the rival university's standards, but Joyce had indeed inherited or acquired in his youth the mentality of an intellectual cornerboy, the type which Shaw stigmatised as satirical onlookers given to 'eternal derision ... envy ... folly ... eternal fouling and staining and degrading' (*John Bull's Other Island*, Introduction).

Stanislaus was, as always, his brother's keenest and truest critic. On 7 August 1924, he wrote : 'you try to shift the burden of your melancholy to the reader's shoulders without being yourself relieved. . . . There is no serenity or happiness anywhere in the whole book'. The book has, of course, a plethora of the comic but it is nearly all satirical. So much for the morbid. As to pornography, *The Pink Un*, itself not notable for journalistic delicacy, remarked 1 April 1922, that 'The main contents of the book are enough to make a Hottentot sick'. One wonders what enterprising member of that moribund and illiterate tribe could have got hold of a copy of *Ulysses* at that early date and, having read it, found, as Justice Woolsey of the United States District Court in New York found ten years later, that it was an emetic rather than an aphrodisiac. And yet, and yet, had not that Hottentot already come ino Joyce's own head when he wrote to Ezra Pound, 9 April 1917 :

There once was a lounger named Stephen
Whose youth was most odd and uneven;
   He throve on the smell
   Of a horrible hell
That a Hottentot wouldn't believe in.

John F. Byrne ('Cranly'), in his *Silent Years*, tells of his asking Joyce, about his use of 'three elemental four-letter words', two questions—what effect did the employment of these words have on the book considered as a work of art; and what effect did the appearance of these three words in the book have on its sales?' 'I found' (he wrote) 'Joyce not at all positive about the artistic value of the words; but inflexibly positive about their sales or popularity value'. Byrne's theory was that while Joyce himself 'rarely, indeed scarcely ever, uttered orally any of these words', he put them in his writing because 'he believed it was becoming for strong men, or strong characters, to talk that way'. They were also, in Byrne's view, Joyce's 'protest against popular insincerity, cant and hypocrisy and against a puritanical prudery which is essentially prurient'. It did not occur to Byrne's slow-moving mind to interrogate Joyce about the larger issue of the general obscene content of *Ulysses*.

About the fact that his book was obscene Joyce himself had no doubts. He wrote to Budgen, 16 August 1921, imitating the unpunctuated text of the last chapter, 'Penelope' : 'Though probably more obscene than any preceding episode it seems to me to be perfectly sane full amoral fertilisable untrustworthy engaging shrewd limited prudent indifferent *Weib. Ich bin das Fleisch das stets bejaht*'.

My own opinion accords with that of Stanislaus who wrote, 26 February 1922 : 'I suppose "Circe" will stand as the most horrible thing in literature. . . . Everything dirty seems to have the same irresistible attraction for you that cow-dung has for flies.'

'Circe' is the dramatic climax of *Ulysses* and it has in it, among other things, the culmination of all forms of obscenity, coprophilia, transvestitism, sadism and masochism. In *Finnegans Wake* it is described as 'obscene matter not protected by copriright' (185). It contains a varied miscellany of the local vernacular :

MARY DRISCOLL : (*Excitedly*) As God is looking down on me this night if ever I laid a hand on them oysters!

FIRST WATCH : The offence complained of? Did something happen?

MARY DRISCOLL : He surprised me in the rear of the premises, your honour, when the missus was out shopping one morning with a request for a safety pin. He held me and I was discoloured in four places as a result. And he interfered twice with my clothing.

BLOOM : She counterassaulted.

MARY DRISCOLL : (*Scornfully*) I had more respect for the scouringbrush, so I had. I remonstrated with him, your lord, and he remarked : keep it quiet! (444)

More heavily embroidered, however, are the scenes in which

Bloom 'desiderates the domination' of transvestist and flagellant society women.

One of them declares:
THE HONOURABLE MRS MERVYN TALBOYS: . . . I'll scourge the pigeon-livered cur as long as I can stand over him, I'll flay him alive.
BLOOM: (*His eyes closing, quails expectantly*) Here? (*He squirms*) Again! (*He pants cringing*) I love the danger.' (449)

This treatment is based on *Venus im Pelz* by Leopold von Sacher-Masoch (the identity of his first name with that of Bloom is scarcely a coincidence). Much more of the 'Circe' material, however, came from a central European lady named Baroness St Leger who lived on an island in Lake Maggiore and whom Joyce visited in May 1919. She was known as the Siren or Circe or Lady of the Lake. She gave him a trunk of books dealing with erotic perversions and a packet of obscene letters. Thus the thongs that sent a pang through the sad heart of Bloom when sick for home he quailed with fears was, in fact, Alien Porn. (This phrase, 'Alien Porn' was, many months after I wrote it here, invented independently by a *Sunday Times* writer in January 1974 to provide a headline for an article on Lord Longford, HOLY FOOL IN ALIEN PORN). This Alien Porn is an extravaganza in esoteric vice which seems inappropriate for staging side by side with the facts of sinful living in Mecklenburg Street in 1904. Structurally it seems to derive from Flaubert's *Tentation de St Antoine*, but there the whole work is a phantasy intended to portray mankind as incorrigibly evil and proof against the teachings of all religions, whereas 'Circe' is an epiphany of evil, which serves only to pursue the characters from the other chapters of this large book into the dark nights of their souls without drawing any moral or other conclusion from the exercise.

In the scenes where Bloom quails, yet loves the danger, and in those where his wife exults in adultery and her lover invites Bloom to act as voyeur, Joyce gets a masochistic pleasure in the painful excitements of his surrogate. It is the same reaction as one senses in the writer of the scene in *A Portrait* where little Stephen suffers exquisite agonies from the strokes of the pandybat and, as regards adultery, it is an overt development of what is already implicit in the experimental play, *Exiles*. Here one may recall Budgen's story about Joyce's effort to persuade Nora 'to go with other men' so that she could thereby provide him with fresh copy for his writing.

'Nausicaa' is a mish-mash of all the contemporary and nine-teenth-century sentimental trash poured out to feed the libido of teenage girls, yet written so as superficially to suggest that the tone is one of high romance. Joyce dresses Gerty's erotic phantasy in the 'poetic' prose of sweet sixteen and does it with such zest as to reveal that he is taking pleasure in the composi-tion, just as he brings the flaming fireworks down to earth in ashes to synchronise with Bloom's part in the scene. This is as much as to admit that he is himself a porn addict, and we are brought back to the conclusion that in *Ulysses* Joyce is 'all in all': he is the dreamy, sex-starved sweet sixteen simultaneously with the middle-aged practitioner of onanism.

All this underlines the fact that *Ulysses* is *sui generis*: it is the unique production of a man by no means unique but the only one of that type who was not alone able and willing but felt compelled to reveal the various devious phases of his nature, and to put them all down in cold print on paper that is metaphorically akin to the copy of *Tit-Bits* which Bloom con-verted to his private use in 'Calypso'. I tender my apologies to Juvenal for similarly appropriating and misquoting a line of his:

Annales Ulixis, cacata carta.

PART II
Sprakin sea Djoytsch

Chapter 15
The Exile of Erin

IN May 1900, the Joyce family made one of their numerous changes of residence—from 13 Richmond Avenue, Fairview, to 8 Royal Terrace, Fairview, where they stayed until 1901. On their arrival in their new dwelling some of the children disinterred two books from the ashpit at the back of the garden. Stanislaus Joyce (*MBK*) describes them:

> One was a song-book, the first pages of which were missing. It contained a large and miscellaneous collection of classical traditional songs, popular ballads and many so-called comic songs, the humour of which always remained a vulgar mystery to me. The other was a closely and badly printed collated edition of the four gospels in a red cloth cover, still quite presentable . . . though the cloth of one cover was detached from the cardboard owing to exposure to weather . . .

Long afterwards when Joyce read accounts of creation myths (geneses or postdiluvian creations) such as that in the Egyptian *Book of the Dead* where the creation of mankind is ascribed to the act of Atem or Tema by an emission on the mudmound at Heliopolis, he must have decided that, as the composition or compilation of his Book of the Night (*Finnegans Wake*) was as much a cosmogony as any of the creations of the gods of old, it must accordingly be related to a mudmound, preferably an ashpit. This would be in line with his youthful symbolisation of himself in the rowan tree and its offspring, the ashplant, which he probably acquired during his trip to Mullingar in the same year as the family move to Royal Terrace.

Again, in 1906, the ashpit found a place amongst the controversial references which Grant Richards sought to have modified before he would finally agree to publish *Dubliners*.

E

Joyce wrote to him on 23 June: 'It is not my fault that the odour of ashpits and old weeds and offal hangs around my stories.'

Joyce, therefore, is returning to old familiar territory when (110-11) he has Belinda, a hen of the Dorans, scratch out 'a goodish sized sheet of letter paper' addressed as described 310 pages later (420-21): 'Letter carried of Shaun, son of Hek, written of Shem, brother of Shaun, uttered for Alp, mother of Shem, for Hek, father of Shaun.' Successive addresses (places at which the Joyce family had lodged) include '8 Royal Terrors', endorsed 'None so strait'—no such street, perhaps, but it does not matter, for henceforth the family will be universalised symbols of mankind, nature and the incessant revolutions of history. The sheet of letter paper scratched out by the hen, expanded to 628 such sheets is, in fact, *Finnegans Wake*, in the course of which the principal characters are subdivided and renamed in successive changes of scene, context and action but remain constantly recognisable as Humphrey Chimpden Earwicker, a Chapelizod publican, whose character is based on that of Joyce's father, John Stanislaus Joyce; Joyce's wife who becomes Earwicker's wife under the name of Anna Livia Plurabelle; their children Shem (i.e. James Joyce himself), his twin brother, Shaun, (symbolising the Irish at home as opposed to Shem himself, the Artist and Irish Exile); and a daughter, Isabel, who is intended to succeed her mother in various capacities but meanwhile represents Iseult, based on that lady's legendary connection with Chapelizod on the Liffey near Dublin in the drama of *Tristram and Iseult*, of which we get a version in the course of the book.

Humphrey, the father's first name, may be interpreted as deriving from Humpty Dumpty, signifying Fall and from the hump, or load of conscience, which man carries since the Fall of our First Parents; his second, Chimpden, appears to suggest an alternative origin, the descent of man from the primates (so sing they 'Charley you're my darwing') (252); his surname, Earwicker, may indicate his Irish location, dweller in Eire, but it also is connected with the earwig, an insect reputed to creep into one's ear. This is important in the structure of the work: the whole of *Finnegans Wake* is planned as a dream dreamt by Earwicker or by either of his predecessors, Finnegan or Finn

McCool. The confusion of the composition may, in exculpation of the author, be notionally attributed not only to the natural kaleidoscopic meanderings of the dreaming mind but also to the tipping of a twig against the bedroom window of sleeping Earwicker or the buzzing and importunate interferences, interjections and interruptions of this intrusive insect known in French as *perce-oreille*. This is translated into Persse (or Pearce) O'Rahilly and, to my mind, is used to suggest the undertones of the national movement in Ireland from 1916 onwards, heard feebly, but nevertheless heard, by the Exile of Erin, listing 'as she bibs us by the Waters of Babalong'. We are not yet done with this great name : its initials H.C.E., stand for Here Comes Everybody, a nickname borrowed from that given to Hugh Culling Eardley Childers, a member of the 1894-95 House of Commons commission on the financial relations between Ireland and Britain. In its application to Earwicker 'H.C.E.' is intended to universalise him as a symbol of all mankind down the ages and back to Adam or to palaeolithic man, whichever one prefers. Joyce regards his father as a worthy candidate for this symbolic post : 'An imposing everybody he always indeed looked, constantly the same as and equal to himself and magnificently well worthy of any and all such universalisation . . .' (32)

He is a god, doomed to periodical sacrifice in the waxing and waning year after the manner of Osiris and the divinity of Frazer's Golden Bough. As a god, he is arbitrary, irascible, unpredictable, lecherous, alcoholic, exculpatory—everything, in fact, which Joyce considered that his father and the godhead had in common.

For all this universality, H.C.E. is Dublin itself ever since he landed there in his Viking days and laid it out as a city : 'I laid down before the trotters to my eblanite my stony battered waggon ways, my norsoud circulums, my eastmoreland and westlandmore, running boullowards and syddenly parading . . .' (553) (The references are to Dublin streets, Stoneybatter, North and South Circular Roads, Westmoreland Street, Westland Row and Sydney Parade.)

H.C.E.'s wife, Anna Livia Plurabelle, also has her overtones of universalisation. She is 'The Log of Anny to the Base All' (105). She represents all the rivers of the world, many of which are woven into the section of *Finnegans Wake* originally published as *Anna Livia Plurabelle*, now Chapter VIII, pp. 196-216, an essay which is at once so cosmopolitan in its geography and elementary in its Irish dimension as not to require detailed explication here. Its contents, excluding the inundation of river names, are used where relevant to the context. While H.C.E. is the masculine creator of artificial things, the Master Builder of cities, A.L.P. is Nature, the daughter of earth and water and the nursling of the skies. She is Alp, the German nightmare, perhaps the nightmare of history from which Stephen (*U* 40) was trying to awake but which now rides rampant through the night of the *Wake*. As to her nuptials, the old washerwomen on the Liffey banks wish to ascertain the precise ritual by which H.C.E. and A.L.P. were wed, citing several forms of irregular marriage services conducted by blacksmiths, tinkers and sea captains : 'who blocksmitt her soft anvil or yelled lep to her pail? Was her banns never loosened in Adam and Eve's or were him and her but captain spliced?' (197)

The answer seems to be given by James Joyce himself, the basis of whose union with Nora Barnacle might be similarly queried. He may or may not have married her as Miss Greta Green. After twenty-seven years' cohabitation, they were married in a London registry office in 1931 for what was officially stated to be 'testamentary reasons'. The answer given to the washers at the ford was : 'For mine ether duck I thee drake. And by my wildgaze I thee gander.' This is a reference to the symbolic role which Joyce has Miss Barnacle and himself assume as twentieth-century 'wild geese' when they eloped in 1904 on their 'wild goup's chase across the katharctic ocean' (185).

A.L.P. and H.C.E. are married for all time but H.C.E. has a new bride each time the Liffey renews itself. The old one, soiled by the stains of city life, broader in the beam than she was when she never dreamed she'd lave Kilbride (576), and Missisliffi (159) is her muddied name, thinks of the time when she was 'water parted from the say', a raincloud in the sky : 'My great blue bedroom, the air so quiet. . . . It's something fails us. First we feel. Then we fall. And let her rain now if she likes. (627) Her successor, Nuvoletta (159),

reflected for the last time in her little long life and she made up all her myriads of drifting minds in one. She cancelled all her engauzements. She climbed over the bannistars; she gave a childy, cloudy cry: *Nuée! Nuée!* A lightdress fluttered. She was gone. And into the river that had been a stream (for a thousand of years had gone on her and she was stout and . . . her muddied name was Missisliffi) there fell a tear, a singult tear, the loveliest of all tears . . . for it was a leaptear. But the river tripped on her by and by, lapping as though her heart was brook: *Why, why, why! Weh O weh! I'se so silly to be flowing, but I no canna stay.*

This Heraclitean succession of streams in the riverbed is, therefore (600): 'the river of lives, the regenerations of the incarnations of the emanations of the apparentations of Funn and Nin in Cleothabala, the king domain of the Alieni, an accorsaired race, infester of Libnud Ocean, Moylamore, . . .' . . . that is, the reincarnation in successive generations of Finn (i.e. Finn Mac Cool represented by Earwicker) and Anna in Dublin (Baile Atha Cliath) the (onetime) kingdom of the alien Scandinavians, a coarsehaired race of pirates (corsairs) in Dublin (Libnud) on the sea, 'the moyles and moyles of it,' from the name of the channel between Ireland and Scotland to which Moore refers in his poem beginning 'Silent O Moyle be the roar of thy water'.

We shall now try to trace the career of Shem, one of the twin sons of H.C.E. and A.L.P. The material bearing on him is important, for Shem is a portrait of James Joyce himself: 'Shem is as short for Shemus as Jem is joky for Jacob . . .' (169) 'Shem was a Sham and a low Sham . . .' (170) 'He even ran away with himself and became a farsoonerite, saying he would far sooner nuddle through the hash of lentils in Europe than meddle with Ireland's split little pea.' (171) That is to say he left the green isle of Ireland (subsequently partitioned) and went to live 'in Europe'.

'All the time he kept on treasuring with condign satisfaction each and every crumb of trektalk, covetous of his neighbour's word . . .' (172) This addiction to eavesdropping is borne out by what many of his associates recalled of Joyce's habit of jotting down key words of conversations or even stray remarks overheard in cafés, venerated pieces of reality to replace 'literary' cliches outworn with use. At the same time he essayed multiplication of meanings by the use of several languages in association—'unconsciously explaining . . . with a meticulosity bordering on the insane, the various meanings of all the different foreign parts of speech he misused.' (173)

We begin to grasp that we are being told about the composition of *Finnegans Wake* itself, interrupted at times by noises off, whether those of insurrections or ambushes echoing from Ireland or that of the Divine Thunderer himself, volleying from the sky (which is a personal terror for Joyce but which also forms the basis of civilisation according to Vico, on whose historical philosophy *Finnegans Wake* depends for its theory of the cyclic patterns of social evolution):

> Now it is notoriously known how on that surprisingly bludgeony Unity Sunday . . . when Irish eyes of welcome were smiling daggers down their backs, when the roth, vice and blause met the noyr blank and rogues and the grim white and cold bet the black fighting tans, categorically unimperatived by the maxims, a rank funk getting the better of him, the scut in a bad fit of pyjamas fled like a leveret for his bare lives . . . kuskykorked himself up tight in his inkbattle house . . . his face enveloped into a dead warrior's telemac, . . . his cheeks and trousers changing colour every time a gat croaked. (176-7)

This passage, spoken presumably by his hostile surrogate, Shaun, accuses Shem of cowardice in absenting himself from Ireland while the War of Independence was at its height and concentrating on playing the part of Telemachus (Stephen Dedalus) in his book, *Ulysses* then in course of being written. The charge that he apparently acted the part of a poltroon does not appear to worry him, for in the next page it is intimated that nobody 'ever nursed such a spoiled opinion of his monstrous marvellosity as did this mental and moral defective'. The hostile account goes on:

> he had flickered up and flinnered down into a drug and drunkery addict, growing megalomane of a loose past, (presenting a) shuddersome spectacle of (a) semidemented zany amid the inspissated grime of his glaucous den making believe to read his usylessly unreadable Blue Book of Eccles

(179) [i.e. *Ulysses*, some of the scenes of which is laid in Eccles St] ...

... but what with the murky light ... the fumbling fingers ... the scum on his tongue, the drop in his eye, the lump in his throat ... the fog of his mind, the buzz in his braintree, the tic of his conscience, the height up his rage ... the squince in his suil the bats in his belfry ... he was hardset to memorise more than a word a week. (180)

These obstacles to composition are echoed in Henry Miller's *Tropic of Cancer* (Panther Books, 1969, p. 96) originally published in Paris, 1934.

Shem persevered 'so as one day to utter an epical forged cheque on the public' (181). The forgery consisted in the purloining of quotations from other writers without the acknowledgment of their use by putting them in inverted commas.

In the intimate den where the composition goes on, with his bad sight and the bad light, he has had to fall back for illumination on 'his gnose's glow as it slid lucifericiously within an inch of his page' (182), that is to say he wrote with the light of heresy (gnosticism) and the phosphorescent light from his alcoholically burnished nose (as Shakespeare says, he carried his lantern in the poop) working at his alphybettyformed verbiage ... 'ineffable tries at speech unsyllabled ... borrowed brogues ... blackeye lenses ... once current puns ... quashed quotatoes, messes of mottage ... stale shestnuts ... thaws ... yeses and yeses and yeses.' (183) 'Yes, the last word in *Ulysses*, is Molly Bloom's affirmation and 'Thaw' (tá) is the Irish for 'yes'.

There he is, in the act of creation—'Tumult son of Thor, self exiled in upon his ego, a nightlong a shaking betwixt white or redder hawrors, noondayterrorised to skin and bone by an ineluctable phantom ... writing the mystery of himself...' (184). The 'hawror' loses some of its frightfulness when one realises that the reference is to hawthorn blossoms, white or red, (an indirect acknowledgment of Nathaniel Hawthorne's being responsible for the suggestion that somebody should attempt to write a book about the dreaming processes of an individual). This book, *Finnegans Wake*, on which Shem is engaged, purports to be the answer: it records the dreams of H.C.E. in

Dublin but they are written down by Shem in Paris and borne by his brother Shaun the Post to his mother A.L.P. in Dublin. This, of course, is a process which demands an act of faith or suspension of disbelief on the part of the reader. The multifarious contents, depending on polyglottic combinations of the languages of the world, the historical and prehistoric records of mankind and the literatures of the world, could not be known to Earwicker in Chapelizod. The real author, James Joyce, trips airily into the dream whenever he wishes, to explain that what he aimed to set down was 'a most moraculous jeeremyhead sindbook' (229) for all the peoples. With the assistance of Vico's theory of the succession and repetition of cultural cycles in history and the theology of Bruno of Nola, who saw conflicts and contrarieties on earth eventually resolved into unity in eternity, we have here a series of opposites, Shem and Shaun, Butt and Taff, Mutt and Jute, Wellington and Napoleon, Blessed Michael the Archangel and Satan ('Mick', 'Nick') 'All Saints beat Belial' (175), Caesar and Brutus, Sitric and Brian Boru, Buckley and the Russian General, Stella and Vanessa and, of course, H.C.E. and his predecessors, Finn Mac Cool and Finnegan, contending and then 'coalescing through the labyrinth of their samilikes and the alteregoases of their pseudoselves (576) . . . in that multimirror megaron of returningties whirled without end to end.' (582)

All this is written for Leimunconnulstria (229)—a place that looks and sounds as if it were some twilight zone in science fiction, but in fact it is made up of abbreviations of the names of the provinces of Ireland: Leinster, Munster, Connacht, Ulster. These provinces themselves have had their sieges and civil wars, patched up, perhaps, by marriages in the bloodied ruins of desecrated fanes:

> Miscegenations on miscegenations . . . They lived and laughed ant loved, end left . . . Thy thingdom is given to the Meades and Porsons. (18) What clashes here of wills gen wonts, oysterygods gaggin fishygods . . . What bidimetoloves sinduced by what tegoteabsolvers! (4)

These passages refer to the conflicts and subsequent mixtures of successive races who gained control of Ireland. In particular, they refer to the confiscation of the lands of Gaelic chieftains in the seventeenth century and their grant to English families such as the Meades and the Porsons. The 'miscegenations' occurred subsequently when Irish Catholics and the new Protestant grantees contracted mixed marriages. The Protestants, girls, are indicated by the portmanteau word 'Bidimetoloves' based on the lines of the poet, Herrick, a contemporary of the confiscations:

> *Bid me to live and I will live*
> *Thy protestant to be:*
> *Or bid me love and I will bring*
> *A loving heart to thee.*

The word for their seducers 'tegoteabsolvers' is based on the Catholic priest's words of absolution in the sacrament of Penance, *ego te absolvo*, which three words are telescoped into one, with the letter 't' prefixed, Teague or Tadhg being the new planters' generic word for a native Irishman, which is still used by their successors in the sectarian squabbles in Northern Ireland. The names 'Meades and Porsons' also conceal a Biblical reference to the Medes and Persians. Supplanting after confiscation or invasion followed by the miscegenation of races did not, of course, commence with Cromwell. A passage (14-15) shows Joyce casting a backward look, while resting from his parody of old Irish annals, on the remembered scenery of Magh nEalta, the Old Green Plain between the river Liffey and the river Boyne which, being the fertile mother of flocks and herds, was the part of Ireland most coveted by the successive waves of invaders and therefore the scene of numerous battles in the Takings of Ireland, the *Gabhála Eireann* recorded in the earliest legendary annals. Nothwithstanding the din of warfare and the turmoil of battles, first between savages and beasts, and then between barbarians and savages, the calm procession of the seasons goes on year after year. As Ferguson remarks in his poem, 'The Burial of King Cormac':

> Round Cormac spring renews her buds
> In March perpetual by his side,
> Down come the earth-fresh April floods
> And up the seafresh salmon glide.

Each spring the flowers bloom again, the doe and the faun

graze side by side, the shepherd reclines near his flock and a pastoral peace replaces the martial storms that erstwhile swept the plain.

This descriptive passage (14-15) is quoted and dealt with at some length because, as in many other parts of the text where the fundamental scene or subject is Irish, many a Yale key fails to open the gate of Dublin. It is a parody of a passage in Edgar Quinet's *Introduction à la Philosophie de l'Histoire de l'Humanité* which is quoted on p. 281.

> Now after all that farfatch'd and peragrine or dingnant or clere lift we our ears, eyes of the darkness, from the tome of *Liber Lividus* and, (toh!), how paisibly eirenical, all dimmering dunes and gloamering glades, selfstretches afore us our fredeland's plain. Lean neath stone pine the pastor lies with his crook; young pricket by pricket's sister nibbleth on returned viridities; amaid her rocking grasses the herb trinity shams lowliness; skyup is of evergrey. Thus, too, for donkey's years. Since the bouts of Hebear and Hairyman the cornflowers have been staying at Ballymun, the duskrose has chosed out Goatstown's hedges, twolips have pressed togatherthem by sweet Rush, townland of twinedlights, the whitethorn and the redthorn have fairygeyed the mayvalleys of Knockmaroon, and, though for rings round them, during a chiliad of perihelygangs, the Formoreans have brittled the tooths of the Danes . . . these paxsealing buttonholes have quadrilled across the centuries and whiff now whafft to us, fresh and made—of—all—smiles as, on the eve of Kill-allwho.

Here the author pauses from his pretended perusal of the Annals of the Four Masters, Fearfeasa O Mulconry, Peregrine O'Clery, O'Duigenan and Michael O'Clery, to vision Dublin and its hinterland in a period of peace.

In the words *paisibly eirenical*, one may detect various meanings: one, peacably peaceful which is tautological; two, peaceably ironical which is within the context; and three, peacefully Irish-victorious, which may also pass muster, as meaning the victorious recovery of the soil and vegetation of Ireland from the destructive forays of its successive invaders. Through the growth of words as well as of grasses we discern the modest shamrock, emblem of the Trinity, as expounded by St Patrick when preaching to the Irish. The bouts of Hebear and Hairyman do, literally, mean the fights of beast and barbarian for the possession of Ireland, but they also relate to the invasion of the Milesians led by Eber and Eireamhon (*anglice*, Heber and Heremon) who, when they had wrested the land from the Tuatha de Danaan, fought each other for the hegemony. Later in the passage, the word 'Formorean' should read 'Fomorian' but the letter 'r' was probably inserted to suggest the greedy character of the sea-robbers. We notice also in the passage our old friends the whitethorn and the redthorn and the 'two-lips' makes for both kisses and flowers at Rush, which supplies Dublin with the earliest bouquets of the year.

I was once asked whether the phrase, 'a chiliad of perihely-gangs' referred to Tim Healy and his Bantry Gang. I was obliged to say that the answer was no; a *chiliad* is a thousand, *peri* (Greek) round, *hely* from *helios* (Greek) the sun, and *gang*, Teutonic for going; thus the phrase means 'for a thousand circuits of the sun' which Joyce could have more simply expressed by saying 'for a thousand years'. 'Killallwho' means Killala, Waterloo, or more generally, the site of any battle anywhere. I should point out, however, that there is no museum to commemorate the battle of Waterloo at the Wellington monument in the Phoenix Park, as is stated in one book on the *Wake*: that was an establishment visited by James Joyce, in September 1926, near the site of the Battle of Waterloo. Finally, for good measure, the words 'pricket's sister nibbleth' conceal the name of one Sister Niblet who was a nurse in the Richmond Hospital when Gogarty was a medical student there.

It will be evident from this review of the main themes that the chief characters and events and the scenes in which they are laid are all primarily Irish. Other books serve to explain the further global and cosmic literary, historical, theological and philosophical universalisations which are overlaid on these fundamental themes and I do not decry the value of their annotations on these airy levels. Such heights however were not attained by Joyce except in the afterthoughts of his association-mania when he got down to work with telescopes and microscopes, galleyslaving on successive proofsheets from the longsuffering printers. He was correct therefore when he described his work as a building (or, in literature, a *bildungs-roman*) which shot up, storey upon storey, till it attained the height of the Woolworth building: 'A waalworth of a skyer-scape of most eyeful hoyth entowerly, erigenating from next to nothing and celescalating the himals . . . with larrons o'toolers clittering up and tombles a' buckets clottering down.' (4, 5)

The word for 'originating' here is 'erigenating' and is based on Eriugena, used in the name of Johannes Scotus Eriugena, the ninth-century philosopher, to emphasise that he was a native of Ireland, and used here similarly to attest to the Irish sources of *Finnegans Wake*. The work of construction is assisted by St Laurence O'Toole and St Thomas à Becket, both of whom clashed with Henry II, the monarch who sponsored the Norman invasion of Ireland.

Chapter 16
Shem and Shaun

HAVING dealt in some detail with Shem as representing James Joyce, I now pass to his very un-identical twin, Shaun, at home in Ireland, where he is known as Shaun the Post, a name borrowed from Dion Boucicault's nineteenth-century melodrama, *Arrah na Pogue*. As postman, he carries news of Dublin and Ireland to Shem in exile and he is also delivering Shem's letter, *Finnegans Wake* (in instalments presumably), to A.L.P. and H.C.E. His postman's outfit includes (404) a classy mac Frieze o' coat (?Macpherson) of far superior ruggedness indigo braw (Erin go braw), tracked and tramped; . . . thick welted brogues on him . . . and his jacket of providence (Providence Woolen Mills, Foxford, Co. Mayo, for whose products Joyce tried to act as agent in Trieste) . . . and the damasker's overshirt he sported inside, a starspangled zephyr with a decidedly surpliced crinkey doodle front with his motto through dear life embroidered over it, in peas, rice and yeggy-yolk, Or for royal, Am for Mail, R.M.D., hard cash on the nail. This motto might be interpreted in Latin as *Da Valorem* embroidered in green, white and orange, the national colours of Ireland. (It could be derived from the *ad valorem* duties levied by Britain during the 1930s.) . . . 'No mistaking that beamish brow . . . Those jehovial oyeglances' (405). He eats a hearty meal with Boland's broth and including in their green free state a clister of peas . . . with rheingenever to give the Pax cum Spiritututu.

When Mr de Valera went to Switzerland to see Dr Vogt, the eye specialist, he was accompanied by Mr Fred Boland and Joyce was also present to consult Dr Vogt. It happened that the two men had lunch in the same dining-room. Mr Boland was attending Mr de Valera, cutting a roll for his soup etc. Mr de Valera was also due to preside at a League of Nations meeting in Geneva and, in his inaugural speech, dwelt on the positive steps required to preserve peace in Europe and throughout the world. 'Spiritututu' therefore combines the meanings of spirit of security and alcoholic spirits. De Valera had had a hand in stirring the original insurrectionary 'Pot of Broth' in Dublin where he commanded the garrison in Boland's Mills during the 1916 Rising.

A change seems to come over the spirit of the dream: the days of the ambulant postman are replaced by the arrival of radio, by which Shem is enabled to hear Shaun who, from being a mere carrier of state mail, is now the national spokesman: 'I heard a voice, the voce of Shaun, vote of the Irish, voise from afar' (407).

Shaun recalls the time when he and his 'other' (i.e. Shem) were growing up together and remarks, 'He looks rather thin, imitating me. I'm very fond of that other of mine.' (408)

His 'other' politely enquires about Ireland and how does she stand (as in the days of Napper Tandy and *The Wearing of the Green* with a sideglance at Red Riding Hood whose grandmother became the prey of the wolf): 'yet one minute's observation, dear dogmestic Shaun, as we point out how you have while away painted our town a wearing greenridinghued.' (411) 'Dogmestic' emphasises at once the insularity and dogmatism of Shem's opposite number at home in Ireland. Shaun agrees that letter boxes, mail cars, etc. inherited in their red hues from the British have been overpainted green: '. . . I will confess to have, yes. . . . Down with the Saozon ruze!' (411)

The rather confused conversation is broken off (414) to permit the recital of the fable of the Ondt and the Gracehoper, in which the Gracehoper is obviously James Joyce but the Ondt seems to be not Shaun, but Wyndham Lewis who in *Time and Western Man* had attacked the Time principle which he found in *Ulysses*. This is answered by the reference (292) to *Spice and Westend Woman*. When the fable is told, Shem intervenes again (419) to enquire whether Shaun has read the letters to Ireland contained in the published instalments of *Work in Progress*.

Shaun dismisses these 'shemletters patent' as 'a pinch of scribble . . . puffedly offal tosh'. He'd write better himself with his eyes shut.

'Kind Shaun' was then asked,
have you not, without suggesting for an instant, millions of
moods used up slanguage tun times as words as the penmarks
used out in sinscript with such hesitancy by your cerebrated
brother—excuse me not mentioning ahem? (421)

CelebrAted! HeCitEncy! These words grate on Shaun's
ears. That his brother should be celebrated for cerebration or
that the Pigott spelling of hesitancy should be used to invoke
the initials H.C.E. almost drives him into impulsory irelitz.
However, he understands that the pixillated doodler (here
confused with the hero of the film *Mr Deeds Goes To Town*)
is 'on his last' and likely to 'dejeunerate into a skillyton be
thinking himself to death'. Pages 423-4 review Shem's career;
his backslidings are castigated until interrupted by a cough,
'the hundredlettered word again'.

It is then put straight to Shaun whether he could write
Finnegans Wake himself and he replies : '. . . it would be a fall
day I could not . . . and by the power of blurry wards I am
loyable to do it (and) far exceed what that bogus bolshy of a
Shame (has written) . . .' (425)

As to any question of Shem's returning to Dublin to set the
Liffey on fire, Shaun swears that he will 'commission to the
flames any incendiarist whosoever or ahriman howsoclever who
would endeavour to set ever annyma roner moother of mine on
fire.' (426)

Shem counters with some flattery : 'Winner of the gamings,
primed at the studience, propredicted from the storybouts, the
choice of ages wise! spickspookspokesman of our specturesque
silentiousness.' (427)

This is the leader who is elsewhere described as 'a genuine
prime, (i.e., prime meat and prime minister) the real choice,
full of natural greace, the mildest of milkstuffs yet unbeaten
as a risicide and, of course, obsoletely unadulterous . . .' (161)

Here we have a composite picture of one who in his youth
came first in all his examinations, excelled at Rugby football,
whose coming was foretold in the old prophecies as the chosen
hero from the sunny land of Spain to lead the Irish to victory;
one, also, who during the long years of Shem's concentration on
his 'shemletters' was the spokesman of his silence. He is the

genuine material of a Chief Minister to be chosen by the people, one whose speeches have filled heavy parliamentary reports and newspapers for some twenty years, 'tun times as words' as those in Shem's 'sinscript', unbeaten as a laughterkiller and, of course, so little given to adultery as to be of archaic austerity.

The next section of the book dealing with the homily of Shaun (now Jaun, perhaps Juan) to the 29 schoolgirls ends with hints of the coming dawn : 'Ay, already the somberer opacities of the gloom are sphanished . . .' (473)

The people lament Shaun's departure as Ambassador-at-large : 'Life, it is true, will be a blank without you . . . ere Molochy wars bring the devil era.' (473). Here, 'Molochy' can be associated with the Phoenician god, Moloch, or with wars prophesied by the Hebrew prophet Malachi or by the Irish prophet St Malachy. It can also mean that Gogarty (Malachi Mulligan's) 'wars' with Joyce and his subsequent hatred of de Valera would bring the latter into the structure of *Finnegans Wake*. There is also in the phrase an imitation of the assonance of 'Malachy wore' in Moore's poem about the 'days of old/when Malachy wore the collar of gold/That he won from the proud invader'. While the primary reference seems to be to the apocalyptic struggle between the forces of good and evil and the reign of Antichrist before the end of the world, the expression 'Devil era', as pronounced if not as read, could refer to a personage entirely different from Antichrist.

Mr de Valera came to power in March, 1932 with the resolve to remove from the Free State Constitution all vestiges of sub-servience to Britain. These included the oath of loyalty to the British King required to be subscribed by Deputies as a precondition of their entering the Dail and the continuance in office of James MacNeill appointed as Governor General by the previous Administration in 1927 on the vacation of that office by Tim Healy. The new Government's attitude to MacNeill as representative of the King was to accord him merely perfunctory recognition in respect of the functions legally vested in him which had to be performed to legalise certain government decisions and enactment of parliamentary statutes : otherwise, his existence was not recognised officially or socially. On his entrance to a reception given by the French Minister, two Irish ministers, Sean T. O'Kelly and Frank Aiken, decamped hurriedly through the french windows of the French legation. MacNeill was removed from office in October 1932 and replaced by Donal OBuachalla (Buckley) who abjured the royal state of the vice-regal residence and performed his constitutional functions with no official pomp and no social publicity. In those days Mr de Valera's outdoor garb included a large, black hat and a long, black overcoat or cloak.

Joyce was bound to take cognisance of Buckley whose name was the same as that of the character in *FW* whose mission was to shoot the Russian General: 'Don Gouverneur Buckley's in the Tara Tribune' (375)—there being no such newspaper, he gets no press publicity—and 'Pardon the inquisition, causas es quostas? It is Da Valorem's Dominical Brayers. Why coif that weird hood? Because among nosoever circusdances is to be apprehended the dustungwashed poltronage of the lost Gabbarnaur—Jaggarnath.' (342) The reference in the last sentence to the 'lost Governor General' who is in no circumstances to be seen or even understood to exist is clearly to Buckley hidden in Suburbia, but the passage also contains an allusion to another sweep by de Valera's new broom. Having won his second General Election in January 1933, he removed from office the Commissioner for Police, General Eoin O'Duffy and replaced him by Colonel Broy who was instructed to recruit a supplementary force of Civic Guards. These were nicknamed 'the Broy Harriers' and were alleged to be organised to chase the Blue Shirt force which O'Duffy headed shortly after his dismissal. 'Dominican', was punningly written *Domini canis* ('dog of the Lord') so that 'Dominical Brayers' is as fair a rendering as can be expected from Joyce of 'Broy Harriers'. The contest between O'Duffy's Blue Shirts and de Valera's forces of law and order is further referred to (305): 'In effect I could engage in an energument over you till you were republicly royally toobally prussic blue in the shirt after.' 'Prussic' is a sideglance at Hitler's contemporary organisation.

'Da Valorem' in the context quoted primarily means de Valera but translated literally from its Latin wording, 'Give Value', it is a further version of Shaun's motto quoted at the beginning of this chapter, 'R.M.D.', 'Royal Mail, Dublin', and 'Ready Money Down' or, as Joyce himself puts it, 'hard cash on the nail'. Thus de Valera as a historical personage with a reputation as a tough negotiator is here explicitly subsumed into the character of Shaun who, as has been shown above, is elsewhere in the book given the accent and various other personal attributes of the quondam Irish Prime Minister. The connection is again indicated by an anagram of 'Valera' (424.26): '—Peax! Peax! Shaun replied in vealar penultimatum.'

Like other characters in the book, Shaun is subjected to various metamorphoses of personality and he must not be deemed to represent Mr de Valera consistently. On page 407 there is a quick change from Shaun as the national spokesman to Shaun as John Mac Cormack singing the *Panis Angelicus* at the Eucharistic Congress in Dublin in June 1932, 'and cert no purer puer palestrine e'er chanted panangelical'.

Shaun may have originally been intended to be based on J. J. Walsh, the first Free State Minister for Posts and Telegraphs, who introduced new postage stamps one of which displayed a map of Ireland (symbolising the claim to an unpartitioned island) while on another was depicted a sword surrounded by light rays, representing the *Claidheamh Soluis* or Sword of Light, a solar symbol borrowed from Irish mythology. Joyce's father knew Walsh's father in his youth in Cork. He is recorded in the *James Joyce Yearbook* (Paris 1949), as having said:

> I remember I used to buy cigars from the father of the present Postmaster General of the Free State. He had a shop in Parliament Street and sold papers and tobacco.

Here the word 'present' suggests that Jack Joyce's remarks were recorded before June 1927, as J. J. Walsh ceased to be a member of the Executive Council of the Irish Free State about that time. By that date Joyce had been four years at work on sections of *Finnegans Wake* and Walsh would naturally come to his mind as a surrogate for Shaun the Post in that he was the Minister responsible for the conveyance of correspondence between the Irish Exile in Paris and the home country. Some such train of thought seems to be responsible for the present (211) of 'a sunless map of the month, including the sword and stamps for Shemus O'Shaun the Post'.

The foregoing series of references would seem to establish

that Shaun in most of his guises represents the Irishman at home, sometimes a stage Irishman, frequently him who wields the highest authority in the state and with whom Shem, at once the prototype of the introvert artist and of the Irish exile, holds a kind of love-hate relationship. They also seem to lead to the conclusion that in many or most of them the actual person referred to as Shaun is, in fact, Mr de Valera. It remains to demonstrate why Joyce made this bizarre selection.

Stephen Dedalus, representing Joyce as a young man, has Malachi Mulligan as his opposite number, in fact, in Stephen's view, his enemy. Mulligan is the fictional representation of Joyce's pal, Oliver St John Gogarty. In the year 1922 and subsequently, Dr Gogarty had some traumatic experiences apart from seeing himself in the cracked mirror of Joyce's art: he was the doctor called to Griffith's deathbed in August, 1922, and, in the same month, he embalmed the body of Michael Collins who had been killed in an ambush in county Cork. Later in the civil war, Gogarty himself was kidnapped, but he escaped during the night by plunging into the wintry waters of the river Liffey and swimming to the other side. In gratitude to the river for its help in his escape he presented swans to the Liffey together with a poem of dedication, 'Offering of Swans'. Later, when Mr de Valera came to power, Gogarty who had been nominated as a Senator by the previous Government denounced him as having been responsible for the Civil War and for the agricultural upheaval created by the Economic War between his government and the British. Gogarty's denunciations were not confined to the Senate chamber alone; his private and unparliamentary cracks about Mr de Valera were well known amongst his friends and it was gradually realised that Gogarty was developing a de Valera fixation. One example of his abrasive witticisms: de Valera hoped to make Ireland a land flowing with milk and honey by crossing a bee with a bull. Another likened the rare smile of de Valera (the 'risicide') to the glint of moonshine on a tombstone.

The temporary fall in cattle exports occasioned by the Economic War, the Government's democratic abandonment of morning dress at social functions such as the reception of the Papal Legate to the Eucharistic Congress, while adhering to sartorial protocol at the Imperial Conference in Ottawa in

1932 were all celebrated in a quatrain probably composed by James Montgomery but attributed to Gogarty:

> We'll raise the price of everything,
>   On pigs and sheep we'll gorge
> We wear slouch hats for Christ the King
> And toppers for King George.

These events and commentaries were well known to Joyce both from perusal of the Dublin newspapers and from gossip brought to him in Paris by his friends. It seems that as Joyce had already fixed on Gogarty as his symbolic enemy at home in Ireland and as he was aware of Gogarty's hatred of de Valera, he decided to complete the cyclic order by choosing de Valera as his twin brother, Shaun, born like himself in 1882. This was all subjective phantasy on Joyce's part, but it was quite cohesive in its lunatic logic. Gogarty had likened de Valera to something uncoiled from the Book of Kells. Very well, Joyce would re-coil him into the modern version of that manuscript, his own 'Book of Kills'—*Finnegans Wake*.

Gogarty's full fictitious name in *Ulysses* is 'Malachi Roland St John Mulligan'; 'Malachi Mulligan' to preserve the dactylic metre of the syllables of 'Oliver Gogarty', 'Roland' as a substitute for Oliver (*à la* Shakespeare) and St John to preserve Joyce's claim that Gogarty was his own Messianic precursor on the analogy of St John the Baptist.

Bearing all this in mind, the following passage in *Finnegans Wake* portrays Daniel O'Connell with a hint of another personality in the shadows of a double exposure:

> . . . his manslayer's gunwielder portended towards that overgrown lead pencil which was soon, monumentally at least . . . to be his mausoleum . . . while olover his exculpatory features, as Roland rung, a wee dropeen of grief about to sillonise his joujous, his ghost of resignation diffused a spectral appealingness, as a young man's drown o'er the fate of his waters may gloat, similar in origin and akkurat in effective to a beam of sunshine upon a coffin plate. (56)

This refers as clearly to Daniel O'Connell as most passages in *Finnegans Wake* refer clearly to any one thing: the gun is that with which he shot D'Esterre in a duel (this is also referred to on p. 2); the overgrown lead pencil is his monument in the shape of a Round Tower in Glasnevin cemetery; his exculpatory features mutely plead absence of malice in his being forced to shoot D'Esterre and 'as Roland rung', as well as referring to a bell in Bruges, is intended to echo the name of O'Connell's political opponent, Sir Robert Peel, whose smile he likened to a beam of sunshine on a coffin plate. But here, as elsewhere, the text may be assumed to carry more than one meaning. From the gratuitous introduction of 'olover' we seem to sense the presence of Oliver Gogarty as in a palimpsest, from which it is easy to recall Oliver's similitude for de Valera's smile— the glint of moonshine on a tombstone (a reference to the Republican ideology of 1922 and the Civil War mortality). 'A wee dropeen of grief' paraphrases Longfellow's reaction to the peal of the bell Roland which made his 'eyes wet with the most delicious tears' and borrows the poet's name for de Valera's nickname 'The Long Fellow'.

The civil war which followed the signing of the 1921 Treaty with Britain caused the Sinn Fein party to split into Pro-Treaty and Anti-Treaty factions. *Finnegans Wake* takes cognizance of this controversy in the reference to the finding by 'Keven' (Shaun) of 'dogumen number one . . . an illegible downfumbed by an uneligible' (482). The Treaty was signed late at night after the wording of the typewritten draft had been altered by amendments of various kinds, 'a multiplicity of personalities inflicted on the document or documents' (107). Mr de Valera submitted an alternative draft designed to substitute a looser connection between Ireland and Britain; this was called Document Number Two, the Treaty signed in London being impliedly Document Number One. In 1932, when Mr de Valera formed his Government, he disinterred the original Treaty showing the penmarks of excision, revision and so on, to suggest unseemly haste and indecision on the part of the signatories.

There are numerous references to Documents No. 1 and No. 2 in *Finnegans Wake* (358.30: 'ducoman's nonbar one'; 369.24: 'decumans numbered too'; 386: 'darkumond number wan'; 390.29: 'Dalkymont nemberto'; 528.33: 'Doggymans' nimmer win!' and 619: 'But she's stillher deckhuman amber too'). Joyce seems to have been more intrigued by the form of the Treaty than by its contents: he may have found a resemblance between the description he read of it and the 'proteiform graph' of any of his own galley-proofs after he had inflicted his endless revisions on it. There is a deliberate confusion between the finding by Shaun of the text of the Treaty and of Shem's letter which is *FW*.

'Dogumen' has the paranoic echo of one feeling himself a fugitive, a symptom of the persecution ('Eatupus') complex which appears so frequently in Joyce's work. 'Illegible' refers to the condition of the Treaty documents which Mr de Valera revealed, while 'uneligible' refers to Document no. 2, in that it did not have the approval of Parliament or Government. The whole sentence is a parody of Oscar Wilde's description of an English fox-hunting gentleman—'The unspeakable in full pursuit of the uneatable'. Joyce was rather taken by this expression: he uses it again in reference to the Turks who were racially and culturally very different from the Greeks and who had become notorious for their massacres of the Armenians. He refers to them as the 'ungreekable in purscent of the armenable' (181).

'Remove that Bible' (71 and 579) refers to the attitude of Mr de Valera and his party to the oath of loyalty to the British king which they were required to take on re-entering the Dail in 1927. They signed the members' roll, having removed the Bible to a distant part of the room. The incident is equated to the Cromwellian 'Remove that bauble.'

The next confrontation between Shem and Shaun will be found in the Academic section (complete with marginal comments and footnotes, after the manner of scholarly text books). In this section it may be possible to ascertain the inborn psychological basis of the antagonism between the twins.

Shem (Dolph) plays on Shaun's (Kev's) interest in geometry to show him a problem touching on the construction of 'ann aquilittoral dryankle' and the concoction of 'an equoangular trilitter' (286). He suggests that he should 'first mull a mugfull of mud, son'. Shaun expostulates, 'what the D.V. would I do that for' and in reply Shem explains that the mud is that of his mother, A.L.P. Gradually the figure is constructed of two intersecting circles, the cardinal points being doubly indicated by the letters A.L.P. in Greek and Roman lettering. The ratiocinative elegance of the successive steps of this geometrical demonstration the virtuoso Shaun enthusiastically applauds.

Dolph (Shem) proceeds briskly to demonstrate with his pointer (Siegfried's sword or Joyce's ashplant from the West-meath midlands): 'I. . . curry nothung up my sleeve. Now springing quickenly from the mudland Loosh from Luccan with Allhim as her Elder tetraturn a somersault.' (295) He is using the Irish words for trees, *Luis, Ailm,* and *Peithe* (rowan, elm and dwarf elder) which signify the letters, l, a, p, in the Irish alphabet, to spell out the cardinal points of his geometrical representation of their mother and, by a 'somersault', correcting the order of the letters to ALP. This, he tells his brother, will make him to 'see figuratleavely, the whome of your eternal geo-mater.' (296) Thus the future Irish leader is being shown as a schoolboy an illustration of the anatomical structure of his mother, ALP, and Ireland also, as his brother has already pointed out (294), 'Modder ilond there too', imitating incident-ally John Mac Cormack's brogue when singing 'Ireland, Mother Ireland'. The exercise is one in realism as against the poetical personification of Ireland as a woman, Dark Rosaleen (Roisin Dubh, the Dark Little Rose) or Kathleen ni Houlihan, of whom Yeats had written that they had 'all bent low and low and kissed the quiet feet /Of Cathleen, the daughter of Houlihan'. Dolph, on the other hand, presents his brother with a picture of his 'eternal geomater', a geometrical figure of his 'earth-mother', given to one who, as a student of geometry, might be expected to appreciate it. But Kev's mathematical enthusiasm gives way to anger when he realises the outrageous intrusion which Dolph is making on his filial piety and he knocks the erring brother down with a blow right through his pergaman— 'and it did for him like it done for many another unpious one' (303).

The artist is doomed to be for ever at variance with his brother, the Irish politician, and so to remain an Irish Exile. When the politician came into his kingdom and could invite his exiled brother to return to Ireland, would he be brought back and crowned with laurel to celebrate his literary triumphs? Not, as we have shown, if his objective was to set the Liffey on fire. St Patrick had returned at the behest of Irish voices heard in his dreams, calling on him from the woods of Foclut by the western shore, 'Come O holy youth and walk once more amongst us.' Patrick became the National Apostle. If Shem returned as the 'National Apostate' and repaired to the woods of Foclut perhaps what he would encounter would be the *wolves* of Foclut on the analogy of Parnell who in his *Manifesto* of 29 November 1890 adjured his colleagues not to throw him to the English wolves. This phrase was first used by Bodkin, William O'Briens' 'scribe' (cf. *U* 575) in the *United Irishman*, before O'Brien cabled him orders to change the paper's policy and oppose Parnell. Bodkin probably knew, but neither Parnell nor Joyce knew, that the name of the author of *Parnellism and Crime* was John Wolfe Flanagan of the editorial staff of the London *Times*, who died November 1929. (He edited the material which Sir John Anderson of the Home Office had collected from his spy, Le Caron, and from other informers through the police—see 496.32).

Joyce did, in fact, imagine that he was officially invited back to Ireland when Desmond FitzGerald, newly appointed Free State Minister for External Affairs, met him in Paris and asked him (perhaps quite casually) if he now proposed to come to Ireland. He rejects the invitation—'Sherlock is lorking for him!' (534) The reference is, not to Sherlock Holmes, but to Lorcan Sherlock, the then City Sheriff, who would by virtue of his office attend an execution. The idea that he would be hanged if he travelled back by 'the highroad of the nation, Traitor's Track' was not all mere humorous exaggeration on Joyce's part; his paranoic fixation led him to imagine that in Ireland his destiny would be to share the fate of Parnell who, he believed, was hounded to his death by the priests and the venal politicians. In fact, Parnell died of double pneumonia.

Chapter 17

Jaun and Yawn

THE second chapter of Book III (429-73) is devoted mainly to
Jaun's longwinded and ambivalent 'sermon' to the girls at St
Bride's academy, a set piece which does not need explication or
detailed analysis. It does, however, contain a small snapshot of
The Artist (443-4) where Jaun declares a strong inclination to
give 'the brother-keeper into custody' or to take the law into
his own hands and swing for him. The 'brother' makes a personal but silent appearance under the name of 'Dave' on pp.
462-4 and the narrator has Jaun refer to him in addressing the
girls and his 'aunt Julia Bride' (perhaps their teacher or the
Catholic Church, or both, as well as a character from a story in
Henry James's *The Altar of the Dead*), in terms that make it
evident that 'Dave' is Shem, returned to take the place of 'Jaun'
(Shaun) who is on his way to foreign parts. He is leaving his
'darling proxy . . . Dave the Dancekerl' for their consolation,
that is, as a Paraclete. 'Here he its, darling Dave . . . on quin-
quisecular cycles after his French evolution'. Dave carries the
'testymonicals' which he had obtained in 'Paddyouare'.

Two five-year periods calculated from Joyce's first departure
from Dublin to Paris in 1902 would date this arrival of Shem-
Dave in 1912—Joyce did in fact visit Dublin in the summer of
1912. A few months previously he had undergone written and
oral tests in the University of Padua to obtain a qualification
to teach in Italy. He passed the tests but was refused the qualification in the absence of reciprocal recognition of University
degrees by the Italian and British authorities.

Jaun continues his commentary : 'He's the sneaking likeness
of us, faith, me altar's ego in miniature . . . Got by the one goat,
suckled by the same nanna, one twitch, one nature, makes us
oldworld kin . . . I love him. I love his old portugal's nose . . .

He is looking aged witt his pebbled eyes, and johnnythin too.'

The 'goat' referred to as their common father is H.C.E. under the name of *Hircus Civis Eblanensis* (215) where Shem and Shaun are said to be 'twins of his bosom'. 'His old portugal's nose' is appropriate to Joyce's rubicund proboscis or to that of Shem which lit the page on which he was writing 'as it slid lucifericiously within an inch' of the paper (182). The 'pebbled eyes' depict Joyce's eyes seen through his thick glasses; 'johnnythin' would also refer to Joyce as meaning 'jolly thin' but, as it almost certainly also means 'Jonathan', this aspect of the reference should properly relate to Jaun in his character of Jonathan, Dave's brother or opposite. The equivocal utterance is continued at the end of p. 463 :

> Bravo, senior chief! Eamose! Sure there's nobody else in touch anysides to hold a chef's cankle to the darling atall for sheer dare with that prisonpotstill of spanish breans on him like the knave of trifles!

This reads much more like a eulogy of Shaun (Eamon de Valera, called 'The Chief' by his followers, with his prison record and Spanish origin) than of Shem, 'Dave', Joyce. Here, as elsewhere, e.g. p. 354, there are suggestions of a merger, or exchange, of personalities. A similar exchange seems to occur on page 288 where 'cunctant that another would finish his sentence for him' seems to refer to Mr de Valera's escape from Lincoln Gaol when the number to escape with him was limited to two of the other four involved.

Next (464) Dave is likened to Lemuel Gulliver (Jonathan Swift) with his 'blackguarded eye' (i.e. Joyce with the black lens on his bad eye) and is seen to be tonsured (as St Patrick?) when he takes off his hat. Jaun shakes hands with him, 'the Claddagh clasp' (two hands clasped on the Claddagh ring), when he 'met with dapper dandy and he shocked me big the hand' ('I met with Napper Tandy and he took me by the hand').

Shem's normal character as seen by Shaun reappears (467) where it is related that the 'Illstarred punster' was 'capped out of beurlads scoel'. This has been taken to mean Berlitz school where Joyce taught but it also means that he taught English there, Béarla (otherwise Béurla) being the Irish word for the English language.

Jaun takes his departure heralded by the usual accompaniment of first lines from Moore's Melodies identified here by 'the moore the melodist': 'Gulp a bulper at parting' ('one bumper at parting') and 'Farewell but whenever', and by the motif words (469): 'I'm going. I know I am. I couldbet I am. Somewhere I must get far away from Banbashore'.

The reference to Ireland under its poetical name, Banba, has an undertone of a chorus of the 1920s:

> A thousand miles I travelled
>   And a thousand sights I saw,
> But there are no sights like the moonlit nights
>   On the Bam-Bam-Bammy shore.

The greater part of the next chapter (474) deals with Shaun, who from 'Jaun' in the preceding chapter has now become 'Yawn' the voice of a sleepy person and also pronounced like the vocative case of Shaun (Gaelic, Seán, a Sheáin). He lies low on a hillock. 'His dream monologue was over . . . but his drama parapolylogic had yet to be': his dreaming sermon to the girls in the preceding chapter will now be succeeded by interrogations conducted in several tongues. Yawn's actual situation is 'on the mead of the hillock . . . up the mountainy molehill' (474), 'ells upon ells of him . . . one half of him in Conn's half but the whole of him nevertheless in Owenmore's five quarters . . . Up to the esker ridge it was, Mallinger parish' (475). The Mamalujo Four, 'three kings of three suits and a crowner' (coroner) approach him 'from the westborders of the eastmidlands . . . from all their cardinal parts, along the amber way where Brosna's furzy' (474) and they find the 'ells upon ells of him, making so many square yards of him (475) . . . a few perch to the weatherside of the knoll Asnoch'. A cross-reference is necessary here to page 293 where mention is made of 'The Turnpike under the Great Ulm (with Mearingstone in Fore ground). Given now ann linch you take enn all.'

The 'knoll Asnoch' with 'Mearingstone' refers to the hill of Uisneach (pronounced as in the English spelling, 'Ushnagh') in the county Westmeath, about 600 feet high, surmounted by a large rock, twenty feet high and twenty yards in circumference, which was the traditional centre, meditallium, navel, umbilicus or omphalos of Ireland and the point at which its four ancient provinces met. In Irish the rock was Aill na Míreann, Rock of the Divisions. The English word 'mere', 'mear' or 'mearing' signifies 'boundary' and 'merestone' a stone which marks a boundary. The Irish word 'mír' is pronounced the same as the English 'mere' but it means, not a boundary, but a section of countryside separated from other sections by a boundary. The Irish genitive plural 'míreann' and the English 'mearin' have become merged in the Irish brogue pronunciation 'maerin' which is now used to connote a boundary between adjoining farms. Aill na Míreann ceased to have its traditional and literal meaning when a new province or 'fifth' was created by detaching sections of territory from the other four. This operation is ascribed to the legendary King Tuathal Teachtmhar, newly restored to the High Kingship after a rebellion of the aborigines, who is said to have formed the new province of Meath by detaching from each of the old provinces sections of them around their meeting-point, thereby creating a mensal kingdom for himself, independently of the provincial kings. The Irish word for province, cúige (fifth) must have come into use after this division and it continues to have this meaning although the country has long since reverted to the quadripartite provincial system. The contradictory use of a fifth for a quarter and a subsequent division of the island into halves, between Conn Ced-cathach (Conn of the Hundred Battles) and Eoghan Mór, explains the references to 'Conn's half' and 'Owenmore's five quarters'. 'Fore ground' (293) refers to Fore, also in Westmeath, site of an abbey founded by St Fechin (d. 664). 'Mallinger' is Joyce's spelling of Mullingar, county town of Westmeath, which is also the name of the inn in Chapelizod where he locates H.C.E. and his family. It would seem that Joyce was inspired by his youthful memories of Mullingar and Uisneach in making his choice of Mullingar Inn as the focus of the Finnegan epic. Lough Ennell, between Mullingar and Uisneach, is referred to on page 293 ('you tek enn all') and on page 475 ('ells upon ells of him', a linear measure of Yawn which might perhaps be written algebraically as 'L^n'). Lough Ennell itself is drained by the river Brosna (474), a tributary of the Shannon, the upper course of which feeds and drains Lough Owel before entering Lough Ennell.

The Inquisition into, or Inquest on, Yawn conducted by the

Four ('Crowner' is the Irish brogue word for 'Coroner' used by Samuel Lover in *Handy Andy*) is a variation on the trial of Festy King (85 *et seq.*) but the process here is much longer, the scene is geographically explicit (the parts of Westmeath to the west and north of Mullingar) and the historical references are intended to be an evocation of 'climes of old times gone by' which the historic hill of Uisneach might well be deemed to hold invisible but imperishable in its aura of sombre and mysterious solitude. It is also a flash-back to Joyce's stay in Mullingar as a youth. Yawn apparently answers his inquisitors from his 'neverstop navel' and, as he is lying on Ireland's navel or omphalos, the intention may be to put Ireland as well as Yawn to the question. Through Yawn we get replies in the voice of St Patrick. This is appropriate as Petra Coithrigi (Patrick's Rock) was an alias of Aill na Míreann. St Patrick says, through Yawn, *Moy jay trouvay la clee dang les champs*, meaning that he used the clover leaf (klee) or shamrock as a key (*clef*) to the mystery of the Trinity in his mission to the people of Ireland. The voice adds 'Hay sham nap poddy velour'. The Inquisitor dismisses this assumed reference to de Valera: 'whur's that inclining and talkin about the messiah so cloover!' This answer seems to disclaim the presence of de Valera in Yawn who now proceeds to assume also the voice of Jonathan Swift: 'The woods of fogloot! O mis padredges!' for example, refers to St Patrick's dream about being recalled to Ireland by voices from the woods of Foclut and also to Swift's parodies of John Partridge's predictions in his almanac. The reference to 'Foclut' and 'partridge' brings the Fourth Master's mind back to his native Mayo, Festy King's country, but Yawn translates 'woods' to 'wolves': 'The wolves of Fochlut! . . . Do not fling-amejig to the twolves!'—a version of Parnell's 'Do not fling me to the wolves'.

St Patrick is heard again where, as he tells in his *confessio*, a pagan offers to initiate him into his tribe, 'Laid bare his breast paps to give such, to suckle me' and he repudiates the 'welsher perfyddye', proclaiming himself a Christian Saint, 'Ecce Hagios Chrisman', but revealing himself at the same time by his initials as a mixed-up H.C.E. (480).

The wolf theme is continued, 'We move in the beast circules', with the addition of the fox whose medieval legend was re-written in Johann Wolfgang Goethe's *Reinecke Fuchs* :—'Hey! Did you dream you were ating your own tripe, acushla, that you tied yourself up that wrynecky fix?' Yawn complains that the cubs are after him, 'the whole totem pack', on which one of The Four suggests that they get out the Fingal Harriers (a county Dublin hunt club) to run them down.

Pages 481-482.4 are concerned with the father figure H.C.E. and a Trinity in which Lewis Carroll (Dodgson) participates and then the fourth gospeller 'Jong of Mayo' is adjured by the first, Matthew of Armagh, to fix up his spreadeagle and pull his weight! St John the Evangelist, whose symbol is an eagle, is here identified with John McHale, Archbishop of Tuam, in the province of Connacht in the arms of which an eagle is also represented. Tuam is spelt 'Chuam', giving the English phonetic effect of the Irish pronunciation. (Joyce had noted in *Scribbledehobble* that W.B.Y. [Yeats] pronounced tune 'chune'.) Matthew asks John whether he knew a young man named Keven 'that found the dogumen number one . . . an illegible down-fumbed by an unelgible'.

John certainly knows 'sinted sageness' but he needs no prodding from Matty Armagh. Mark takes a hand and points out that the inventor of the ultimate writing (Shem) is he who discovered the original script: 'That's the point of eschatology our book of kills reaches for' (482). This refers to St Columcille's prophecies (not primarily to the Book of Kells) and to the evil times at the end of the world and of Ireland in particular. It goes on to suggest that Yawn's style seems indebted to the amanuensis Shem: 'The gist is the gist of Shaun but the hand is the hand of Sameas.' (483) The meaning is as Shaun intended but it is expressed by Shem (Shemus, Seamas) or by somebody identical with (same as) Shem. Yawn denies the connection: 'Been ike his kindergardien?' (This question was already raised at 305.16 and 443.4). In the eloquence of his *apologia* Yawn becomes quite self-assertive, exchanging his Goidelic 'c' for the Brythonic 'p'—I'm of the ochlocracy with Prestopher Palumbus and Porvus Parrio [*cf.* 496, 'Christy Columb' and Le Caron Crow'] . . . Ha look at my jailbrand Exquovis . . .' He boasts of his national record as a freedom fighter who had suffered imprisonment. You do not meet one like him every day: *Ex quovis ligno non fit mercurius* (a statue of Mercury cannot be hewn from the first log you stumble on).

St Luke is not impressed. With a passing reference to 'Rose Lankester and Blanche York' to indicate Shem's educational background of schoolroom competitions where the teams were made up of those ranked under the Red Rose of Lancaster and the White Rose of York, he puts Yawn the leading question: 'Are we speachin d'anglas landage or are you sprakin sea Djoytsch!' (485)

This is a momentous question which could have had the effect of shattering the dream on which the book is theoretically based, awakening the dreamer and bringing Joyce himself before the court to admit responsibility for the writing of 'That letter selfpenned to one's other, that neverperfect everplanned' (489) in a specially invented language, 'Djoytsch', but the examination of Yawn continues: he is called back, like Paddy Reilly to Ballyjamesduff, to speak in his old fellow's accent, stutter and all. He is submitted to a T square test in which he sees 'a blackfrinch pliestrycook' (Huysmans), very like Shem, (486) and it is suggested to him (487) that he could 'be very largely substituted . . . by a complementary character'. His reply earns no conviction and one of the examiners says, 'The voice is the voice of Jokeup, I fear'. Yawn's reply (488-9) ends with a sentence in which, following on all the suggestions of Shem's taking his place, I am inclined to regard as the voice of Shem: 'I call you my halfbrother because you in your soberer otiumic moments remind me deeply of my natural saywhen brothel in feed'. This points to a comparison of Eamon de Valera and Stanislaus Joyce—two risicides (laughter-killers), monolithic personalities, total abstainers, obsoletely unadulterous.

A.L.P. intervenes in the discussion (492) on behalf of H.C.E. and, in the course of her statement, refers to A.H.A. Borumborad, the name by which an Irishman named Patrick Joyce masqueraded as a Turk in eighteenth-century Dublin and introduced Dubliners to Turkish baths. Her account is dismissed as 'Fantasy! funtasy on fantasy, amnaes fintasies! And there is nihil nuder under the clothing moon. When Ota, weewahwificle of Torqualls, bumpsed her dumpsydiddle down in her woolsack . . .' (493) Here we are back in Westmeath, with historical echoes of the Norse invader, Torgils, whom the Irish called

Turgéis and Latinised Turgesius, a tyrant who made promiscu-
ous use of the *jus primae noctis* or, in default, the financial
composition known as *luach impidhe*. Keating records that
Turgéis was in the Abbacy of Armagh for seven years and
also in the monastery of Clonmacnoise on the altar of which
his wife, Oda, was accustomed to promulgate her oracles, judg-
ments and commands to all. 'A.D. 843. Turgesius was taken
prisoner by Maelseachlainn, the son of Mulrony, who afterwards drowned him in Loch Uair (Lough Owel).' This translation by Connell Mageoghegan of an entry in the Annals of
Clonmacnoise is considered more reliable than the account
given by Giraldus Cambrensis and copied by Keating, who say
that he was drowned in Lough Ennell.

The examination is diverted to A.L.P.'s animadversions on
Sully : 'If they cut his nose on the stitcher they had their siven
good reasons . . . when Lynch Brother, Withworkers, Friends
and Company with T. C. King and the Warden of Galway is
prepared to stretch him sacred by the powers to the starlight,
L.B.W. Hemp, hemp hurray! says the captain in the moonlight.' (495) The name of Sully, 'Sully the Thug' (212), seems
to be borrowed from James Sully, author of *Illusions, A
Psychological Study* (4th ed. 1895) which contains (Chapter
VIII, 'Dreams') some sixty pages on the Dream as Illusion,
the Dream as Hallucination, the Form and Structure of Dreams
etc.

'Stretch', in Dublin eighteen-century slang meant 'hang' (cf.
The Night before Larry was stretched), and is associated with
Lynch, the Warden of Galway who hanged his son for the
murder of a Spanish visitor. ('L.B.W'. qualifying 'Hemp' means
'Lynch Brother Withworkers' thus unifying the executioner and
his rope). 'Captain Moonlight' was a generic name for leaders
of midnight marauders.

A.L.P.'s version of the charges against H.C.E. involving a
character named Magrath and his thug the aforesaid Sully and
his 'skirriless ballets in Parsee French' and the 'lady perform-
ers' Elsebett and Maryetta Gunning with motto 'O'Neill saw
Queen Molly's pants,' carries references to Percy French's songs,
the two beautiful Gunning sisters from Roscommon who
married into the British aristocracy in the eighteenth century
and a version of the motto on the British Royal Crest (*Honi*

soit qui mal y pense, elsewhere rendered as 'Honey swarns where mellisponds'.

Pages 496, 497, 498 review the preparations for the death, wake and resurrection (499) of H.C.E. which brings us back to Uisneach and the inquest on Yawn, who is now a mere receiving and broadcasting set for the voices which come up out of the historic hill on which he lies. These purport to represent the racial memory of the Irish and their leaders and conquerors but Joyce's effort to give effect to this is very superficial and the cries from the earth portray only the stock characters who appear or are symbolised elsewhere in *FW* :—Dovegall and finshark (dark and fair foreigners); the yeomen (the 1798 militia); Crum abu! Cromwell to victory! (warcries of the Earl of Desmond and Oliver Cromwell). Christianity or Puritanism in the editorial controls of Dublin newspapers, the *Irish Times, Irish Independent, Freeman's Journal* and *Daily Express*; racial and sectarian riots (rape the daughter! choke the pope!); Sold! I am sold! Brinabride! I sold! (Iseult); Pipette dear! (Swift and Stella); Fort! Fort! Baysoyt! March! ('Fort' is FERT, *Fortitudo eius Rhodum tenuit*, ('his courage held Rhodes' or *Foemina erit ruina tua*, 'woman will be your ruin'): when you sell get my price (Parnell). In the Galway bye-election of 1886 when Parnell nominated Captain O'Shea as his party's candidate in spite of local opposition, Joe Biggar proposed to telegraph him, 'Mrs O'Shea will be your ruin.' Tim Healy changed the first words to 'The O'Sheas'. This seems to explain the repeated use in *FW* of FERT but various versions of the words involved subserve other literary devices.

SILENCE (501) stands for the Indian *sandhi* or the Yawning Gap of the Norse Edda, marking the pause or gap between two cycles, here referred to as a 'justajiff siesta', after which the inquest continues. The questions relate to a 'fair day' followed by a 'lukesummer night' which echo the cross-examination in the Trial of Pegger Festy (85 *et seq.*). Witness agreed there was also snow, 'By snaachta clocka', by seven o'clock or by hailstones. There were also gales and frost. Yet the moon was shining (502) that nackt (*nocht*, Ir. night), 'and not one but a pair of pritty geallachers', i.e. there were two moons (Ir. *geallach*, moon) or two Gallaghers or a pair of breasts and

F

whitecaps foamflaking from Foxrock to Finglas. According to the 'Dublin Annals' in Thom's *Directory*, two moons appeared in the sky in 1339.

There are descriptions of places where 'the illassorted couple first met' which evoke the remark, 'Godamedy, you're a delville of a tolkar!' (503) Delville was the name of Mrs Delaney's house near the river Tolka on the north side of Dublin where Swift's attack on the contemporary members of the Irish Parliament was printed. The questioning passes on to the 'overlasting eshtree' or everlasting ashtree, that grew in the vicinity. The vicinity of north Dublin is, however, clouded by a reference to a river and a mountain in Tipperary: 'Beside the Annar. At the ford of Slievenamond' while 'With a snoo-drift from one beerchen bough' relates the ashtree, in passing, to a metaphorical beech tree used by C. J. Kickham in his poem:

> She lived beside the Anner
> At the foot of Slievenamon,
> A gentle peasant girl
> With mild eyes like the dawn,
> Her cheeks were dewy rosebuds
> And her teeth were pearls rare
> A snowdrift neath the beechen bough
> Her neck and nutbrown hair.

This ashtree is the Teutonic mythological Yggdrasil, the steed of ygg and woden ('woodin'), our 'beingstalk' or 'quickenbole' (tree of life) and also 'crossbones' where 'tyburn fenians' (Irish rebels condemned to death) snore. It is frequented by all the birds of the air and climbed by 'Borstol Boys' from Erasmus Smith's charity schools for the origin of spices and charlotte darlings, i.e. students of Darwin's *Origin of Species* and *The Descent of Man*, i.e. agnostics and also saints (hermits of the desert barking their infernal shins over her triliteral roots'— St Jerome, perhaps, studying Hebrew). 'Nobirdy aviar soar anywing to eagle it.' Being both male and female, this ashtree represents the ultimate union of H.C.E. and A.L.P. (505), and near by is the stone of the unchanging Law. Thus Tree and Stone, the dumb whom Shem made speak (195), are here static and finally fixed. 'Were you there when they lagged um through the Coombe?'

Joyce portrays Stephen in *Stephen Hero*, on a visit to Mullingar, staying with his 'godfather' or 'guardian' at a house near Lough Owel. (*Stephen Hero*, revised edition, 1956). Later he has Stephen Dedalus follow false Hellenic gods into a martello tower, which Mulligan unjustifiably dubbed their 'Omphalos'. In this chapter of *Finnegans Wake*, Joyce returns to his youth and his 1900-1901 memories of the country around Mullingar as the scene of the confrontation with Yawn on a real Omphalos fixed by the Ice Age imperishably on Uisneach, a theatre for communion between skygods, men and earthspirits.

Here he had a real rock, the enormous Ail na Míreann, as a justification for his symbolic stone of unchanging law. Here, too, in ancient times there grew that huge tree, *Craeb Uisnig*, an Ash. 'Due northward fell the Ash of Uisneach as far as Granard, in the time of the sons of Aed Sláine.'—*Book of Leinster*. This would mean that the tree was about twenty-five miles high and thus a cosmic rival of Yggdrassil.

A small Latin tag, *ex ungue leonem*, is put into Joyce Latin, *Ex ugole lenonem* (513), in revenge for Mick Lennon's hostile article in a Canadian periodical, the *Catholic World*, March 1931. Referring to a supposed invitation to return to Ireland, Joyce had said, 'No, *hic sunt lennones*.' The personal antagonism of the eccentric Lennon was ascribed to Ireland as a lion, her claw red with Joyce's blood. The phrase appears in 179.2.

In the concluding portion of the Inquest on Yawn, the responses are relayed through him from H.C.E. himself, who recites an *apologia pro vita sua*. An edition of this section (532-54) entitled *Haveth Childers Everywhere* was published by Faber and Faber in 1931 as an instalment of 'Work in Progress'. It is for the most part fairly easily deciphered. Parts of it have already been used in explicating H.C.E. and various references in it will be covered in the chapter, 'Permutations and Combinations' below. The pages based on B. Seebohn Rowntree's *Poverty, A Study of Town Life*, (543-5), are dealt with in the 'Ashplant' chapter in Part I. Yawn appears to remain the medium of communication but he has ceased to participate in the dialogue. The Four have ceased to be interrogators but remain as audience with an occasional comment, e.g.—'He's not all buum and bully.' (550) All that needs to be dealt with here is an interpolation (535-6) in H.C.E.'s monologue:

—Old Whitehowth he is speaking again. Ope Eustace tube! Pity poor whiteoath! Dear gone mummeries, goby! Tell the woyld I have lived true thousand hells. Pity, please, lady, for poor O. W. in this profundest snobbing I have caught. Nine dirty years mine age, hairs hoar, mummery failend, snow-drift to my ellpow, deff as Adder . . . Pity poor Haveth Childers Everywhere with Mudder!

Here are echoes of Mangan's 'The Nameless One' of which the following is the penultimate quatrain:

> And lives he still then? Yes! Old and hoary
> At thirty-nine, from despair and woe
> He lives, enduring what future story
> Will never know.

One gathers from the beginning of the interpolation that Finn Mac Cool, disguised as Howth Head wearing a white cloudcap, is taking control of the seance, using Mangan's words to lament decay and decrepitude similar to the conditions be-wailed in 'The Nameless One'. But the reference to O. W. in this profundust snobbing' seems to transform Old Whitehowth to Oscar Wilde and the accents of his dolorous despair in *De Profundis*. Wilde's conduct 'bycause of what he was ascend into his prisonce on account off' are deplored in the words 'Mongrieff! O Hone!' (536) but the first exclamation is a play on Moncrieff, the name of a character in *The Importance of Being Earnest*, while 'O Hone!' though it sounds like the Irish for 'alas!' could also be interpreted phonetically in that language as an invocation of a posterior. Wilde is clearly identi-fied as the 'Communicator' where he is called (535-6) 'A dis-incarnated spirit, called Sebastion', Sebastian Melmoth, a character from Charles Robert Maturin's *Melmoth the Wanderer*, being the *alias* adopted by Wilde on his release from prison.

Other references to Wilde in *FW* are also hostile. The 'great white caterpillar' (33) is a borrowing of Lady Colin Campbell's description of him and he is referred to (350) in the Butt and

Taff episode as 'Mr Lhugewhite Cadderpollard' at Oldbally Court, i.e. the Old Bailey where he was tried.

Joyce had previously treated Wilde with a somewhat condescending sympathy. In section 40 of the edition of his *Critical Writings*, he used Wilde as a weapon with which to attack British puritanism and hypocrisy. Writing to Stanislaus, 19 August 1906, he suggests that *The Picture of Dorian Gray* failed because of Wilde's not having the courage to name the sin which is the theme of the book (*Letters*, II). *The Importance of Being Earnest* was staged by Joyce's company, the English Players, in Zurich in 1918 and it was Joyce's quarrel with Henry Carr, the English consular official who played the part of Algernon Moncrieff, that resulted in Carr and his colleagues, Bennett and Rumbold, being accorded derogatory parts in *Ulysses*, the first two as foulmouthed British Tommies in 'Circe' and Rumbold as the hangman in 'Cyclops'.

Joyce's hostility to Wilde seems to have been a later development arising from remarks about *Ulysses* attributed to Wilde's spirit in *Psychic Messages from Oscar Wilde* (1924) by Hesther Travers Smith who, Joyce wrote to Miss Weaver, 1 January 1925, was 'a daughter of Professor Dowden of Trinity College, Dublin'. Wilde had conveyed from the Otherworld the view that it was singular 'that a countryman of mine should have produced this great bulk of filth'. Joyce seems to have borrowed Wilde's spirit from Mrs Travers Smith's seance in order to hold him up to obloquy and contempt.

When Joyce abandoned Catholicism in his youth, he retained, and gradually added to, his stock of superstitions, superstitious fears, taboos and observances of dates, omens and accidents. It is quite possible that he believed that the hostile verdict on *Ulysses* had actually come from Wilde in the psychic message described by Mrs Travers Smith. Alternatively, or perhaps additionally, he may have come to develop towards him the type of jealous intolerance that he displayed towards any writer, Irish or otherwise, who had shown signs of venturing into literature akin to the *risqué* writing in which he deemed himself a specialist. His hostility in this respect was reserved in special measure for D. H. Lawrence but it also extended to Proust and George Moore. It seems to have been based on a psychopathology originating in his solipsism and of the same pattern as the sense of alienation from his near relations which he had early on divined in himself. This latter sense is expressed in *U* 196: 'The images of other males of his blood will repel him. He will see in them grotesque attempts of nature to foretell or repeat himself.'

Chapter 18

The Trial of Festy King

THE first three chapters of Book I of *Finnegans Wake* are mainly concentrated on investigations into the origin, name, deeds and misdeeds of Humphrey Chimpden Earwicker as a citizen of Dublin and, in his universalised capacity (H.C.E., Here Comes Everybody) as a symbol of all mankind, bearing the burdens of the first man's disobedience and the sins, crimes and torts of all his breed. This provides wide expanses of space and time for charges and exculpations, trials and errors, but in the fourth chapter the sleeping Earwicker, sinking into a deeper stratum of slumber, dumps his burden on the shoulders of his son, Shaun, narrowing at the same time the conudrum of his own crime to simple charges of assault and battery. Shaun defends himself under the name of Festy King, but Shem seems to be also involved and ultimately there is an amalgamation of their personalities.

> . . . a child of Maam, Festy King, of a family long and honourably associated with the tar and feather industries, who gave an address in old plomansch Mayo of the Saxons in the heart of a foulfamed potheen district, was subsequently haled up at the Old Bailey on the calends of Mars under an incompatibly framed indictment of both the counts (from each equinoxious points of view, the one fellow's fetch being the other follow's person). . . . (85)

The accused 'deposing for his exution with all the fluors of sparse in the royal Irish vocabulary' is apparently defending himself through the medium of Irish.

> . . . it was attempted by the crown (P. C. Robort) to show that King, *elois* Crowbar, once known as Meleky (went to a

fair) under the illassumed names of Tykingfest and Rabworc
. . . with a pedigree pig.

'Tykingfest' is a crude anagram of the accused's name;
'Rabworc' is crowbar written backwards, while 'Meleky' is a
version of 'Melecky', Arabic for 'king' and refers back also to
Malachy, High King of Ireland before and after the reign of
Brian Boru.

The next sentence begins, 'They were on that sea by the plain
of Ir nine hundred and ninetynine years . . .' This has no
relevance to the context. It is an echo of a fragment of the old
Irish tale, The Fate of the Children of Lir, three brothers and
their sister, Fionnuala, who were metamorphosed into swans
by a cruel stepmother and doomed to dwell on the seas around
Ireland for three periods of 300 years, one such period to be
spent on the sea of Moyle between Ireland and Scotland. Elsewhere I have shown that Joyce uses on several occasions the
first line of Moore's lyric on this theme—*Silent, O Moyle, be
the roar of thy water*—and, in fact, adopts the word 'Moyle'
as a generic name for ocean ('the moyles and moyles of it'; 'the
moylean main').

The injection of a fragment of this tale into the context of
a narrative about an Irish-speaking character may be an attempt
to evoke the Gaelic background of the accused, so utterly alien
to the principles and practice of English legal procedures under
which he was being tried. Joyce may also have considered the
reference relevant to his general theme of Crime and Punishment, with the associated versions of false accusations or
trumped-up charges.

The fair to which Festy King had gone was held in 'Mud-
ford', possibly an anglicisation of Ballinamuc which in Irish
would mean 'town of the ford of pigs' while in English the
sound of the last syllable would convey the meaning of mud
or dirt. The fair is described as a 'gathering, convened by the
Irish Agricultural and Prepostoral Ouraganisations, to help the
Irish muck to look his brother dane in the face' and, 'when the
ballybricken he could get no good o', Festy later sold 'the
gentleman ratepayer' in order to pay off 'six doubloons fifteen
arrears' of rent. The first reference here is to contemporay efforts
to bring Irish pig production up to a standard which would

enable Ireland to compete effectively with Denmark in the British market for bacon. 'Ballybricken' is a reference to a district in Waterford City which was inhabited by large numbers of pigjobbers who purchased pigs for bacon factories. They were an inbred community but their suburb was not a ghetto; they lived well on pigs' heads and crubeens and, like Mr Bloom, they ate with relish the inner organs of these animals. The reference to 'gentleman ratepayer' and the sale of the pig to liquidate arrears of rent are based on the nineteenth-century 'joke' about the Irish pig being called 'the gentleman that pays the rint', rendered later in this chapter as 'a gent who prayed his lent'.

The account of the trial goes on to detail evidence by one W. P. ('Wet Pinter') whose initials are apparently a reversal of P. W. which, in summaries of testimony given at the inquiry into Parnellism and Crime, stood for 'Parnell Witness'. 'Wet Pinter' is itself an alias for Shem, twin brother of Shaun, who testifies as to what he and two others had seen, 'though ours not to reason why.' Here the previous preoccupation of Earwicker with charges against himself is breaking through the current of his dream about the charges against Shaun, something attempted or committed by Earwicker having been observed by a trio who have different identities in different contexts in the book. The quotation from Tennyson's 'Charge of the Light Brigade' also anticipates a subsequent section on the Crimean War, which will be dealt with in Chapter 19 below.

'W. P.'s' evidence goes on to recite the slaughter, by one Hyacinth O'Donnell, B.A., 'a mixer and wordpainter', on the fair green of 'two of the old kings' and to explain that the litigants, 'local congsmen and donalds, kings of the arans, and the dalkeys, kings of mud and tory, even the goat king of Killorglin, were egged on by their supporters'.

Here Joyce purports to explain the name of Festy King. In fact, he probably found the name 'Festus King' on a shopfront in Clifden when he went there in August 1912, in an effort to interview Marconi at the new Wireless Station. Festus is an anglicised version of the Irish name Feichin, patron saint of Cong, and the introduction of Cong in this context, although it is not an island, may have been, apart from its contiguity to Maam, due to Joyce's associating it with the thriller film *King*

Kong which was being shown about the same time as Joyce was writing this section of his book.

The other 'kings', all of islands, except King Puck of Killorglin, are or were authentic survivals of old tribal titles, but Dalkey is a light-hearted creation of eighteenth-century Dublin while 'Mud' was a so-called island at Fairview, Dublin, kingship of which might appropriately be claimed by Joyce's father who lived in the vicinity. A he-goat is still annually elevated to autumnal eminence as King Puck in Killorglin, county Kerry. The reference to 'donalds' seems to cover both the Mac Donnells, Lords of the Isles off the west coast of Scotland, and John Macdonald, a journalist who reported the proceedings before the Parnell Commission and published in 1890 *The Diary of the Parnell Commission Revised from the 'Daily News'*. He is also represented by the 'Hyacinth O'Donnell, B.A.' already mentioned.

The general tenor of the passage seems to have been inspired by Sir William Wilde's *Irish Popular Superstitions*, (Dublin, James Mc Glashan, after 1850), on page 34 of which reference is made to 'Burgesses and 'prentice boys of Atha-Clea, kings of Dalkey, and Mud Island, sweeps of Kevin's Port and the Cabbage Garden [the Capuchins' garden, both terms combined by Joyce on page 568 as 'cabbuchin garden', an old burial ground opposite the Meath Hospital], you have either voluntarily surrendered or been deprived of, your festal days and civic shows'. Reading this passage Joyce would have quickly fastened on the words 'kings' and 'festal' whereupon it was inevitable that Wilde's sentences should be incorporated in his account of Festy King.

In view of W. P.'s evidence the mixer, O'Donnell, is questioned and a string of eighteen names is put to him, the initials of which in succession spell, 'Here Comes Everybody', thereby again involving Earwicker. The examination goes on to matters irrelevant to the Trial until, on page 91, Festy King is re-introduced to give direct evidence under the description of 'the senior king of all, Pegger Festy' who, through an interpreter on oath, deposed that he had thrown no stones since he was born. 'This the sockdologer had the neck to endorse with the head bowed on him'—notwithstanding his nickname 'Pegger' which means stonethrower.

'Sockdologer' is defined in the dictionary as '(American slang), a conclusive argument; a knock-down blow; anything very big, a whopper; a form of fish-hook; a corruption of *doxology*, as the closing act of a service'. It may be recalled that the adjectival form of the word occurs in the play, *Our American Cousin*, and was being used by the actor, Hawk, as Dundreary, in the sentence : 'Society, eh? Well, I guess I know enough to turn you inside out, old woman, you darned old sockdolonging mantrap'—just as John Wilkes Booth shot Abraham Lincoln in 1865 in the President's box in Ford's Theatre on 10th Street, Washington. Immediately after 'sockdologer', and in the same sentence, the word 'trelawney' appears, recalling the sentencing of Trelawney to death in the 1685 Bloody Assizes following the rebellion of the Duke of Monmouth against King James II. Thus other crimes and trials are written into the narrative of Festy King's Trial.

It then emerged that Festy King (Shaun) and Wet Pinter (Shem) were 'equals of opposites . . . polarized for reunion'. Shem had already deposed that at the time of the alleged ocurrence, twixt dusk and dawn, 'there was not as much light from the widowed moon as would dim a child's altar' (88). The identical appearance of the twins, Shem and Shaun, was also no doubt taken into consideration : 'The four justicers laid their wigs together, Untius, Muncius, Punchus and Pylax but could do no worse than promulgate their standing verdict of *Nolans Brumans* whereonafter King, having murdered all the English he knew, picked out his pockets and left the tribunal scotfree' (93). This merciful decision may have been the result of the dreaming Earwicker's wishful thinking but it is also analogous to Bloom's philosophical dismissal of Boylan without any re-enactment of the bloody vengeance which Odysseus meted out to the suitors.

The references to Maam and to evidence being given through an interpreter recalls an article entitled 'Ireland at the Bar', written by Joyce in 1907 for a Trieste newspaper, *Il Piccolo della Sera*. The misrepresentation of Irish claims by foreign journalists is symbolised by a tale of mistrial in Ireland several years before :

In an isolated district . . . called Maamtrasna, a murder was committed. Four or five local men, all belonging to the ancient tribe of the Joyces, were arrested. The oldest of them, the seventy-year-old Myles Joyce, was the prime suspect. Public opinion at the time considered him innocent and to-day they regard him as a martyr . . . The court had to have the services of an interpreter. The interrogation was sometimes funny and at times tragic. On one side was the excessively ceremonious interpreter, on the other the patriarch of a poor tribe unused to civilised practices, who seemed stupefied by all the judicial ceremony . . . He was asked a leading question put to him in Irish and the old man broke out into an involved attempt at exculpation, gesticulating, appealing to the others accused and to God. Then he became quiet, exhausted by his effort, and the interpreter turned to the magistrate and said: 'He says no, your worship' . . .

When the interrogation was finished, the guilt of the poor old man was declared proved, and he was remanded to a superior court which condemned him to the noose. On the day the sentence was executed, the square in front of the prison was crowded with kneeling people praying aloud in Irish for the repose of Myles Joyce's soul. It was said that the executioner, unable to make the victim understand him, kicked at the miserable man's head in anger to push it into the noose.

Joyce must have obtained the bones of the material which he used in this account from Nora Barnacle. Even the 'bones' are inaccurately articulated and they are fleshed with the folklore growth of twenty years. Seventeen years after Joyce wrote his story (further touched up, no doubt, by his artistic pen) I was given a version of part of the folk tale when I was a student in University College, Galway. My landlady was a thin, elderly spinster, her naturally lively intelligence coloured by superstition and a penchant for the sensational. Of the execution of Myles Joyce she had this to say:

The Governor of the jail he was a Captain Mason and the night before the hanging didn't his wife wake up in a sweat and she woke the Governor and let you, says she, have nothing to do, says she, with the death of that innocent man.

From the awful mixings I had in my sleep, says she, I warn you agin having any hand, act or part in his execution, says she. But the Governor wouldn't budge and Myles Joyce was hung. With that Myles Joyce's widow stripped her stockings down from her knees and she knelt on the bare ground and she keened her man and she cursed the captain and she keened and she cursed so high and so hard that he met an idiot's death within in his quarters, shouting and roaring and bidding the dead man's ghost to keep away from him.

It is easy to relate this story of the dream of the Governor's wife to St Matthew, 27:19-20: 'and even as he (Pilate) sat on the judgment seat, his wife had sent him a message, Do not meddle with this innocent man. I dreamt today that I suffered much on his account.' The content of folklore is constantly evolving, adapting the scripture and tradition of thousands of years to current *memoria hominum*. Past and present merge in folklore just as they coalesce in the artistic continuum of *heri, hodie, cras* (546). It seems that the folk version of Myles Joyce's end, as told to me in Galway in 1924 was known to Nora Barnacle twenty years previously, that she related it to Joyce, as her most memorable association with his name before she met him and that he used the praying crowd scene and the hangman's allegedly brutal *coup de grace* for his 1907 journalism, reserving the phantasy for *Finnegans Wake* where he used it obliquely in the expectation that the bespoke 'ideal reader suffering from an ideal insomnia' would align his version of 'Pontius Pilate' with the dream of the Governor's wife. In the *Trial of Festy King* alone the Four Old Men are given the names Untius, Muncius, Punchus and Pylax. Elsewhere they bear the names of the Four Masters, the Four Evangelists ('Mamalujo'); the Four Provinces; the four waves of Ireland and so on. Even here, 'Untius, Muncius' are used for 'Ulster, Munster' but the ordinary sequence is broken to bring in the Joycean version of 'Pontius Pilate'. A motif indicating the projected introduction of Pilate may be found in the word 'eolithostroton' (73) where without the prefix 'eo', the word 'lithostroton' is based on St John, 19:13, where Pilate is said to have 'brought Jesus out and sat down on the judgment seat, in a place which is called Lithostrotos'. With the prefix, the first part of the word, 'eolith' is an archaeological term for the earliest chipped flints, the artefacts of Palaeolithic man.

Accounts of the Maamtrasna murders from contemporary sources record that in the early hours of 18 August, 1882, a man named John Joyce, his wife, his mother and two of his children were killed in their cabin in the Joyce Country, two being shot and the other three bludgeoned to death. The motive for the murders was not explicitly indicated during the course of the trial. In the following November there were charged with the murders, Patrick Joyce, Patrick Joyce (John), Thomas Joyce, Martin Joyce, Myles Joyce, Michael, John and Thomas Casey and Anthony Philbin. The two last named turned informers ('approvers') and their names were withdrawn from the indictment. The murdered people and all the accused lived in Joyce's Country, then a wild and isolated district in the north-west of county Galway, lying south-west of Lough Mask, the lake being the first area that presented a comparatively easy mode of travel or transport (by boat) to Ballinrobe or Cong. 'Mayo of the Saxons' is a small village some miles from the lake on the county Mayo side, the site of one of the early Irish schools in which St Colman housed his Anglo-Saxon monks when they left Northumbria on his case against the Celtic mode of computing the date for Easter being rejected in favour of the Roman method at the Synod of Whitby.

A true bill against the accused having been found by the Dublin grand jury, they were arraigned before the Commission Court. The evidence of successive witnesses was to the effect that of the ten men who went to John Joyce's cabin on the night in question, Patrick Joyce, Patrick Casey and Myles Joyce were those who entered and participated in the killings or were legally presumed to have done so. These three were each tried separately and were each sentenced to death by Mr Justice Barry. There was an interpreter available for all the accused and there is no record of Myles Joyce's having failed to understand the proceedings at his trial or of his having indulged in passionate pleas to have his defence better presented to the judge and jury. The reporters described him as 'between forty and fifty years of age, with short brown whiskers and moustache'.

The remaining five prisoners were prevailed on to withdraw their pleas of Not Guilty and to allow a joint and several plea of Guilty to be entered. They were then tried summarily, found guilty and sentenced to death but were afterwards reprieved. One of these was Michael Casey, said to be the oldest of all the accused; he was sixty-five but looked older because of the whiteness of his hair and beard. He was tall, with regular features and was described as 'more prepossessing than any of the others'. It would seem that the description of Michael Casey was applied to Myles Joyce who was not, as James Joyce described him, 'seventy years old', 'prime suspect' or 'patriarch' of his 'tribe'.

The morning of the execution of Patrick Joyce, Myles Joyce and Patrick Casey in Galway gaol, 15 December, 1882, was cold and dark. In the contemporary reports it was stated that 'scarcely a dozen people assembled around the prison even when the black flag was run up'. This clearly negatives James Joyce's statement, that 'the square in front of the prison was crowded with kneeling people', which, in any event, is cut out by Occam's Razor—there was no square in front of the prison; its gateway faced only a narrow road leading to a bridge across the Eglinton Canal.

Inside the prison Marwood, the hangman from England, pinioned and capped each of the three men and placed them on the drop. Two of them submitted passively but Myles Joyce was very restive and kept up a series of protestations of innocence. A local journalist who knew Irish took down his last words on the scaffold, which may be translated as follows:

I am going.
Why put me to death?
I am not guilty.
I had neither hand or foot in the killing.
I don't know anything at all about it.
God forgive the people who swore against me.
It's a poor thing to die on the scaffold for what I never did.
I never did it and it's a poor case to die.
God help my wife and her five orphans.
I hadn't hand or part in it.
But I have my priest with me.
I am as innocent as the child in the cradle.

As he uttered the last words, Marwood drew the bolt and the three men dropped from view. While two of the ropes scarcely quivered, that from which Myles Joyce was suspended continued to oscillate violently. It seems that the unfortunate man, in throwing himself about, got the rope under his wrist so that when he fell he was left hanging crossways. The hangman gave the rope a vigorous kick to enable it to complete its descent. Joyce's neck was not broken and death was from strangulation.

Myles Joyce's was a posthumous fame and, at that, mainly due to the presence at the execution of a journalist whose literate knowledge of Irish enabled him to give the condemned man's last words to the Irish-speaking population of the west of Ireland. The version of the hangman's act which was in circulation amongst the people for 25 years was probably correctly reported by James Joyce in 1907—that he 'kicked at the miserable man's head in anger to push it into the noose'. But the act thus described was a physical impossibility. Marwood apparently used his foot as best he could to adjust the rope so that it would make a full descent. In doing so, his face quite possibly betrayed some professional distaste at the 'bothersome fellow' with the unintelligible 'lingo', whose antics at the end prevented his hanging 'straight and proper like the others'.

James Joyce seems also to have known at least the first phrase of his namesake's last words, tá mé ag imtheacht (I'm going), and to have appropriated it (with variations) as a motif of departure at successive changes of scene in *Finnegans Wake*:

p. 215—I'm going (Anna Livia).
p. 228—I'm breaving (Shem).
p. 469—I'm going. I know I am (Jaun the Boast).
p. 528—I'm fading! (Iseult, 'Issy').

The informer, Thomas Casey, subsequently retracted his evidence at the trial and exonerated Myles Joyce as one of the party concerned in the murders, whereupon the matter was investigated by Timothy Harrington, M.P. (whom we have already met in Chapter 6 'The Flower in Bloom'). In *The Maamtrasna Massacre, Impeachment of the Trial* (Nation Office 1884), Harrington cites the Attorney General as quoting the statement of a witness that 'The new moon was about her fourth day and therefore there was not much light.' This is the source of Joyce's treatment of the moonlight in 'Festy King' (88) and in the 'Inquest' on Yawn (502 and 519).

Chapter 19
Popes and Paschs

THE parable of 'The Mookse and The Gripes' (152-159), apart from references to the Great Eastern Schism and the Old Catholics of 1870, is primarily devoted to a confrontation between Ireland and the Irish Church, on the one hand, and, on the other, England and the Church of Rome represented in 'The Mookse' by Pope Adrian (Nicholas Breakspear), the only Englishman ever to attain the Triple Crown of the papacy. Adrian reigned from 1154 to 1159 and is said to have given the papal bull *Laudabiliter* (154) to John of Salisbury in 1156, authorising Henry II to occupy Ireland in order to bring the standards of religion and morality there into accord with current Roman Catholic practice. The bull is said to have been confirmed by Alexander III, first when he succeeded Adrian, and again in 1172, following on Henry's going to Ireland in 1171 in the wake of his Norman-Welsh vassals who started the invasion in 1169. Thus Joyce retains Adrian as the symbol of Roman-English orthodoxy although he had been dead ten years when the Norman invasion of Ireland began.

On the analogy of Greene's calling Shakespeare 'the only Shakescene' and by virtue of Breakspeare's unique position as an English pope, he is called 'our once in only Bragspear . . . from veetoes to threetop, every inch of an immortal' (having vested in him the right of veto in matters of faith and morals and wearing the 'threetop' triple crown). He had come from the Vatican, '*De Rure Albo* (socolled becauld it was chalkfull of masterplasters . . .)' but he had also come from 'Ludstown' (London) (152). He travels 'cheek by jowel with his frisherman's blaque *Bellua Triumphanes*' (153). There follow (154) references to 'telesphorously' 'the concionator,' 'zozzymusses' and 'an animal rurale'. The Gripes asks 'what is the time',

thereby trying to turn the discussion on to the ancient controversy of the mode of calculating the date for observing the
festival of Easter, but the Mookse dismisses the question
'rapidly by turning clement, urban, eugenious and celestian in
the foremose of good gregory humours'. There are subsequent
references to 'cannos' (154) and (155) *sus in cribro* and 'crucycrooks' and then to 'Malachy the Augurer' who is thus indirectly
acknowledged as one source of Joyce's documentation.

Thomas E. Connolly, *The Personal Library of James Joyce*,
includes in his lists P.-V. Piobb's *Le Sort de l'Europe d'après
la célèbre prophétie des papes de Saint Malachie ... 1939*. But,
as Mr Atherton has pointed out, this publication was too late
for its contents to be used in *Finnegans Wake*. There was, however, a book published in Dublin by John O'Daly in 1856 containing 'The Prophecies of Saints Colum-Cille, Maeltamlacht,
Ultan, Senan, Bearcan and Malachy, as compiled, translated
and annotated by the late Mr Nicholas O'Kearney'. This was
re-published in 1932 by James Duffy & Co. Ltd, Dublin, but
Joyce must have had access to the previous edition or some
other edition of Malachy's prophecies prior to 1914 when
Dubliners was first published, as he has the characters at the
sick bed in 'Grace' discourse ignorantly about the 'mottoes' of
Pope Leo XIII and Pope Pius IX which Mr Cunningham gives
as *Lux upon Lux* and *Crux upon Crux (recte, Lumen in Coelo*
and *Crux de Cruce)*.

Joyce appears to have become acquainted with at least the
title of the sixteenth-century work in which St Malachy's prophecies were first printed. This was a two-volume book compiled by
a Benedictine monk, Arnold de Wion and published in Venice
under the title *Lignum Vitae*. This term Joyce uses (84) as
meaning a cudgel of selfdefence, a 'humoral hurlbat or other
uncertain weapon of *lignum vitae*'.

Another early printed version of the 'prophecies' to which
Joyce might have had access in Dublin or Paris was a volume
the title page of which runs as follows :

Florilegium Insulae Sanctorum seu Vitae et Acta Sanctorum
Hiberniae. Quibus accesserunt non vulgaria monumenta. Hoc
est *Sancti Patricii Purgatorium, S. Malachiae Prophetia de
Summis Pontificibus, Aliaque nonnulla quorum Elenchus*

post Praefationem habetur. Omnia nunc primum partim ex MS. codicibus, partim typis editis collegit & publicabat Thomas Messinghamus *Sacerdos Hibernus, S.R.E.* Protonotarius, nec non Seminarii Hibernorum Parisiis Moderator. [Here follow figures depicting 'S. Columba', 'S. Patricius', and 'S. Brigida Hiberniae Patroni'.]

Parisiis, Ex officina Sebastiani Cramoisy, via Jacobaea, sub Ciconiis.

M. DC XXIV.

cum privilegio et approbatione.

Each of the 'prophecies' attributed to St Malachy consists of a few words or brief phrases in Latin, purporting to describe successive popes, their coats of arms or the circumstances of their accessions or reigns from his own time, 1143, to the end of the world when he declares that 'Peter the Roman' will become Pope amid many tribulations, after which the City of the Seven Hills will be destroyed and the Terrible Judge will judge the people. Between the regime of Paul VI and that of Petrus Romanus whose advent to the Roman See will signalise the predicted end of the world, only three more popes remain to complete St Malachy's list; these are indicated by the phrases, *De medietate lunae, De labore solis* and *Gloria olivae.*

The eschatological denouement is suggested in the Mookse-Gripes colloquy, following on a paragraph stuffed with Russian and Greek terms about the schism between the Roman Catholic and Eastern Orthodox Churches regarding the addition of *Filioque* to the Creed and other theological disputes:

—Efter thousand yaws, O Gripes . . . yow will be belined to the world, enscayed Mookse the pius.

—Ofter thousand yores, amsered Gripes the gregary . . . Yours may be still, O Mookse, more botheared.

—Us shall be chosen as the first of the last by the electors of Vale Hollow, obselved the Mookse nobily . . . as when that brokenarched traveller from Nuzuland . . .

—Wee, cumfused the Gripes limply, shall not even be the last of the first, wee hope, when ouse are visitated by the veiled Horror.

The foregoing pieces of wishful thinking about their respective places at Jehosophat have been reinforced by an echo from Lord Macaulay's essay on Von Ranke's *History of the Popes* where he foresees the survival of the Vatican down to a time 'when some traveller from New Zealand shall, in the midst of a vast solitude, take his stand on a broken arch of London Bridge to sketch the ruins of St Paul's'.

Meanwhile, Joyce's use of the names and mottoes of the popes calls for explication. His name for the Vatican, *De Rure Albo*, is borrowed from Malachy's motto for Pope Adrian himself and is appropriate to that Pope whether translated as 'from England' or 'from St Albans', where Breakspear was born. Adrian's 'fisherman's blaque, *Bellua Triumphanes*', comes partly from the description of Innocent XI (1676-1689) as *Bellua Insatiabilis*, 'insatiable beast', which may refer to a lion and a vulture on his coat of arms or (as Joyce would surely prefer) to the Pope's constant counsellor, Cardinal Cibo, whence he was said to be never without food (*sine cibo*). The words are also an echo of Bruno's *Bestia Trionfante*. *Concionator* (preacher) and *animale rurale* were the mottoes laid down for Innocent V (1276) and Benedict XIV (1740-58). The papal names applied adjectivally to the Mookse (in p. 154 quoted above) conceal the identities of Clement III (1187-1191), Urban III (1185-1187), Eugene III (1145-1153), Celestine II (1143-1144), and Gregory VIII (1187).

In addition, the motto of Urban III, *sus in cribro*, (sow in a sieve), is also quoted. It has been interpreted as referring to the Pope's family name, Crivelli, which means a sieve, this article appearing on his coat of arms, the supporters of the crest being two sows. The Mookse, however, uses the motto pejoratively in bullying the Gripes as if it meant 'pig in a creel' and the commentator sneers contemptuously, 'Poor little sow-sieved subsquashed Gripes!' (155). The Mookse also calls him 'barbarouse' (154) from the name of the Emperor, Frederick Barbarossa, his (i.e. Adrian's) enemy and 'crucycrooks', the *crux de cruce* motto of Pio Nono with which Joyce had already made play in *Dubliners*.

Finally the two washerwomen carry away the Mookse and the Gripes as laundry items, one to her dwelling *Aquila Rapax* (158) and the other to her shieling, *De Rore Coeli* (159).

Aquila Rapax was the term assigned to the pontificate of

Pius VII 1800-1823) who was brought a prisoner to Paris by Napoleon Bonaparte. He officiated at the coronation of Napoleon as Emperor, to the extent of being allowed to hand him the crown but Napoleon reserved to himself the right to don it. 'A rapacious eagle' is an excellent description of Napoleon as well as a literally accurate reference to his emblem, the eagle. Similar names are given to Napoleon in the *Centuries* of Nostradamus: *Aigle*, III.37, and *Rapax*, IX.76.

De Rore Coeli ('from the dew of the sky') was the motto foretold for Pope Urban VII (1590) who had served as bishop of Rossano in Calabria. 'Manna' or 'dew of Heaven' is a sweet secretion gathered from trees in the area.

References to popes reigning earlier than the date at which Malachy's list commences include (154) Telesphorous, (126-7) Zozimus (fifth century) and (155) Hildebrand (1020-85) who in 1073 became Pope Gregory VII and, bending his energies towards the advancement of papal power, compelled the Emperor Henry IV to make humble submission to His Holiness in the snow at Canossa, in 1076. This is referred to by the Gripes (154): 'If I cannow make my submission, I cannos give you up.'

The controversy is concluded with learned citations by the Mookse from ecumenical but anachronistic authorities, the Dutch Arminius (1560-1609) and Erasmus, Anaxagoras, a Greek philosopher of 500 B.C., Hildebrand, Mommsen etc. What was proven 'to the extinction of Niklaus altogether' is not clear. The Gripes's question, 'what is the time', remains unanswered and as this is an important matter it requires further elucidation.

The question posed by the Gripes had already been raised (35) with H.C.E. by 'a cad with a pipe' who saluted him with: Guinness thaw tool in jew my dinner ouzel fin?' which seems to be Joyce's version of the Irish, *Cionnas tá tú indiú mo dhuine uasal fionn?* which in turn means, How are you today my fair-haired gent? The cad went on to ask could H.C.E. tell him how much a clock it was. A Cad (or cadet), being a young man aspiring to promotion, the elderly H.C.E.'s subliminal reaction to his question appears to have been fear of displacement on the ground that his time was up. This fear expressed itself in a lengthy exculpatory addendum to the information (tolled out simultaneously

by a church clock) that it was twelve. The reply suggested secret
guilt, perhaps that of keeping the wrong time but 'Gaping Gill',
the cad, thanked him and went on his way 'not a little token
abock allthe same that that was owl the God's clock it was'
(37). The rumour of H.C.E.'s having committed a nameless crime
fans out from Gill across the city and amongst a representative
cross-section of the men of Leinster (42-3), which included 'a
particularist prebendary pondering on the roman easter, the
tonsure question and greek uniates, plunk em'. Later (76), when
H.C.E. is inhumed in an 'underground heaven or moles' paradise' under Lough Neagh, he found 'the ground battery fuse-
boxes all differing as clocks from keys since nobody appeared
to have the same time of beard, some saying by their Oorlog it
was Sygstryggs to nine, more holding with the Ryan vogt it
was Dane of pfife' (77).

One of the Christmas boxes distributed in the A.L.P. episode
is 'a niester egg with a twicedated shell' (210) and Shem has
been reminded of his origin 'in this two easter island' (188)
while on page 130 there is a death notice of H.C.E., 'after a
lenty illness the reeverand Mr Easterling of pentecostitis, no
followers by bequest'. Of Finn Mc Cool it is stated (134), 'he
can get on as early as the twentysecond of Mars but occasionally
he doesn't come off before the Virgintiquinque Germinal'. (The
dates are March 22 and April 25.)

The question is put to Yawn (512) during his interrogation:
'are you solarly salemly sure, beyond the shatter of the canicular
year? *Nascitur ordo seculi numfit.*' (The order of the age is
not being born, is it?) The last question is based on Virgil's
Eclogue IV: *magnus ab integro saeclorum nascitur ordo.* This
is translated by Shelley, *The world's great age begins anew,*
but in Joyce's version there is a mixture of the Paschal controversy with Vicos' *ordo* and *ricorso.*

The answer (513) is: '—Siriusly and selenely sure behind the
shutter. *Securius indicat umbris tellurem,*' probably meaning,
referring to the phases of the moon, 'it surely indicates the earth
by its shadows'.

The text following in page 513 includes the words, 'an easter
sun round the collander'. The calendar references are to the
solar calendar, the lunar year and the 'canicular year', that is
the year based on the rising of Sirius, the dog-star.

By the end of the sixth century St Columcille had evangelised Scotland from Iona and in the first half of the seventh, his monks had converted the Angles of Northumbria and founded the see of Lindisfarne. They followed the method of calculating the date for the celebration of Easter Day which was practised by Irish churchmen in Armagh and Iona, and their tonsure was frontal, leaving the hair at the back untonsured. There had been differences in the mode of computing the date of Easter as between Rome and Alexandria, but these had been settled for a century when the controversy came to a climax in Northern Ireland, Iona and Lindisfarne. The agreed Universal Church formula laid down that Easter Sunday should be celebrated on the next Sunday after the 14th day of the moon on or next after the vernal equinox, 21 March. The Irish, however, observed the feast on the date of the full moon, if that day was a Sunday, thus leaving it sometimes aligned with the Jewish festival, a practice which had been prohibited by the Council of Nice. The reasoning was that the Pasch occurring in the year of Christ's death fell on Friday, so that Easter Day must have been two days later.

As early as 629, Pope Honorius had admonished the pastors of the Irish Church for persisting in their erroneous practices and generally those in the southern half of the country adopted the Roman usage. On their behalf St Cummian wrote to Segienus, stating that the southern Irish pastors had changed their ancient observances after they had been to Rome and there seen representatives of all nations celebrating Easter on the same day 'which differed a month from our own'. Thus Ireland had become what Joyce calls a 'two easter island'. The saint pointed out that the northern Irish and their associates in Britain were but a fragment living at the end of the world and forming a conventicle separated from the communion of the Church. This Joyce refers to Finn Mac Cool (138) as 'an excrescence to civilised humanity and but a wart on Europe'.

St Colman, an Irish monk from Iona, became Bishop of Northumbria in 661 and continued to observe Easter after the old Irish fashion. At the Synod of Whitby (664) presided over by the Abbess Hilda, Colman made his case, citing the authority of St Columcille, but a local abbot, Wilfrid, later Archbishop of York, espoused the orthodox side, quoting the authority delegated to St Peter and his successors in the see of Rome.

When the conference decided against Colman, he left Britain, taking with him all the Irish of Lindisfarne and about thirty of the Anglo-Saxons who sided with him. He founded an abbey for them in Inisbofin, an island about six miles from the Connemara coast of County Galway. The English monks soon had occasion to complain that their Irish brethren were too fond of visiting the mainland, leaving them to work the land and harvest the crops, and later returning to claim their share of the food. Thereupon, Colman founded a separate monastery for the Angles and Saxons at Mayo, a place in the south of the county of that name and north of Lough Mask and Carra Lake, which was thereafter known as Mayo of the Saxons. This is referred to (85) as the address of Festy King and 'the heart of a foulfamed potheen district'.

In dealing with the Festy King episode, I traced some of the folklore background to Joyce's wife, Nora Barnacle, and it seems probable that she derived her information from her father, Tom Barnacle, the 'Gobra Goney' of Jim Tully's reminiscences about the family. Mrs Barnacle was parted from her husband when Joyce took her daughter abroad. On 3 December 1904, Joyce wrote to his brother Stanislaus:

> Nora's father is a baker . . . Papa had a shop but drank all the buns and loaves like a man . . . (Now he) bakes and drinks in a distant part of Connacht.

The place to which the father had withdrawn was probably that which I believe to have been his native place, at or near Mayo Abbey in county Mayo, adjoining the Joyce country in county Galway. Here his family wishing to anglicise their original name Ó Cadhain (Coyne) had changed it to 'Barnacle' because of its real or fancied identity with the Irish *cadhan*, a barnacle goose. Nora lived with her grandmother before going to Dublin but she must have sometimes visited her mother and seen and listened to her father, even if to his neighbours he was an invisible man in his bed, in his bakery and in his beer. Her estimate of his character should not be based entirely on Joyce's version retailed to Stanislaus in the 1904 letters. In *James Joyce*, p. 565, Ellmann quotes Kathleen Barnacle as having been told by Nora in 1923 that she wished she was married to a man like her father rather than to a 'weakling' such as she found her own husband to be. It may be assumed that it was from her father that Nora learned and subsequently told Joyce the facts of the Maam Cross murders and the facts and folklore of the executions. Similarly, he must have apprised her of the ancient fame of the local abbey, Mayo of the Saxons. Its fame was resurrected and featured in the nationalist poetical propaganda of Anglo-Irish writers in the nineteenth century. Anglo-Saxon students, they claimed, swarmed to Ireland for the learning afforded by *Insula Sanctorum et Doctorum*, traditionally translated as 'the Isle of Saints and Scholars' but retranslated from Joyce's Italian writings in Trieste, 'the Isle of Saints and Sages'. Those who came to Mayo for their education in the seventh century were probably confined to followers of the Anglo-Saxon dissidents who went with Colman, first to Inisbofin and then to Mayo. Of these, Aldfrid of Northumbria, later king of that region, is remembered for his poem in Irish celebrating the hospitality, holiness and scholarship of the Irish. The Northumbrian students of that era, educated in or from Iona were Irish speakers even before they came to Ireland. Aldfrid appears to have been a student at Lismore and also at Armagh and Cluanmacnois. It seems clear that he also attended at Inisbofin, as appears from James Clarence Mangan's reference to 'island' in the translation of his poem about his Irish itinerary :

> I found in each great church moreo'er
> Whether on island or on shore,
> Piety, learning, fond affection,
> Holy welcome and kind protection.

Mangan's poem mentions 'Leinster the smooth and sleek from Dublin to Slewmargy's peak'; 'Munster unfettered of any'; 'Connaught the just' in 'Cruachan's land of heroic name'; 'Armagh the splendid'; and 'the noble district of Boyle'.

Joyce knew this poem—and used passages from it in the *Cyclops* episode, inserting the word 'Eblana' for Dublin, which was misprinted 'Elbana' in the first edition and left uncorrected ever since :

And heroes voyage from afar to woo them, from Elbana to

Slievemargy, the peerless princes of unfettered Munster and of Connacht the just and of smooth sleek Leinster and of Crucahan's land and of Armagh the splendid and of the noble district of Boyle, princes, the sons of kings. (*U* 292)

Arnold Toynbee regarded the submission of the Celtic Church at the Synod of Whitby as the abortion of a potential Great Western Civilisation. The Church of Northern Ireland-Iona-Northumbria, however, was remote, isolated from the governmental traditions of Imperial Rome and from the new growth of western civilisation fed from Rome. It was a lamp that lighted the west in the dark ages when Roman teaching was well-nigh extinct, but it could not withstand the Catholic Renaissance of Hildebrand and his successors. Joyce saw fit to supplement his theme of East-West Schism with this outline of the clash of the Irish Church with Roman Catholicism, the better to universalise this portion of his 'history of the world'. But, as ever, his theme had also a local habitation. Nora's memories of her father's Mayo gossip must have reinforced what Joyce had learnt from Mangan and from church histories in his decision to highlight the Paschal controversy which led to the foundation of Mayo Abbey. She may even have had childish memories of a visit to her father's natal spot: 'The woods of fogloot!' (Foclut has been identified as Foghill, near Killala Bay, north of the site of Mayo Abbey, which is north of George Moore's Carra Lake on the northern side of Lough Mask). 'I know that place better than anyone. Sure, I used to be always overthere on the fourth day at my grandmother's place Tear-non-Ogre, my little grey home in the west, in or about Mayo' (478-9).

Chapter 20

Bruinoboroff

THE incidents based on the Crimean war and the story of
Buckley's efforts to shoot the Russian General (pp. 338-55) are
part of the second section of Book II, the whole of which (pp.
309-82) relates to the brawls, story-telling and newscasting
which occur in H.C.E.'s tavern. These, including the Crimean
war material, are all nearly inextricably intermingled. The radio
(which sometimes becomes television) adds to the confusion
and even the mezzotint on the wall which is fairly clearly stated
to portray the charge of the Light Brigade seems fated to turn
occasionally into an illustrated calendar (almanac), presented by
Messrs Findlater at Christmas, the top picture showing John
Peel's hunt in full career. A foretaste of this latter metamorphosis is given on page 334, five pages before the Crimean
episode proper commences :

> On the mizzatint wall. With its chromo for all crimm
> crimms. Showing holdmenag's asses sat by Allmeneck's men,
> canins to ride with em, canins that lept at em, woollied and
> flundered.

> Yes, we've conned thon print in its gloss so gay how it
> came from Finndlader's Yule to the day and its Hey Tallaght
> Hoe on the king's highway with his hounds on the home at a
> turning.

Butt and Taff (Shem and Shaun) participate in the narrative
of the Crimean episode. Taff, the compere, calls on Butt:
'Rassamble the glowrings of Bruyant the Bref' and, again,
'Lets hear in remember the braise of. Hold!' (338). The context
suggests a reference to Bruin the Bear, symbol of the Russian
imperial might, but the wording is in fact an echo of the first

lines of two of Thomas Moore's poems, one dealing with Brian Boru and the other referring to Malachi who both preceded and succeeded Brian as High King of Ireland:

> *Remember the glories of Brian the Brave*
> *Though the days of the hero are o'er*
> *Though lost to Mononia and cold in the grave,*
> *He return to Kincora no more.*

and

> *Let Erin remember the days of old,*
> *Ere her faithless sons betrayed her;*
> *When Malachi wore the collar of gold,*
> *Which he won from her proud invader.*

Thus, from the very start of this episode, we gather that the progress of the Crimean War (1853-56) between Russia and the allied forces of Britain and France is to be related to Brian Boru and his wars with the Norse invaders of Ireland and that it also includes possibly the deposition of Malachi by Brian in 1002. This was, according to orthodox Irish annalists, the third 'usurpation' by Brian, his first being his seizure of the kingship of Munster (976) and the second his becoming king of the southern half of Ireland by agreement with King Malachi in 998. Early on in the book (p. 16) we find a reference to Brian as a 'usurper' (the word Joyce reserved for Malachi Mulligan in *Ulysses*): 'Urp, Boohooru! Booru Usurp! I trumple from rath in mine mines when I rimimirim!' (The last sentence contains a punning reference to Rathmines, a suburb of Dublin).

Butt proceeds to describe the Russian Czar's position enveloped or, as it were, clothed with enemies: 'He was enmivallupped. Chromean fastion. With all his cannonball wappents. In his raglanrock and his malakoiffed bulbsbyg and his varnished roscians and his cardigans clousejagged and his scarlett manchokuffs and his treecoloured camiflag and his perikopendolous gaelstorms.' (339)

The names of the articles of clothing are borrowed from Lord Raglan, the English commander at Sevastopol—a raglan coat (German and Swedish, *rock*) Malakoff, the fort near Sevastopol captured by the French under Marshal MacMahon; the Earl of Cardigan who commanded the charge of the Light

Brigade (and who gave his name to the garment); Sir James Yorke Scarlett, another British commander; and the Russian commanding general, Prince Menshickov. The articles of clothing are 'Obriania's beromst! From Karrs and Polikoff's, the latter being the name of a Dublin clothier.

Butt goes on to describe the Czar of all the Russias: 'A bear raigning in his heavenspawn consomation robes.' But he entitles him 'Erminia's cape-cloaked hoodooman', which read backwards bears the initials H.C.E., thus leaving us uncertain whether we view Czar Nicholas in the Crimea or Earwicker in the Phoenix Park where the 'Mizzatint Wall', from which we started, would end up as the Magazine Wall. A more general picture of battlefields is given (350) and the end result 'lomondations of Oghrem' for the felled, i.e. the farewell after the defeat at Culloden Moor, 1745, of the condemned Highland Chief through the prison bars to his weeping wife:

> O ye'll tak' the high road and I'll take the low road
> And I'll be in Scotland afore ye,
> But me and my true love will never meet again
> On the bonnie, bonnie banks o' Loch Lomon.

—that is, his spirit would be in Scotland travelling by way of the grave, before his widow reached it overland. Towards the conclusion of this chapter we shall see how 'lomondations' or lamentations relate to 'Oghram' or Aughrim.

These references make Taff repeat in effect the comment already quoted from page 16 on 'Boru Usurp'. 'Oh day of rath! Ah murther of mines! Eh, selo moy! Uh, zulu luy, Bernesson Mac Mahahon from Osro bearing nose easger for sweeth prolettas on his swooth prowl!' (340) Here Taff associates Brian Boru with 'Bernesson' Mac Mahon and Butt rejoins with 'Bruinoboroff' which unifies the two characters. A variation of the alternative names in another context appears in 529.16 as 'O'Bejorumsen or Mock Macmahonitch'.

Bruinoboroff is not the same bear as that symbolising the Czar. It is Marshal MacMahon of France, commander of the assault on Sevastopol, who is here called a son of a bear (Bernesson) and, doubling with Brian Boru, a bear himself (Bruinoboroff). 'Bernesson' and Mac Mahon (Irish, Mathgamhna) both mean the same thing, 'son of a bear' the Irish word for bear being identical with 'Mathgamhain' the Irish personal name, Mahon. Another consideration which Joyce would regard as justification for his associating the Marshal with a bear was that his grandfather, John Count d'Equilly son of Patrick Mac Mahon, one of the Wildgeese who left Ireland for France after the Siege of Limerick, had his genealogy registered with the Ulster King of Arms in Dublin Castle in 1749 where he (John) is described as the son of Patrick Mac Mahon of Terrodile, county Limerick, and of his wife, Margaret, daughter of John O'Sullivan of Bantry, county Cork, of the House of O'Sullivan Beare. The fact that the word Beare in the tribal name 'O'Sullivan Beare' is a place name would not deter Joyce from regarding Marshal MacMahon as having a second bear for his great-grandmother.

Brian Boru was the younger brother of Mahon, chieftain of the Dalcassians, and he rose to greatness when Mahon was killed. Joyce may have reasoned that Brian could thereby be deemed to have succeeded to the name as well as the title of his brother. As far back as 1907, in a lecture on Ireland in Trieste, Joyce had referred to Brian Boru as a usurper. The word 'usurper' could, however, have been suggested by *ursus* (Latin, a bear) and this may have been in Joyce's mind from the name of Reginald Fitz Urse, the ringleader of the knights who murdered Thomas a Becket at the behest of Henry II. Fitz Urse is said to have gone to Ireland and to have founded a family of the Mac Mahons. Fitz Urse is a form of the Norman family name Fitz Ursula. It may have been Gaelicised Mac Mathgamhna but, if so, its founder was not the ancestor of the whole Mac Mahon Clann. It seems also to have been anglicised Hurson.

Fitz Urse's name does appear in *FW* (96-7) where H.C.E. 'bestly saved his brush . . . which Mr Loewenteil Fitz Urse's basset beaters had first misbadgered for a bruin of some swart'. This seems to end in one of the real or imaginary killings of H.C.E.: 'the Mac Mahon chaps, it was, that had done him in' (99).

The reference on page 343 to 'camp, camp, camp to Saint Sepulchre's march' relates to the nominal cause of the Crimean war, a controversy between the Orthodox and Catholic Churches as to the custody of the Church of the Nativity at Bethlehem and the Holy Sepulchre at Jerusalem. The real occasion of hostilities was British and Russian rivalry in the Near East, which hinged on the question whether to preserve or liquidate Turkey, 'the sick man of Europe'.

Page 344 details Butt's efforts to screw his courage to shoot the Russian general or the Czar. He goes on (345) to make excuses, 'I met with whom it was too late' (a reference to the supposed remark of Joyce to Yeats that he had met Yeats too late to influence him and also to Oscar Wilde's remark in *De Profundis*, 'But I met you either too late or too soon.' 'And think of that when you smugs to bagot', has been interpreted as a reference to Bagehot, an English journalist who reported the Crimean war. Joyce, however, also uses the words in the context of some seventeenth-century lines about tobacco, a note of which (*Scribbledehobble*, 8) runs, 'tobacco is like a soul in sin, fair without and foul within, so think of that when you smoke tobacco'. Joyce probably took this from the following lines in Samuel Lover's *Handy Andy*:

> Tobacco is an Indian weed
> Alive at morn and dead at eve;
> It lives but an hour,
> Is cut down like a flower
> Think o' this when you're smoking tobacco.
> A pipe it learns us all this thing—
> 'Tis fair without and foul within
> Just like the soul begrimed with sin
> Think o' this when you're smoking tobacco.

The *Scribbledehobble* extract from these lines inaccurately likens tobacco instead of a pipe to a soul in sin, but *Handy Andy* nevertheless seems to have been Joyce's source as he unquestionably uses another item from the same portion (Chapter VI) of Lover's book. Escaping from the irate victim of one of his blunders, Andy has taken refuge in his mother's cabin and fallen asleep under the bed in which she and her niece, 'Oonah', slept. They are awakened by Andy's shouting in a nightmare and rolling and heaving against the bottom of their bed. The screaming women set the dog against the supposed robbers, the dog attacks the pig, the squealing pig escapes under the bed from which Andy has dislodged himself, the frightened hens fly against the dresser and knock the plates on to the floor; even when a light is lit and Andy is recognised Oonah insists that there is another person under the bed, 'a dirty blackguard without any clothes on him'. This, of course, turned out to be the pig.

Joyce echoes this scene of chaotic bedlam in 64.7-9: 'hammering on the pandywhank scale emanating from the blind pig and anything like it (oonagh! oonagh!) in the whole history of the Mullingcan Inn he never.' Lover's spelling of Una, the girl's name, was designed to convey the proper pronunciation to his English readers who were not conversant with the sound of the open initial vowel U in the Irish language.

Another echo from Handy Andy is found in 171.15, 16, where 'the tragic jester sobbed himself wheywhingingly sick of life on some sort of . . . applejack'. This derives from a lively set of verses in Chapter V of *Handy Andy*, entitled 'Love and Liquor' and dealing with the desertion of Ariadne by Theseus and her rescue by Bacchus:

> Oh sure 'twould amaze yiz
> How one Misther Theseus
> Deserted a lovely young lady of owld
> On a dissolute island
> All lonely and silent
> She sobbed herself sick as she sat in the cowld.

And if Joyce pilfered material from Samuel Lover, he in his turn, lifted his 'dissolute island' from Maginn.

But we must return from Crete to the Crimea. Butt's comment as he partakes of communion, 'There's scares knud in this gnarlworld a fully so svend as dilates for the improvement of our foerses of nature by your very ample solvent of referacting upon me like is boesan fiennd.' (345) is annotated by Campbell and Robinson: 'There are cares enough in this old world, so send us delights for the improvement of our forces of nature by reacting upon me like is bosom fiend.'

Whether this interpretation is correct or not, the original on which Joyce's wording is based is the opening of Moore's lyric 'The Meeting of the Waters':

G

There is not in this wide world a valley so sweet
As that vale in whose bosom the bright waters meet.

The Russian general is shot at last (352) and this deed is equated to the (353) 'abnihilisation of the etymn' which has been translated 'Annihilation of the Atom'. This is an over-simplified interpretation: the words are intended to signify the kind of surgery to which Joyce was subjecting the English language in his campaign to 'wipe alley english spooker, multa-phoniaksically spuking, off the face of the erse' (178) and to his creation of a new language from nothing (*ab nihil*).

The episode ends on page 355 : 'Nightclothesed, arooned, the conquerods sway. After their battle thy fair bosom.' The first word seems to refer to nightclothes (appropriate to a book which is a dream) and to soldiers resting, warfare o'er, but it is in fact Moore again, in the 'lomondations of Oghram' which I quoted earlier. These are the lamentations after the Battle of Aughrim where the Irish were defeated by the forces of William of Orange :

> *Night clos'd around the conqueror's way,*
> *And lightnings show'd the distant hill,*
> *Where those who lost that dreadful day*
> *Stood few and faint, but fearless still!*
> *The soldier's hope, the patriot's zeal,*
> *For ever dimm'd, for ever cross'd—*
> *Oh! who shall say what heroes feel.*
> *When all but life and honour's lost?*

What Joyce quoted, however, is not from the text of the poem but from the table of contents of an edition of Moore's *Irish Melodies* containing the title and first line of each poem and, in most cases, the name of the Irish air to which the poem was set. The title of this particular poem is 'After the Battle'; the first line has been quoted above and the English version of the name of the Irish air is 'Thy Fair Bosom'. Thomas E. Connolly lists this edition of Moore as being one of the books in *The Personal Library of James Joyce* and adds : 'Table of contents heavily marked with crayon of various colours seemingly to indicate some order of mastery of the pieces.' The 'mastery' designed and executed was the inclusion in various parts of

Finnegans Wake (indicated by the colour of the crayon marks) of a reference to the title, first line and air of every poem in Moore's *Irish Melodies*. This seems a rather crudely mechanistic and superficial exercise in 'the human disposition of sensible or intelligible matter for an esthetic end', to quote Stephen's definition of art.

While it has been shown that the passage from 64.7-9 cited above is based on a noisy scene involving a pig and a girl (Ooonagh) in *Handy Andy*, it must be recorded that here, too, Joyce is indebted to the names of two airs placed one after the other in the Moore's *Melodies* table of contents, viz., 'Oonagh' as the air for 'While gazing on the Moon's Light' and 'Paddy Whack' as that for 'While History's Muse'. Joyce changed 'Paddy Whack' to 'pandywhank' in memory of the occasion on which he was unjustly punished with a pandy (Lat. *pande*, 'hold out') in Clongowes.

Many other 'first lines' of books are used in *Finnegans Wake*, as may be seen from the examples cited in the following paragraphs.

In his preface to *Le Morte D'Arthur* Caxton wrote: 'It is notoriously known throughout the universal world that there be nine worthy and the best that ever were.' Joyce has (176): 'Now it is notoriously known how on that surprisingly bludgeony Unity Sunday . . .'

On page 378 'In the buginning is the woid', the opening words of St John's Gospel, are transformed into an account of an insectival genesis based on the void.

The first words of St Luke's Gospel, 'Forasmuch as many have taken in hand to set forth a declaration of those things', are used by Yawn in his contention with his Inquisitors (who include St Luke himself): 'forasmuch as many have tooken in hand to' (484). Later on the same page, the beginning of St Matthew's gospel is translated into Irish and English as 'the leabhour of my genrations'.

The first words of the first line of Virgil's *Aeneid* are (389.19) given as *Arma virumque romano*.

Chapter 21

Permutations and Combinations

In addition to the themes of Irish origin or having Irish connotations examined in the preceding six chapters, there are some others of such significance as to merit explication but more briefly than those already dealt with. These are examined under separate subheadings in this chapter.

1. *The Partition of Ulster*

The co-existence of two hostile ethnic and sectarian elements in the population of Ulster stems from the plantations of English and Scots settlers in that province following the abandonment of their territories by O'Neill and O'Donnell in 1607, an event known as 'The Flight of the Earls'. Rebellion against the new order, which broke out in 1641, was finally subdued with ferocious cruelty by Oliver Cromwell in 1649. Wholesale confiscation and plantation of the rebels' lands ensued. Cromwell's name became synonymous in the Irish folk mind with evil and destruction so that 'the curse of Cromwell' wished on one was deemed a fiendish malediction. So the popular historians would have us believe but there was a more antique figure whose curse might have been inherited by Cromwell : this was Crom Cruach, the god to whom the firstlings of families had to be sacrificed in pagan times in order to preserve cattle and crops from pestilence and blight. By accident or with a greater insight into the obscurities of history than one might expect, Joyce uses one of his telescopic words to unify the god and the Lord Protector by having the prankquean punch 'the curses of cromcruwell with the nail of a top into the joining' thus converting Shem into a 'tristian' (22).

The next effort to oust the planters was made in 1689-91

when the Irish army of King James's Lord Lieutenant, Richard Talbot, Earl of Tyrconnel, tried to capture the city of Derry and subsequently to resist the invasion of William of Orange. The invaders and their Anglo-Irish supporters sang a song which is said to have sung a king (James II) out of three kingdoms.

> Dere was an old prophecy found in a bog,
>> *Lillibulero bullen a la,*
> Dat our land would be ruled by an ass and a dog,
>> *Lillibulero bullen a la*;
> So now dis old Prophecy's coming to pass
>> *Lillibulero bullen a la,*
> For James is de dog and Tyrconnel's de ass.
>> *Lillibulero bullen a la.*
>> *Lero, lero, lero, lero,*
>> *Lillibulero bullen a la.*

There is a reference based on this refrain to 'allenalaw' (83) and a variation of it (206), 'Liltabolero, bulling a law'.

The slogans of Orangemen of a later day are reflected on page 53: 'Chee chee cheers for Upkingbilly and crow cru cramwells'. The history of subsequent centuries is reflected in the understatement that the Pope is not popular in Portadown and similar strongholds of Orangemen. 'To hell with the Pope' has been their usual benison for this potentate and a legend to this effect is said to have been chalked on the *Titanic* when that liner made its first and last effort at an Atlantic crossing in 1912. Joyce gives it an appropriately nautical touch by rendering it 'to hull with the poop' (416), preserving incidentally the phonetics of the Ulster accent.

In an effort to meet the Irish demand for Home Rule and at the same time to soothe Protestant intransigence in north-east Ulster, the British Parliament passed an Act in 1920 for the government of Ireland which for this purpose was divided into two parts, Northern Ireland and Southern Ireland. The former consisted of the six north-eastern counties of Ulster and the latter of the other twenty-six counties of Ireland, including counties Cavan, Donegal and Monaghan, being the remaining three counties of Ulster. One of these, Donegal, contains the most northerly point in the island, but under the

Act of 1920 it formed part of what was grotesquely called
'Southern Ireland'. The provisions of the Act were accepted in
Northern Ireland and a Parliament was convened in Belfast
to form a government for the six counties. The Act was ignored
in the twenty-six counties which recognised the assembly known
as Dáil Eireann, set up in 1919, as the only legitimate legis-
lature for Ireland as a whole. When the Treaty of 1921 was
made between Dáil Eireann leaders and the British Government, the Irish Free State was the name decided upon for the
whole of Ireland or, if the Northern Ireland government opted
out, for the twenty-six counties of 'Southern Ireland'. The
Belfast government exercised their right to opt out and Ireland
then became what Joyce tersely described (78) as 'New South
Ireland and Vetera Uladh', the latter phrase indicating correctly that the six counties now separated from the rest represented more closely the ancient tribal territory of Uladh than
do the nine counties which have comprised the province of
Ulster for the last four hundred years. Joyce goes on to associate
the newly re-named territories with 'the ferment With the
Pope or On the Pope'. De Valera ('the Long Fellow') is asked
(82): 'Was six victolios fifteen pigeon takee offa you, tell he
me, stlongfella.' This pidgin English is followed by the racy
account of an encounter apparently with de Valera during the
1922-23 Civil War: 'There were some further collidabanter
and severe tries to convert for the best part of an hour and now
a woden affair in the shape of a webley (we at once recognise
our old friend Ned of so many illortemporate letters) fell from
the intruser who, as stuck as that cat to that mouse in that tube
of that christchurch organ. . . .' There is a change of attitude
when the 'intruser' becomes friendly and asks whether the other
party could change a tenpound note, 'addling that hap so, he
would pay him back the six vics odd'.

The 'illortemporate letters' appear to be contemporary (*in
illo tempore*) or alternatively illtempered publications of 'our
old friend', so numerous as to be equated to the words of Shem,
'tun times' as many as 'the penmarks used out in sincript with
such hesitancy' by Shaun's 'cerebrated brother', Shem (421),
which have been already touched on in Chapter 16. As to being
'stuck', de Valera once complained that he was imprisoned in
the strait jacket of the republic and the simile is literally true

to the fact that a mummified cat was found in one of the pipes of the Christ Church Cathedral organ and then, in a narrower part of the pipe, a mummified mouse.

While the six vics fifteen might be stretched to refer to vi vic. 15, an 1842 statute about the sale of spirits, the six vics odd (82.27) are the Six Counties, written perhaps twice—'six' and 'vi'cs—either to assist or confuse identification.

An aftermath of the Six County decision to opt out of the Free State was the appointment of a Boundary Commission to consider and make recommendations on any necessary or desirable alterations in the border between the two areas. The Irish Free State (Saorstat Eireann) representative on this commission, the findings of which proved abortive, was Mr Eoin Mac Neill. *'Just a Fication of Villumses*, this Mr Heer Assassor Neelson, of sorestate hearing' (241-2) appears to relate to this episode. Mac Neill, in an over-conscientious concept of the confidential nature of the commission's business, was considered to have been too slow in revealing to his colleagues the prospect of an unfavourable recommendation on the Free State claims. Joyce appears to suggest that his attitude was justification of the claims of those whose patron was William of Orange whose attitude in 1690 was still a fixation in the minds of the 1925 Orangemen. The findings of the commission were left in abeyance (1925) and the Free State government received financial compensation by the abatement of a portion of the liabilities which they had assumed under the Treaty of 1922. The verdict appears (264): 'A phantom city, phaked of philim pholk, bowed and sould for a four of hundreds of manhood and three-score fylkers for a price partitional of twenty six and six.' In other words, a schizophrenic country mirroring Joyce's disunited kingdom (188).

2. *Saint Colmcille and the Book of Kells*

Saint Colmcille (Columba Cellae i.e., Dove of the Cell or Church) *anglice* Columbkille, Columba etc. died in his monastery on the island of I or Iona in the year 597. The monastery of Ceanannus Mor (Kells) was a daughter of the Columbine foundations but was not established until many years after the saint's death. The task of writing and decorating The Book of

Kells was not undertaken until some years before 800 and was probably in course of preparation for several decades thereafter. Joyce has succeeded so well in coiling the saint and his name into the iconography of the manuscript that students of *Finnegans Wake*, who have never studied the life of Colmcille or the details of the Book of Kells, tend to think that the saint was the author, or at least the amanuensis of the book, and that he worked at it in the Kells monastery which they assume was founded by the saint himself. It is only fair to add that issues such as these may be clouded even without Joyce's aid. A fairly recent visitor to Trinity College, Dublin, having inspected the page of the Book of Kells then on view and wishing to extend her research, asked where could she interview Mr Kells, the owner!

Joyce was perfectly well aware of the confusion which he was creating. He states (50) that 'the prophet . . . disappeared (in which toodooing he has taken all the French leaves unveilable out of Calomnequiller's Pravities)'. The 'French leaves' refer to the missing leaves from the beginning of the Book of Kells, probably destroyed when the book was stolen and its cover of wrought gold wrenched off. Again, having described the 'letter' pecked out of the ashpit by the hen of the Dorans with its 'airy plumeflights all tiberiously ambiembellishing the initials majuscule of Earwicker'—i.e., *FW* itself, (119), he proceeds preposterously to suggest (122) that his text is plainly that which inspired 'the tenebrous *Tunc* page of the Book of Kells' and calls the panels provided on that page for illustrations 'the marginal panels of Columkiller'.

These are two instances in which the Book of Kells is clearly ascribed to Colmcille. But where the work is called 'Calomnequiller's Pravities' Joyce is re-writing the title of works really ascribed to the saint, i.e., Colmcille's *Prophecies*. The title is re-written in the phrase (347) 'that's told in the Bok of Alam (? Bog of Allen) to columnkill all the prefacies of Erin gone brugk' and again with further variations in Shaun's statement of his predestined mission abroad (409), 'I have it from whowho but Hagios Colleenkiller's prophecies.'

The works attributed to St Colmcille are contained in the Collectanea of prophecies of various Irish saints, which was published in Dublin in 1856, the full title of which is quoted in Chapter 19, 'Popes and Paschs', above, in connection with the prophecies of St Malachy. St Colmcille is credited with a series of five prophecies which appear on pages 2-78 of this little volume, the Irish version in rhymed quatrains and the English translations on alternate pages throughout. The last prophecy (pp. 60-78) commences,

> *How prosperous Eire is this night*

in order to contrast the destitution which will come upon the country from the invasions of Norwegians and Danes, continuing until 'their doom shall be sealed' at the battle of Clontarf. Next, the invasion of the Normans is foretold. The editor, Nicholas O'Kearney, endeavouring to fix the term of 690 years for which these invaders would hold the country, states in a footnote that he is aware that the extent of the Norman Conquest in 1170 was limited when they effected a landing at Baganbun, near Bannow, county Wexford, but he quotes a popular rhyme which conceded the sovereignty to them at their first landing :

> *At the creek of Bag-an-bun*
> *Ireland was lost and won.*

Joyce's version of this rhyme appears (294.fn.4) as 'At the foot of Bagnabun Banbasday was lost on one'. This provides further evidence of his having used John O'Daly's publication of 1856 or Messrs Duffy's reprint of 1932, probably the former, as argued in Chapter 19, above. The term put to the tenure of Ireland by England after the Norman invasion hurries the reader on from Clontarf (1014) to the time of O'Kearney's translation of the prophecies :

> *In both north and south iron wheels shall support*
> *Fiery chariots which shall resemble druidical deception.*

On this O'Kearney notes that 'it was always traditionally recorded (? by way of prophecy) that Carbaid gan eachraidhe ag taisdiol na tire—chariots without the aid of horses would traverse the country—' and equates the phenomenon with 'our railway carriages'. (This may be compared with Bloom's use of a similar expression, coisde gan capall : see Chapter 12 above.)

The prophecy goes on to foretell the rise to power of a man from Munster, 'to whom every person will send tribute to Dublin', who is clearly Daniel O'Connell, and of 'a pure Cleric . . . who will prohibit the use of intoxicating drinks'—obviously Fr Mathew.

That, as Joyce says (482) being 'the point of eschatology our book of kills reaches', we may safely leave the rest to Nicholas O'Kearney who had by this time manifestly taken over from St Colmcille, being enabled to add to his text with the benefit of hindsight.

The Book of Kells is a transcription of the Four Gospels from the Latin (Vulgate) of St Jerome. Some leaves are missing and the copy is inaccurate in places as in the first lines of the *Tunc* page *Tunc crucifixerant XPI cum eo duos latrones* where XPI (Christos) is an interpolation in the sentence, 'Then they crucified (were crucifying) with him two robbers.' Joyce's knowledge of the book and his acquaintanceship with its beautiful colouring and intricate designs are derived from *The Book of Kells* described by Sir Edward Sullivan, Bart., and illustrated with twenty-four plates in colour. The first edition of this book is dated 1914, the second 1920. Joyce's use of the names and symbols of the Four Evangelists, Matthew, Mark, Luke and John, the 'Mamalujo' of *FW*, is derived from Sullivan's reproductions of pictures of the Evangelists from the Book of Kells. Their symbols are the man (*homo*) for Matthew whose gospel commences with an account of Christ's human descent. The 'man' is sometimes portrayed with wings and hence, perhaps incorrectly, termed an 'angel'. The lion (*leo*) is Mark's symbol to suggest the fauna of the wilderness (in connection with Mark's quotation of Isaiah's 'voice crying in the desert'). The calf or ox (*vitulus*) is the symbol of Luke in reference to his account of the sacrifice of Zacharias. The eagle (*aquila*) relates symbolically to John who flies back to First Beginnings, *In principio*. Finally, all the symbols are related to Christ, as being born a man, as a (sacrificial) calf in his manner of dying, a lion in his resurrection and an eagle in his ascent. (*Christus erat homo nascendo, vitulus moriendo, leo resurgendo, aquila ascendendo.*)

Their symbols are checked (367): 'An angel prophetethis? that eyriewinging one?'

It will be recalled (Chapter 11 above) that Joyce used variations on these symbols in his mock heroic account in *Cyclops* of the Citizen's facecloth where the four evangelists are depicted presenting them to the Four Masters. In *FW* these two quartets are merged and are accredited to the archbishopricks in the four provinces as follows: Matthew, Ulster, Armagh; Mark, Munster, Cashel; Luke, Leinster, Dublin; and John, Connacht (Mayo), 'Chuam' (482) i.e. Tuam. Portrayed as part of the Celtic decor in the Book of Kells, but allowed to retain their version of the Vulgate, the Four Evangelists translated to *FW* are obliged to contain themselves within their allotted local habitations and their vernacular is compulsory Djoytsch. Even this complex and eccentric medium can be made still more unintelligible by mistranslation: the last of the Four, John, is invariably accompanied by a small ass whence this gospeller is referred to as 'Jonny na Hossaleen' (476), Johnny of the Little Ass (Ir. *h-asailin*), which one commentator, relying on the superficial similarity of pronunciation, pronounced to mean 'Johnny of the Little Horse'.

3. Dublin Corporation

'Ceadurbar-atta-Cleath became Deblena tertia' (57) is a linguistic and historical mixture suggestive of the succession of names borne by the Hibernian metropolis. *Céad* is Irish for 'first', 'urbar' representing Latin *urbs* is 'city'; 'atta Cleath' is Joyce's version of *Atha Cliath*, Irish for 'ford of hurdles' with *Baile* (city) understood to be prefixed as *ath* (ford) is in its genitive form, *Atha*; 'Dablena' is a mixture of another Irish name for the city, *Dubh Linn* (black pool) from which the name Dublin is derived and 'Eblana' a city on the east coast of Ireland named by Ptolemy and generally identified as Dublin. 'Leann dubh' which Joyce (553.27) regards as a reversal of 'Dubh Linn' is the Irish for 'porter' and this may explain why H.C.E. and his family are given the alternative name of Porter (560 and 561).

The motto on the Dublin Corporation coat of arms, *Obedientia Civium Urbis Felicitas*, is rendered (23), 'Thus the hearsomeness of the burger felicitates the whole of the polis' and further versions of varying clarity appear on page 76 and elsewhere.

In 1924 the Minister for Local Government directed that a Local Inquiry be held into the administration by the City Council of the affairs of Dublin Corporation and on 20 May 1924 a letter was addressed by the Ministry of Local Government to the Dublin Town Clerk intimating that on consideration of the administration of the Corporation as detailed in the report of the recent public inquiry the Minister had 'conceived it to be his duty to dissolve the Corporation', and that an Order to that effect and appointing Commissioners to perform the duties of the Corporation was enclosed.

A further paragraph in the letter ran as follows:

> The Minister desires me to add that he has been impressed by the sense of duty and civic spirit displayed by individual members of the Corporation. It was evident, however, that the efforts of such members to secure efficient and economical management of the City were unavailing in the absence of support from the majority of the Council.

In the Sealed Order accompanying the letter, the City Commissioners appointed to perform the duties of the Council were named as Seamas O Murchadha (*anglice* Murphy), Dr W. Dwyer and P. J. Hernon. The letter was read at a *Special Meeting of the Commissioners of the County Borough of Dublin, held in the Council Chamber, City Hall, Cork Hill, on Thursday, the 29th day of May, 1924, at 11 a.m.* and it was resolved 'That the Order be placed on the minutes'.

The City Council's alleged maladministration and the fact that the Commissioners' meeting, at which the Minister's rather vague condemnation of their inefficiency and extravagance was read, had been held on a Thursday (Thor's Day) were subsumed in *FW* into the first, rather vague suggestions of culpability on the part of Finnegan: 'What then agentlike brought about that tragoady thundersday this municipal sin business?' (5)

Whatever it was, it brought about Finnegan's Fall and his reincarnation as Earwicker, just as it also sent the City Fathers packing and their replacement by the City Commissioners or in other words, 'this ignorant [maid] sweeps it out withall the rather old corporators' (586).

The City Commissioners held office from 20 May 1924 until 14 October 1930. They are referred to (446): 'Up Murphy, Henson and O'Dwyer, the Warchester Warders! . . . We'll circumcivicise all Dublin country'. They are expected to have Dublin, 'crawling with mendiants in perforated clothing, get its wellbelavered white like l'pool and m'chester . . . who'll brighton Brayhowth . . .? The rampant royal commissioners!' (448) They are given a variation in their names and titles (529): 'the doughboys, three by nombres, won in ziel, cavehill exers or hearts of steel, Hansen, Morfydd and O'Dyar, V.D.'. Hernon's name is altered in each case to relate it to the hen of the Dorans who found the script of *FW*, 'Henson' son of a hen, and Hansen, son of a cock (German, *hahn*).

The commissioners undertook various reorganisations of administrative processes designed to improve efficiency, including the employment of a firm of French street cleaners whose motorised trucks with mechanical rotary sweepers did much to eliminate the word 'dirty' from the slogan 'dear dirty Dublin'. They would have wished to proceed with a new electricity generating scheme, 'The Kettle-Griffith-Moynihan Scheme for a New Electricity Supply' (307). This contemplated a hydro-electric plant on the river Liffey at Poulaphouca waterfall to supplement the Corporation's coal-fuelled plant at the Pigeon House (197). Larry Kettle, a brother of Joyce's U.C.D. colleague Tom Kettle, was the chief engineer of the Corporation's electricity undertaking. Moynihan was the city's Borough Engineer. Sir John Purser Griffith was the consulting engineer for the scheme; the reference to Arthur Griffith in this context by Mrs Glasheen is incorrect. The scheme as projected for Dublin City was not proceeded with; instead the Free State Government set up an Electricity Supply Board to deal with the generation of power on a national basis: they started with a hydro-electric generating plant at Ardnacrusha on the river Shannon near Limerick, the contract being carried out by a German firm named Siemens Schuckert. This firm in a previous generation had provided the electrification of the Arklow lighthouse and they are referred to twice in this context in similar language (245.8, 549.18) and, in each case with a pun on 'seamen'.

The employment of the French street-cleaners and the

German electrical engineering firm left Dublin (H.C.E.) with 'a frenchy to curry him' and 'a fritz at his switch' (138) and Joyce was enabled to amend the prayer for the dead, *Requiem aeternam dona eis* by a rather artificial appeal for artificial light: 'Erdnacrusha, requiestress, wake em! And let luck's puresplutterall lucy at ease!' (262)

'And how long was he under lock and neagh?' one of the washerwomen asked (196). The answer is seven years: 'You'd think all was dodo belonging to him how he durmed adranse in durance vaal. He had been belching for severn years' (199). During that period Larry O'Neill who had been Lord Mayor when the Corporation was dissolved in 1924 continued to use the mayoral style and title, albeit illegally, and he is accordingly given the qualified or disqualified title 'Outlawrie O'Niall' (550).

Numerous Lords Mayor of Dublin are woven into the text of *FW* but here we need concern ourselves only with him who was elected by the new city council when they were returned to office in October 1930 under the provisions of an Act passed in that year extending the area of the city by the inclusion of the urban districts of Rathmines and Rathgar and Pembroke and certain added rural areas ('addled areas', 205). This was Alfred Byrne who succeeded in holding the mayoral chain and chair continuously from 1930 to 1939. He was an adept at keeping in the public eye and cultivating popularity: his hand was freely available to be shaken at any time by all and sundry—all of which may assist anyone who wishes to take one of the subjects that Joyce has set for an essay (307): 'Why we all Love our Little Lord Mayor'. Joyce also works Alfie Byrne into a parody of the Greek alphabet: 'alfie byrni gamman dealter etcera zezera eacla treacla youghto kaptor lomdom noo' (568). Alfie is apparently here incited to emulate Dick Whittington's feat: 'youghta capture London now'.

4. *Bruno of Nola into Browne and Nolan*

The bisection of the Italian philosopher into the double names of the Dublin bookselling firm, Browne usually representing Shaun and Nolan Shem, may be found in *FW*, *passim*. Yawn, when hard pressed by his interlocutors (488) as to the 'indwellingness' within him of the shameful Shem, has recourse to the Nassau Street partners who are credited with familiarity with the philosophies of the Arabian Ibn Sen (Avicenna) and Ipanzussch (Ibn Rushd, Averroes) the Moslem :

—Dearly Beloved brethren : Bruno and Nola, leymon bogholders and stationery lifepartners off Orangey Saint Nessau Street, were explaining it avicendas all round each other ere yesterweek out of Ibn Sen and Ipanzussch. When himupon Nola Bruno monopolises his egobruno most unwillingly seses by the mortal powers alionola equal and opposite brunoipso, *id est*, eternally provoking alio opposite equally as provoked as Bruno at being eternally opposed by Nola. Poor Omniboose, singalow singelearum : so is he !

So, too, one might opine was Lucia, Joyce's daughter, whose malady, as Gillet said, was 'crucifying' him. If the foregoing mad description of a schizoid reconciled her symptoms with those 'opposites' which Bruno claimed could be 're-amalgamated', he was entitled to lay that soothing unction to his soul. In the Night Lessons, opposite the marginal note, *The Twofold Truth and the Conjunctive Appetites of Oppositional Orexes*, the phrase *Trionfante di bestia!* is interpolated (305). This invokes the title of Bruno's book, *Il Spaccio di Bestia Trionfante*, 'The Expulsion of the Triumphant Beast' in a conversation immediately following Kev's hitting Dolph whom Issy (doubling for Lucia) described in fn. 1, 303, as 'Mr Tellibly Divilcult'. Here Joyce has Lucia, through her surrogate Issy, say about him (Dolph, Shem) the exact words (in *FW* language) which Joyce, on 20 April 1932, had written to Miss Weaver about Lucia : 'She is terribly difficult.' (*Letters*, I) On 13 May 1932 (Letters, III) he explained to Valery Larbaud, 'Lucia had a bad *crise de nerfs* at the Gare du Nord so I had to take the trunks off the train (and) abandon our journey to London.' Another of her antics is suggested (304) : 'That might keep her from throwing delph.'

In other respects also Joyce found philosophical support in Bruno's theories. His idea that all that could possibly have happened in the universe but did not is as valid as what historically occurred when considered *sub specie aeternitatis* justified his pillaging mythology, fiction and history and merging his spoils as material for the universalism of *FW*, without any qualms as to the relative validity of his sources. This was an even more liberal and comprehensive postulate than that of Stephen Dedalus in 'Aeolus' when he visualised the 'dead noise' of O'Connell's oratory, gone with the wind, preserved by 'Akasic records of all that ever anywhere wherever was'.

Bruno had fled from his Dominican monastery in Naples and, visiting Paris and London, endeavoured to popularise a philosophy which would reconcile Protestants and Catholics, 'their contrarieties eliminated' (107). This was based on a nonsensical mixture of Pythagorean magic with the new Copernican theory of the cosmos which, without understanding it, Bruno tried to reconcile with the Platonism of Nicholas of Cusa, picturing a world with its centre anywhere and its circumference nowhere, a theory which in fact dated back to Empedocles. A world where man—a man—was the microcosm and the universe the macrocosm appealed to Joyce who would naturally conceive himself as the centre. Joyce was not being deliberately obscure or fanciful when thirty years previously in his paper, *The Day of the Rabblement* (1901), he had referred to Bruno as 'The Nolan', for this was Bruno's own description of himself (*Il Nolano*) when publishing the views which he had expressed in a series of dialogues with Oxford scholars at the house of Sir Fulke Greville in London in 1583. He might be described as the first apostle of Ecumenism, but he was intellectually ill equipped to reconcile the theological conflicts of his time. After years of wandering around Europe he returned to Rome in the hope of persuading Pope Clement VIII to adopt his views. Not surprisingly, he failed in his mission, was imprisoned and in 1600 he was burnt at the stake in the Campo dei Fiori, Rome, for heresy and monastic apostasy.

Bruno's eccentric philosophical theories, like Vico's philosophy of history, form part of the theoretical justification for the structure of *FW* and also profoundly influence the style. Examples of conflicting or contrasting clauses may be found in any page : 'Caseous may bethink himself a thought of a caviller but Burrus has the richly roundered head that goes best with thofthinking defensive fideism.' (162) Or, 'O thaw bron orm, A' Cotraige, thinkinthou gaily?' (54) This is a rendering of the

Irish for 'O, I am sorry, St Patrick, do you understand Irish?'.
The words in the sentence are so structured as to be balanced
between an expression of sorrow (Ir. *brón*) and gaiety ('gaily'
being a pun on Ir. *Gaedhilge*, the Irish language), thus afford-
ing an example of the antithesis personified in the Shem and
Shaun characters Tristopher and Hilary (21). These 'opposites'
who are capable of exchanging identities are based on Bruno's
maxim, *in tristitia hilaris hilaritate tristis* ('*Il Candelajo*').

The interchange of identities and the amalgamation of dis-
cordant personalities may be considered mathematically and,
accordingly, in the academic pages of the Home Lessons chapter
we are given formulae for combinations NCR (284) and permutations MPM (285).

These latter and similar items may also stem from the other
half of the Bruno of Nola dualism, Browne and Nolan. When
Joyce was a schoolboy and a university student, these Dublin
booksellers supplied the exercise jotters and their own editions
of the texts prescribed for Board of Education examinations.
It is in keeping with the theory of the workings of a dreaming
mind that the worries of schooldays and the nervous tensions
of examinations should recur to the adult memory in dreams.

Acknowledgement is made of the booksellers' texts: 'Soon
jemmijohns will cudgel about some a rythmatic or other over
Browne and Nolan's divisional tables.' (268)

A footnote (275 fn. 6), 'Traduced into jinglish janglage for
the nusances of dolphins born' is annotated by Professor Harry
Levin *James Joyce a Critical Introduction* by refence to 'the *in
usum Delphini* of an edition of the classics notorious for its
expurgations'. This gets only half of the reference, the other
moiety, the south Dublin suburb of Dolphin's Barn, being
overlooked.

The children at their Night Lessons, or Joyce remembering
his, know that a noun is the name of a person, place or thing,
as 'man', 'town', 'book', 'goodness'. Thus a noun may denote
anything and everything in the world. The universalism is
accordingly reduced (278) to 'A letters from a person to a place
about a thing'—*FW* in short. Similarly, the words Tom, Dick
and Harry under various guises are used by Joyce to represent
'all men', as in *U* (25):

*Goodbye, now, good bye, write down all I said
And tell Tom Dick and Harry I rose from the dead.*

Here (291) the expression is 'tomthick and tarry' while already the Maynooth Catechism has been consulted on the definition of 'neighbour' in the context of 'thy neighbour as thyself' and 'Nebob' (270) is defined (fn. 4): 'He is my all menkind of every desception', the original 'all mankind of every description' being 'traduced' by Issy with the intent of seducing men with her 'kickshoes on the algebrars' (270).

The word 'Furniss's (289) is annotated by Mrs Glasheen (*Second Census*) as 'Furniss, Father — author of *Sight of Hell* (1861) a book for scaring children'. I think that the reference is more likely to be to Harry Furniss, author of *M.P.s in Session 1882-90, Five Hundred Sketches of Eminent Members of the House of Commons 1882-90*. The caricatures include one of H. C. E. Childers which is sub-titled 'H(ere) C(omes) E(verybody) CH — LD — RS', bringing us 'by a commodius vicus of recirculation back (3) to Hugh Culling Eardley Childers from whose 'Here Comes Everybody' nickname, as explained in Chapter 15 above, Humphrey Chimpden Earwicker (H.C.E.) was evolved in Joyce's mind as the universalised hero of *FW*. Rory O'Connor and Erskine Childers were executed late in 1922 when Joyce was considering his first outline scheme of *FW* and this seems to have been the immediate occasion of his selecting their names for his hero.

5. *The Ass and the Hen*

The ass which, led by Johnny Mac Dougal, follows The Four ('Mamalujo') in their travels, is the narrator of III. 1, where he says, 'but I, poor ass, am but as their fourpart tinckler's donkey' (405). At the end of this episode when Jaun's speechifying is over and he prepares to set out as 'Embrassador-at-Large', the ass manages to get in a few pages of description, exhortation and farewell, in the course of which he pulls up short, saying 'but sure where's the use my talking quicker when I know you'll hear me all astray?' (472) This remark clearly identifies him with 'the ass of the Dorans' (*U* 491), an animal borrowed from a Dublin street ballad, a version of which is given in song 84 of Colm O Lochlainn's collection, *Irish Street Ballads*, (Dublin, 1939, 1946). This describes one Paddy Doyle setting out to meet his love, Betty Toole—

> That day Paddy took some liquor
> Which made his spirits light and gay,
> Says he, 'What use my walking quicker,
> Sure I know she'll meet me on the way.'

Paddy fell into a drunken slumber by the roadside and, unknown to him, an ass lay down beside him. In his dream he embraced the ass mistaking him for his sweetheart, but when the ass began to bray he woke up in terror and fled for refuge to Betty's door.

> So he up and told her all quite civil
> While she prepared a brimming glass
> About how he hugged and smugged the devil:
> Says she, 'Sure that was Doran's ass.'

In a version of the song which I heard long before the publication of the O'Lochlainn edition the girl's name was Biddy, not Betty.

The name of Doran is not associated with the ass in *FW* but, as shown above, the ass mimics a couplet from the song and so identifies himself with the animal in the ballad.

Mrs Glasheen suggests that the ass may be Joyce himself and also says that there is 'a strong possibility' that he may be Christ. The only reference to the latter possibility that I could find is one not indexed in the *Second Census*, viz., 'the puisny donkeyman and his crucifer's cauda' (477), but 'crucifer' here means the carrier of the cross which every ass bears in the pattern of his hide and hair and not a description derived from any reference to Christ.

The only association of importance, apart from that with the Dorans, which I can find with the ass is that discovered by Mr Atherton in St Jerome's letter to Asella, 'Gratias ago Deo meo quod dignus sum quem mundus oderit' (I thank my God that I am held worthy for the world to hate). This he correctly references to 'Hanner Esellus' (478) meaning the ass. Mr Atherton finds St Jerome's name 'used once without any mutation (252.11)' but he seems not to have noticed that the passage to which he refers is followed by one which also ties in with the letter to Asella. The two sentences are:

—And may Saint Jerome of the Harlot's Curse make family three of you which is much abedder!
—Grassy ass ago.

Here the reply is at once an echo of St Jerome's 'Gratias ago' and a play on the association of the ass of *FW* with the name of the saint's pious friend. 'Jerome of the Harlot's Curse' also refers to a church and cemetery called Mount Jerome in the suburb of Harold's Cross in Dublin.

The function of the hen, as briefly described at the beginning of Chapter 15 above, was to scratch out a sheet of letter paper from an ashpit or orangery which was later to be expanded into the text of *Finnegans Wake* and it was explained that this artifice for the finding or the coming into existence of Joyce's act of creation was to link it with the acts of oriental cosmocreators. It also brings *FW* into line with the history of the Book of Kells which was stolen and subsequently found embedded in the earth from which it was dug up minus its diamond encrusted and wrought gold cover.

The hen is clearly identified with the farm from which Doran's ass was borrowed: she is referred to as 'Belinda of the Dorans' (111) and 'the hen in the doran's shantyqueer' (584). Efforts (Mrs Glasheen, *Second Census, sub* 'Doran, Biddy') to derive her name from Greek *doron* (gift) or to identify her with Artemis must therefore be relegated to the field of secondary associations. Her given name, Biddy (112), seems also to stem from the farm, if not of the Dorans, then from that of Biddy Toole who identified her neighbour's ass as the origin of the Satanic spectre which had terrified Paddy Doyle.

Joyce, as distinct from his symbolising commentators, treats the role of the hen lightly: all her activities are examples of what the new man (or woman) may become, wherefore her motto is borrowed from Cardinal Newman and parodied, 'Lead, kindly fowl!' What a bird such as Biddy has done man may yet emulate, 'be it fly, be it moult, be it hatch, be it agreement in the nest'. After some further socio-scientific journalism and science fiction, we are informed:

No, assuredly, they are not justified, those gloompourers who grouse that letters have never been quite their old selves again since that weird weekday in bleak Janiveer (yet how palmy date in waste's oasis!) when to the shock of both, Biddy Doran looked ad literature. (112)

The hen here represents the reading public doomed to be stupefied when confronted with the corpus of *Finnegans Wake*; meanwhile the hen's discovery, a single sheet of paper, contains a letter from Boston (Mass.) which is illiterate but not, as Professor Tindall suggests, in the style of Nora Joyce. The style is that of Nora's relatives whose communications, presents of wedding cake and laconic 'hope you liked the drake' usually evoked more laughter than enlightenment in the Joyce household (see *e.g.*, Ellmann, 717n.). The letter, impenetrable as it may seem, was carefully worked over by Joyce to introduce the case of multiple personality dealt with in *The Dissociation of a Personality* by Morton Prince where the clinical history of a schizoid patient in Boston, Mass., is detailed. Joyce's treatment of this topic, particularly in relation to Isabel (Issy), is an important factor in the structure and style of *Finnegans Wake*. Thus the remainder of this chapter is devoted, first, to a rather disingenuous analysis of the letter and then of the book as a whole.

The hen is also associated with Madame Blavatsky who rejoiced in the maiden name Hahn-Hahn. Madame's writings on oriental theosophy are used extensively by Joyce but he cannot resist misusing her name (66) where 'Cox's wife, twice Mrs Hahn pokes her beak into the matter'.

Ultimately she is back in Doran's yard now seemingly adjacent to Earwicker's inn, where she acts as a Greek chorus to the closing scene of his bedroom dream (584), 'While the dapplegray dawn drags nearing nigh for to wake all droners that drouse in Dublin.' (585)

6. *Scissors and Paste*

The heading of this section refers to Joyce's 'scissors and paste' system of inserting allusions of Irish origin arbitrarily throughout his text. The previous sections of this chapter deal separately with references which require explication at some length; those reviewed here admit of briefer treatment and are annotated by reference to the pages of *FW* where they appear. The items dealt with have not heretofore been correctly explicated.

'This is the Willingdone, bornstable ghentleman' (10) and variations in other parts of the text have their source in a remark ascribed to the Duke of Wellington, whose place of birth was claimed by several localities in Ireland. Wellington did not wish to be called an Irishman and his comment was, 'If a gentleman happens to be born in a stable, it does not follow that he should be called a horse.'

'The shortlegged bergins of Corkhill' (12) refers primarily to Little Alf Bergan (*U, Cyclops*). As a law clerk to the sub-sheriff, Long John Clancy, he did business in the City Hall on Cork Hill, Dublin.

'So this is Dyoublong?' (13) is taken from the title of a book by M. J. Mac Manus, illustrated by Sean O'Sullivan, *'So this is Dublin!'* (Dublin and Cork, The Talbot Press, 1927.) In the part of the book entitled 'Literary Gossip' the first paragraph runs :

> Mr James Joyce has been paying a visit to Dublin for the new book which he has planned, to be called *An Irish Odyssey.* He has spent a considerable time visiting the Corporation Sewage Farm, the Wicklow manure factory, and the sloblands at Fairview. Before returning to Paris he stated that he had derived keen satisfaction from his visit to his native city.

In the next part, 'Irish Biography', the following occurs :

> MR JAMES JOYCE
> Of the books of Mr Joyce
> *Ulysses* is not my choice;
> I think—You may not credit it—
> That it should be sub-edited.

Pages 13-14 contain parodies of extracts from Irish annals, recording amongst other things the birth of two sons to 'a goodman and his hag'. This is a humorous entry to mark the birth of Joyce and his 'mighty opposite' in 1882. It was a portent of 'Blotty words for Dublin', that is, it forecast the writing in due

course of the obscure text of *Finnegans Wake*. The affinity with
the song 'The Rocky Road to Dublin' suggested by Hodgart
and Worthington seems rather slim.

'Bower Moore' (24) derives from the Irish *Bothar Mor*, Big
Road. 'There's a bower of roses by Bendemeer's stream' is the
first line of a lyric in Thomas Moore's *Lalla Rookh*. Bohermore
is a road outside Galway once used by lovers, including James
Joyce's future wife, Nora Barnacle, and her boyfriend Willie
Mulvey, who is mentioned in the 'Penelope' chapter of *Ulysses*.
This is the residence (Bohermore) of Johnny Mac Dougall who
represents Connacht and John the Evangelist. It was also the
birthplace, 14 February 1856, of Frank Harris.

In the phrase 'the millioncandled eye of Tuskar sweeps the
Moylean Main' (25), Tuskar is a lighthouse and Joyce was
correct in suggesting that it had a millioncandled power. 'The
Moylean Main' is the narrow channel that separates Ireland and
Scotland, the name being taken from the Irish *Sruth na Maoile*,
the stream of Moyle. Joyce uses it in several places as a generic
name for sea or the ocean (see, e.g., 'the moyles and moyles of
it' p. 628). He borrowed the word from Thomas Moore's poem
on the Children of Lir who were metamorphosed into swans
and doomed so to live for nine hundred years, of which three
hundred were spent on the ice cold waters of the sea of Moyle :

> *Silent, O Moyle, be the roar of thy water,*
> *Break not, ye breezes, your chain of repose,*
> *While, murmuring mournfully, Lir's lonely daughter*
> *Tells to the night-star her tale of woes.*

(See also the interpolation on page 86: 'They were on that
sea by the plain of Ir', etc.)

On page 25, 'Hoist high the stone that Liam failed' is a
reference to a stone, the Lia Fail, at Tara. Joyce's punning use
of the term is based on mispronunciation of the original (pronounced 'Leeah Faw-ill'). In its context here it may be an
exhortation to Shaun (de Valera) to raise Ireland's destiny
higher than Liam (Cosgrave) had achieved. There is a further
reference to it in the phrase 'his Tiara of scones was held un-
fillable till one Liam Fail felled him in Westmunster' (131). It
is said to have been the practice to crown kings of Ireland on
this stone at Tara, and it was held that when the rightful

aspirant to monarchy ascended it the stone shrieked. It was lent for a similar ceremony at Scone in Scotland and kept there until brought away by the English and inserted in the coronation chair in Westminster Abbey. The 'stone of destiny' (40) is an English version of the name.

On page 27, 'White of gold with a tourch of ivy' refers to Ireland's national colours: green, white, and orange. As to red lips, 'Were I a clerk designate to the Williamswoodmenufactors I'd poster these pouters on every jamb in the town' (27) refers to Messrs Williams and Woods, manufacturers of jam (cf. 'William's jam' in *Gas From a Burner*). Red lips as a substitute for strawberry jam on every jamb in town is suggested to be used as an advertisement; it is also a reference to the biblical use of a substitute for human blood in the Passover. '(Cf. though every doorpost in muchtried Lucalizod was smeared with generous erstborn gore'—p. 178.) The first words of this extract 'Were I a clerk' are given in the Moore's *Melodies* volume as the air for 'You Remember Ellen'.

Mention of 'the redritualhoods of Maccabe and Cullen' (33) refers to two nineteenth-century Irish cardinals, who are also named on page 200. The phrase 'his *duc de Fer's* overgrown milestone' (36) is a reference to the monumental obelisk in memory of the Duke of Wellington ('the Iron Duke') in the Phoenix Park. This reference seems to be based on Chart, *The Story of Dublin*, where the memorial is described as 'a huge obelisk with an unfortunate resemblance to a gigantic milestone'. On page 56, the O'Connell monument in Glasnevin cemetery is called 'that overgrown leadpencil'.

(37) 'mawshe dho hole' is Joyce's version of the Irish *má sé do thoil é* (if you please).

The phrase 'Primewer Glasstone setting a match to the march of a maker (last of the stewards peut-être)' (41) refers to the quotation from Charles Stewart Parnell inscribed on his monument in O'Connell Street, Dublin: 'No man has a right to fix the boundary of the march of a nation: no man has a right to say to his country—thus far shalt thou go and no further.' Here the saying is written so as to refer to Gladstone whose intervention in Irish party politics in 1890 put an end to Parnell's career. It is re-written as 'No mum has the rod to pad a stub to the lurch of amotion.' (365)

On page 42, the words 'seinn fion's araun' mean Sinn Féin's song, i.e. 'The Soldier's Song', with an echo of the party slogan Sinn Féin Amháin (Ourselves alone). The Irish words, however, seem also capable of meaning 'the playing of music, wine and bread' (*seinm, fíon 's aran*). Since identifying the latter meaning, so appropriate to celebrations at an Irish wake, I have been pleased to observe that the same explication has been made in Brendan O Hehir's *A Gaelic Lexicon to Finnegans Wake* which has come rather belatedly to my notice.

'The Ballad of Persse O'Reilly' (44-7), much admired of some but in my opinion 'still today insufficiently malestimated' (125), may nevertheless be noticed for its verse—

> It was . . . while admiring the monkeys
> That our heavyweight heathen Humpharey
> Made bold a maid to woo . . .
> Begob, he's the crux of the catalogue
> Of our antediluvial zoo,

—which is an extension of Bloom's reference (*Circe*, 452) to 'Girl in the monkeyhouse', itself a reference to Caruso's getting into trouble over his advances to a girl in the New York monkey house.

The statement 'and the gauntlet upon the hand which in an hour . . . had struck down the might he mighthavebeen d'Esterre' (52) refers to Daniel O'Connell's duel with d'Esterre and his show of remorse for having had to shoot him (shown by his wearing a glove on his hand).

'It scenes like a landscape' (53) is 'prigged' from Joyce's own Bull Wall scene in *A Portrait*.

'The house of Atreox is fallen indeedust' (55) is a verbally economical way of saying 'indeed in the dust'. Joyce continues:

> The scene, refreshed, reroused, was never to be forgotten . . .
> for later in the century one of that puisne band of factferret-
> ers, (then an excivily (out of the custom huts) (retired) . . .
> under the sixtyfives act) . . . rehearsed it . . . (55)

This might tempt me, had I sufficient superstition and vanity in my composition, to think that Joyce, like Nostradamus, could look into the future and cast his prophetic eye upon me, thirty years afterwards, retired when under the age of sixty-five, out of the Custom House, 'rehearsing', i.e. putting Finnegan back into his hearse for a rehearsal of his wake. He seems, incidentally, to have rehearsed his own interment on page 488 : '. . . One might hear in their beyond that lionroar in the air again, the zoohoohoom . . . Dustify of that sole, you breather! Ruemember, blither, thou must lie!' This could be the zoo near Fluntern where Joyce is buried 'within sound of the lions'.

The parenthetical statement on page 63 '(for ann there is but one liv and hir newbridge is her old)' refers to a bridge across the Liffey, called the New Bridge, when it was built nearly seven hundred years ago. It is located some miles upstream from Lucan. Five Dublin bridges may be discerned in 130.28,29 — Rialto, Annesley, Binn's, Ballsbridge and Newcomen.

The phrase 'hickicked at the dun and dorass' (67) plays on the Irish *Dun an Doras*, meaning 'shut the door'.

The phrase 'which our own little Graunya . . . dished up to the greatsire of Oscar, that son of a Coole' (68) refers to Finn Mac Cool to whom Grainne, daughter of Cormac Mac Airt was affianced. Finn was already the father of Ossian and the grandfather of Oscar and he thus takes his place with Lewis Carroll, King Mark and other elderly lovers of young girls. The elopement is again referred to (137): 'Miss MacCormack Ni Lacarthy who made off with Darly Dermod' and on page 146 in the words 'dear mot's . . . our granny?' as well as on page 369, 'when her daremood's a grownian'. The mythological genesis of Cormac Mac Airt has been dealt with in Part I, Chapter 12, above.

The words 'wilde or the' (69) derive from Padraic Colum's poem 'The Poor Scholar of the 'Forties' :

> *But what avail my teaching slight?*
> *Years hence, in rustic speech, a phrase,*
> *As in wild earth a Grecian vase.*

'Peannlueamoore' (69) means the same in Irish and is in the same context as 'overgrown leadpencil' on page 56.

'faminebuilt walls' (71) were walls built around landlords' demesnes during the 1846-47 Famine, with the cheap labour of hungry tenants.

'Man Devoyd of the Commoner Characteristics of an Irish

Nature' (72) refers to Mr de Valera. The apostrophe before the 'M' indicates the omission of the 'E' of Eamon.

'Kimmage Outer' (72): a district to the south of Dublin, now a suburb of the city.

Here (93) are listed some words borrowed from selected Anglo-Irish writers: 'From dark Rosa Lane a sigh and a weep', is from 'O my dark Rosaleen, do not sigh, do not weep!', the first lines of Mangan's *Dark Rosaleen*. The phrase 'from lone Coogan Barry his arrow of song', alludes to 'There is a green island in lone Guagane Barra/Where Allua of song rushes forth like an arrow' (Callinan), already parodied (88): 'there—is—a—pain—aleland in Long's gourgling barrel', and 'from Sean Kelly's anagrim a blush at the name' is from John Kells Ingram's 'The Memory of the Dead' which begins:

> Who fears to speak of ninety eight?
> Who blushes at the name?

The phrase 'from I am the Sullivan that trumpeting tramp', seems to refer to A. M. ('am') Sullivan, but, in fact, it was his brother T. D. Sullivan who wrote a song to commemorate the 'Manchester Martyrs', Allen, Larkin and O'Brien, hanged as the aftermath of Fenian disturbances in 1867. The chorus commences: 'Tramp, tramp, tramp, the boys are marching'.

The phrase 'from Kathleen May Vernon her Mebbe fair efforts' is based on 'it may be for years and it may be for ever' from the song 'Kathleen Mavourneen'. The words 'from Suffering Dufferin the Sit of her Style', refers to Lady Dufferin's 'Lament of the Irish Emigrant':

> I'm sitting on the stile, Mary
> Where we sat side by side
> On a bright May morning, long ago,
> When first you were my bride.

This is parodied (445): 'You're sitting on my style maybe, whereoft I helped your ore'. Two other lines from this song, 'And the red was on your lips, Mary / And the lovelight in your eye' are echoed on page 441, 'for the wish is on her rose marine and the lunchlight in her eye . . .' Joyce also refers to this song on pages 190-91 where Shem is being abused as 'an Irish emigrant the wrong way out' (i.e., going to Europe instead of to America) 'sitting on your crooked sixpenny stile, an unfrill-frocked quackfriar, you . . . semisemitic serendipitist, you . . . Europasianised Afferyank!'

Page 93 is quite exceptional in giving the sources from which Joyce purloined his material. As a general rule, as he himself says, it would be a mistake to infer 'from the nonpresence of inverted commas (sometimes called quotation marks) on any page that its author was always constitutionally incapable of misappropriating the spoken words of others' (108).

The hundred-letter pastoral conglomerate on page 113 contains the words 'ink ank'; they do not represent, as has been suggested, the tinkling of cowbells—they are part of a riddle well known in rural Ireland years ago:

> Ink ank,
> Under the bank,
> Ten drawing four.

The answer is a cow being milked.

'olmond bottler' (118) is a variation on the name of the Butler family who hold the title of Marquis of Ormond.

In the 1930s, new editions of some of Joyce's works were being published by the Albatross Press. This may have turned his mind to 'The Rime of the Ancient Mariner', for on page 137 we find 'by stealth of a kersse her alburntress abaft his nape she hung.' The content here is related to Nora Barnacle's auburn hair, but the form is borrowed from the 'Mariner': 'Instead of the cross the albatross / About my neck was hung'. Joyce, how-ever, seems to have had a more fundamental preoccupation with Coleridge's 'Kubla Khan':

> *In Xanadu did Kubla Khan*
> *A stately pleasure dome decree:*
> *Where Alph, the sacred river, ran*
> *Through caverns measureless to man*
> *Down to a sunless sea.*

Joyce's sacred river, ALP, the nightmare of H.C.E.'s sunless sea of sleep, may be equated to Coleridge's Alph. It is also the initials, read backwards, of Portrane Lunatic Asylum, a county Dublin haven for the chronic insane.

'If you met on the binge a poor acheseyeld from Ailing,

when the tune of his tremble shook shimmy on shin, while his
countrary raged in the weak of his wailing, like a rugilant
pugilant Lyon O'Lynn' (148), is based on a poem by Thomas
Campbell, the first verse being :

> *There came to the beach a poor exile from Erin,*
> *The dew on his thin robe was heavy and chill,*
> *For his country he sighed when at twilight repairing,*
> *To wander alone by the windbeaten hill.*

'all the kules in Kroukaparka' (78) means all the goals
(Irish, cul) scored in Croke Park, the central arena of all-
Ireland matches in Gaelic football and hurling.

The phrase 'all lock and no stable for Honorbright Merreytrickx' (211) refers to Honour Bright, a prostitute, who was
murdered in 1925 in the Dublin mountains, at the crossroads
of Ticknock. 'Honour Bright' was a nickname derived from her
use of the phrase in reply to most remarks, wise or wild, made
by her customers. Joyce's addition 'Merreytrickx' is a disguised
rendering of the Latin *meretrix* which, as an adjective, means
bright, shiny, while as a noun it means a prostitute. Thus his
single verbal addition (which may have been borrowed from Sir
John Harington's *Nugae Antiquae*) signifies both her nickname and her vocation. Her present, ('all lock and no stable')
apart from a possible reference to the firearm which killed her,
probably refers to the reason for her being murdered—her
having infected some relation of her slayer. In the Lock Hospital
in Townsend Street, women were treated for venereal disease.
It was said to have got its name from a belief that the patients
were chained to their beds to restrain them from escaping to
the streets.

We encounter this hospital again in H.C.E.'s claim (542):
'in my bethel of Solyman's I accouched their rotundaties and I
turnkeyed most insultantly over raped lutetias in the lock'.
Bethel Solomons (1885-1965) was a gynecologist and quondam
Master of the Rotunda Maternity Hospital. The references to
the 'Rape of the Lock' and the 'Rape of Lucrece' are backed
by this further allusion to the Lock Hospital.

'treerack monatan' and 'the divlun from his punchpoll' (227)
refer to two Irish mountains, the Three-Rock near Dublin and
the Devils' Punchbowl in Kerry. The 'Mutther Masons' (223)

was a shebeen run by a lady called 'Mother Mason' in South King Street.

'Wildrose La Gilligan' (229) relates to the title of a popular Irish historical novel, *The Wild Rose of Lough Gill*, by Patrick G. Smyth, Gill 1883, 5th edition 1904. It is a love story set in the period of the Insurrection of 1641 and the subsequent warfare down to 1652.

The mention of 'the papal legate from the Vatucum, Monsaigneur Rabbinsohn Crucis' (243) is a reference to Monsignor Robinson who was Papal Nuncio in Dublin in the 1930s, containing also a reference to Robinson Crusoe. Monsignor Robinson seems to be confused here with the Papal Legate, Cardinal Lauri, who was the personal representative of the Pope at the Dublin Eucharistic Congress in 1932.

References to the 'moon' and 'mud cabins' on page 244 are from the ballad 'The Rising of the Moon' by John Keegan Casey—

> *Out from many a mud-wall cabin*
> *Eyes were watching through the night;*
> *Many a manly heart was throbbing*
> *For the blessed warning light.*
> *Murmurs passed along the valleys*
> *Like the Banshee's lonely croon*
> *And a thousand blades were flashing*
> *At the rising of the moon.*

Dolly Brae (246) is not Dolly Gray to whom Mrs Glasheen references 'Good bye' but Dolly's Brae, the site of some Orangemen's fracas with their enemies and duly celebrated in a ballad.

'Charley you're my darwing!' (252) includes not only Charles Darwin and *The Descent of Man*, but also an ape in the Dublin Zoo known as Charley the Chimp, as well as the Jacobite song, 'Charlie Is My Darling'.

'Move up, Mackinerny! Make room for Muckinurney!' (264) was annotated in *A Skeleton Key to Finnegans Wake* (1944; New York, Viking Press 1961) as 'Move up, you great Archetypal Man, and make room for our local example' (p. 168n.). The local example is otherwise : in August 1922, after General Michael Collins was buried in Glasnevin cemetery, a note was found on his grave, 'Move over, Mick, make room for Dick.'

General Richard (Dick) Mulcahy was Collins's successor as Commander-in-Chief in the Civil War of 1922-23.

'Daft Dathy of the Five Positions . . . is still . . . on the Madderhorn and . . . daring Dunderhead (thunder) to shiver his timbers' (274) refers to Dathi, King of Ireland, who is reputed to have invaded Gaul and in an Alpine thunderstorm challenged the god who killed him with lightning. Joyce, who was chronically scared of thunder and lightning, naturally thought the King's defiance foolhardy. (A reference to Hannibal, son of Hamilcar, naturally follows.)

The references on page 303 to Steele, Burke, Sheridan, Swift, Wilde, and Shaw conclude with 'Doubbllinnbbayyates' which sounds like somebody calling fresh fish but really means W. B. Yeats.

'Our Allies the Hills' on page 307 was a saying of Mr de Valera's when 'on the run'.

The statement 'the barmaisigheds, when my heart knew no care' (387) is based on Mangan's poem, 'The Time of the Barmecides':

> *My eyes are filmed, my beard is grey;*
> *I am bowed with the weight of years;*
> *I would I were stretched in my bed of clay*
> *With my long-lost Youth's compeers!*
> *For back to the past, though the thought brings woe,*
> *My memory ever glides—*
> *To the old, old time long, long ago,*
> *The time of the Barmecides!*

In the next line on page 387, 'the official landing of Lady Jales Casemate' refers to the legendary Lady Ceaser who led a colony of ladies and three men to Ireland before the Deluge, to Julius Caesar's landing in Britain and to Sir Roger Casement's landing in Kerry in 1916.

'Exeunc through a darrus Kram of Llawnroe' (388) means Mark of Cornwall goes out through a door, (darras being used for *dorus*, the Irish for 'door').

'Fish hands Macsorley! . . . We're the musichall pair that won the swimmyease bladdhers at the Guinness gala in Badeniveagh' (408): 'Shake hands as a swimmer, my twin.' (From the song, 'Mac Sorley's two little Twins'.) These twins came first at the swimming gala in the Iveagh Baths, Dublin.

'Rere Uncle Remus' (442), referenced (Census) to Joel Chandler and Romulus, relates in fact to a children's column, The Irish Fireside Club, in the *Weekly Freeman* where the young essay competitors addressed their letters to 'Dear Uncle Remus'.

On the same page, the phrase 'coomb . . . the libs round Close Saint Patrice' refers to three Dublin areas : the Coombe, the Liberties, and Saint Patrick's Close.

The words 'whatyoumaycormack' and 'I'm athlone in the lillabilling of killarnies' (450) refer to John Mac Cormack, the famous tenor who was born in Athlone. His repertoire featured 'By Killarney's Lakes and Dells' and 'I'm Alone' from the *Lily of Killarney*.

'di'yegut?' (455) and the following two sentences are parodies of salutations in Irish meaning, God with you; God and Mary with you; and God and Mary and St Patrick with you.

'When Lapac walks backwards he's the darkest horse in Capalisoot' (487): 'Lapac' spelled backwards is Capal or Capel street. 'Capall' is also Irish for a horse, and 'Capilisoot' is intended to mean Chapelizod.

On page 491, the statement 'our straat that is called corkscrewed . . . the finest boulevard billy for a mile . . . Patrick's, if they took the bint out of the mittle of it' refers to the reply given to an American visitor to Cork who asked a boy if Patrick street was an important thoroughfare. 'Man, dear', he was told, 'it would be the grandest street in the world if dey could only take the bind outa the middle of it'. It also refers to the crooked strait of the 'Wandering Rocks 'in *Ulysses*.

Nile Lodge (494) is the name of a villa at a crossroads in Galway city on the road to Salthill : its primary meaning has therefore no connection with Cleopatra, as suggested by Mrs Glasheen.

Mac Smashall Swingy of the Cattlelaxes (516) is as strikingly picturesque a name for a butcher as is that for the wielder of the 'sledded poleaxe' in *Ulysses*, but it is also as false, for it is really a play on the English translation of the name of a Donegal chieftain, Mac Suibhne na dTuath (Mac Sweeny of the Tuath, the name of North Donegal territories) which was rendered 'Mac Sweeny of the Battle Axes' from confusion of the word *Tuath* with *Tuagh*, a battleaxe. The mistake was probably made because some of the Mac Sweenys acted as commanders of the mercenary forces of Gallowglasses hired by Ulster Chieftains, whose traditional weapon was the battleaxe. As regards 'Smashall', cf. 'Sweeney Agonistes' by T. S. Eliot.

'half hang me, sirr' (516) is an alteration of a colloquial expostulation to recall one of the delicate methods of military interrogation in 1798. The witness was half-hanged and then lowered to ascertain whether he wished to add anything further to his testimony. Major Sirr was the officer who, as Town Major of Dublin, was in charge of these investigations. A successor of his, Frank Thorpe Porter, a Dublin Police Magistrate and author of *Twenty Years' Recollections* is probably the source of H.C.E's name as a Chapelizod publican.

'Beet, peat, wheat' (521) are the raw materials of sugar, fuel and flour which the de Valera Government aimed to produce at home, thus reducing imports.

The statement 'the lion's shire' (528) refers to Ireland. When Henry VIII renounced the Pope as head of the Church he had himself declared King of Ireland, instead of *Dominus Hiberniae*, his title in a papal donation given to his ancestor, Henry II. 'Share' in Cockney English is pronounced 'shire'.

'With a slog to square leg I sent my boundary to Botany Bay' (543) refers to cricket being played at Trinity College, Dublin—from College Park to Botany Bay, the latter being the name of another part of the campus.

Professor Tindall thinks that 'a depression called Holl Hollow . . . the pentapolitan poleetsfurcers bassoons into it on woodensdays their wellbooming wolvertones' (565) is a 'Wagnerian hollow'. It is in fact a natural theatre in the Phoenix Park where the Dublin Metropolitan Police band once gave performances, as well as a play on 'All Hallows', a Dublin seminary.

'Urloughmoor with Miryborough, leaks and awfully' (577) refers to Maryborough (now Portlaoise) and Tullamore, the county towns of Leix and Offaly.

'Callhalton eatwords!' (569) refers to Hilton Edwards, a Dublin Theatre actor.

'Peeter the Picker' (616) is not based on 'Peter Piper', as stated in *Song in the Works of James Joyce*. The reference is to

H

Lord Peter O'Brien, a nineteenth-century judge who was nick-named 'Peter the Packer' on account of the nice discrimination which he displayed in the selection of persons to act on juries in criminal cases, invariably accepting the objections raised by counsel prosecuting for the Crown to jurymen likely to be sympathetic to the case of the accused.

'Recitating . . . pearse orations' (620) refers to the memorable oration delivered on 15 October 1915, by Patrick Pearse at the grave of O'Donovan Rossa whose body had been brought back from the United States for burial in Glasnevin cemetery. The speech carried undertones which suggested that the speaker and his comrades would, in their generation, follow the path of insurrection marked out for them by that 'unrepentant Fenian' at whose grave they stood. When Pearse and his friends were executed after the Easter Insurrection in the following year, his oration became part of the bible of revolt which inspired the subsequent war of independence.

'Still I'll take me owld Finvara for my shawlders' (621): 'Finvara' is Joyce's variation on 'Kinvara' from Frank Fahy's song, 'The Ould Plaid Shawl', the first line of which is, 'Not far from ould Kinvara in the merry month of May'.

'Les go dutc' (622) apart from suggesting that they 'go dutch,' each paying for himself, can also mean that they should travel by the Dublin United Tramways Company, i.e., by tram.

'I'm in everywince nasturls. Even in Houlth's nose' (624). The Nose of Howth is a promontory on the north side of the peninsula. The smell of the Liffey was not usually perceptible at the Nose of Howth in Joyce's time but, in the 1950s, this particular point of the coast was chosen as the site of the outfall works for the new North Dublin Main Drainage Scheme. The nose of Howth now shares with the mouth of the Liffey the 'priestlike task of pure ablution' around Dublin's shores.

> Yes, you're changing, sonhusband, and you're turning, I can feel you, for a daughterwife from the hills again . . . Just a whisk brisk sly spry spink spank sprint of a thing there-somere saultering. (627)

Here is the young Liffey stream coming from her headwaters to succeed her mother, the old river Liffey as she prepares to 'slip away before they're up'. There is something icy and heartless about the description of her successor 'diveltaking on me tail' which contrasts with the lissom sweetness of A.L.P. herself when she started out 'on the spur of the hill in old Kippure, in birdsong and shearingtime'—'She was a young thin pale soft shy slim slip of a thing then, sauntering, by silvamoonlake . . .' (202)

With this 'mamemormee' (628) of her youth we see her go her 'way a lone a last a loved a long the (628) riverun, past Eve and Adam's, from swerve of shore to bend of bay, brings us by a commodius vicus of recirculation back to Howth Castle and Environs.' (3)

PART III
Ricorso

Chapter 22
Ricorso

EACH of Joyce's prose works up to and including *Ulysses* seems to form part of a preplanned *magnum opus*, each leading intrinsically and chronologically to the next. *Dubliners* contains introductions to various minor characters in *U* such as Lenehan, Bob Doran, Joe Hynes, Mr O'Madden Burke, Hoppy Holohan, McCoy, and Messrs Cunningham, Power and Kernan. The Stephen Dedalus of *U* is at once a more melancholy and more sophisticated version of the youth who is poised at the end of *A Portrait* to forge in the smithy of his soul the uncreated conscience of his race. The whole corpus of these writings is primarily autobiographical, the *ego* in *U* being divided between Stephen and Bloom and, possibly, Blazes Boylan, the minor characters (including The Citizen) acting as foils to Stephen or Bloom and sometimes pinpointing an alternative destiny awaiting Stephen if he did not elect for exile, such as that of Bob Doran, forced into marriage with Polly Mooney of 'The Boarding House' in *Dubliners*, whom we meet in 'Cyclops' 'snoring drunk, blind to the world' (*U* 297) on one of the periodical binges to which he was driven by the stress and strains of cohabitation 'with his little concubine of a wife' (*U* 312).

That Joyce intended to continue the interrelationship of his works into *FW* is evidenced by the format of his 1922-23 notes in *Scribbledehobble* the greater part of which is separated into sections referring to *Chamber Music*, each of the stories in *Dubliners*, the five parts of *A Portrait*, the three Acts of *Exiles* and the eighteen episodes of *U*. A considerable number of the words and phrases in this notebook appears in *FW* but in contexts that reveal no effort to retain any relevancy to the headings under which they were originally noted. Thus, under

'Hades', there appears the phrase 'and I stepped into Nelly coming home from the wake'. This (with the word 'stepped' written or miscopied for 'slipped') is based on a line from a set of verses in oral circulation in Ireland about 1922-23, one of which runs:

> You may go, darling Nelly, to the wake in Kildare,
> You may go, darling Nelly, for our lodger will be there.
> He is kind and he's true and good care of you he'll take,
> But keep your legs together coming home from the wake.

Another line is 'He'll fill you up with wine and he'll fill you up with cake' while the next repeats the author's admonition to Nelly which ends the quatrain quoted above. (Cf. my note on *FW* 42 in Chapter 21, Section 6, above, regarding music, wine and bread at a wake.) Joyce obviously intended that the phrase would be used in connection with some of the wakes of H.C.E. but it actually appears in Juan's 'sermon' to the girls of St Bride's in a form so obscure as to be unintelligible to anybody without prior knowledge of the original—'And beware how you dare of wet coctails in Kildare or the same may see your wedding driving home from your wake' (436). The 'sermon' then contains a warning to the girls about lodgers (437), but the relevance of this to the reference to 'cocktails in Kildare' remained hidden in Joyce's memory.

In the section of *Scribbledehobble*, entitled 'Words', the phrase 'hoht wahta bottle' is noted. Variations on this appear in *FW* as 'whotwaterwottle' (176-7) and 'hordwanderbaffle' (610). All three versions are onomatopoeic renderings of a subaqueous reverberation from a bath. When his batman returned to the bathroom with a hot water bottle the old colonel furiously denied having ever asked for it.

Another unexplained quatrain disguised as prose is—'He could claud boose his eyes to the birth of his garce, he could lump all his lot through the half of her play, but he jest couldn't laugh through the whole of her farce becorpse he weren't billed that way.' (509) This is a variation on a vulgar quatrain the first two lines of which are:

> A man may laugh through the whole of a farce,
> A man may laugh through the whole of a play . . .

'A coil of cord, a colleen coy, a blush on a bush turned first man's laughter into wailful moither. O foolish cuppled!' (433) seems to refer to Cain and Abel and the Fall (*O felix culpa*), but in fact it is based on Oliver Wendell Holmes's stricture on punning in *The Autocrat of the Breakfast Table* : 'Homicide and *verbicide* . . . are alike forbidden. Manslaughter, which is the meaning of the one, is the same as man's laughter which is the end of the other'. Joyce's abbreviated version of this passage is rendered in Americanese, obviously in recognition of the country of origin, while the book from which it was borrowed receives mention on the next page (434) as 'the autocart of the bringfast cable'. Sometimes an Americanism is left to the reader to recognise: 'for every dime he yawpens that momouth you could park your ford in it' (*FW* 364). Sometimes the very local reference that I recognised housed by coincidence a more personal meaning of which I was not aware. I was explaining to Robert Briscoe, then (1962) Lord Mayor of Dublin, who had been quizzed about Joyce in the United States, that a local allusion could accurately reflect the signature of the Almighty, I AM THAT I AM (*Exodus* 3 : 14), and be topographically correct even in the repetition involved in 'Hyam Hyam' (*FW* 455) because Hyam had two shops each bearing his name, one in Westmoreland Street and the other in Dame Street, when I was interrupted by Mrs Briscoe's exclaiming that that was her father: the Hyam premises were, in fact, the property of her father, but his name was Isaacs.

It is a difficult task to sort out the various items of building material in the following heap of ruins of The House that Jack Built :

Or may the maledictions of Lousyfear fall like nettlerash on the white friar's father that converted from moonshine the fostermother of the first nancyfree that ran off after the trumpadour that mangled Moore's melodies and so upturned the tubshead of the stardaft journalwriter to inspire the prime finisher to fellhim the firtree out of which Cooper Funnymore planed the flat of the beerbarrel on which my drandydad's lustiest sat his seat of unwisdom with my tante's petted sister for the cause of his joy! Amene. (*FW* 439)

Tub-thumping Shaun is apparently warning the girls of St

I

Bride's not to follow the example of Nora Barnacle in running away with the parodist of Moore's *Melodies*, thus inducing the 'stardaft' author of *The Tale of a Tub* and *Journal to Stella* to have Fenimore Cooper make the barrel on which Shaun is travelling in the Liffey. The passage is still 'circumveiloped with obscuritads' (*FW* 244), but as regards what we do understand we should question the propriety of applying the epithet 'stardaft' to Jonathan Swift. This is an echo of the purple patch in 'Proteus' (*U* 45):

> The hundredheaded rabble of the cathedral close. A hater of his kind ran from them to the wood of madness, his mane foaming in the moon, his eyeballs stars. Honyhnhnm, horsenostrilled.

The attribute of misanthropy is probably borrowed from Macaulay's 'heart burning with hatred against the whole human race', a generalisation which can be discounted by the abundant evidence of Swift's philanthropy, his charitable donations and his unstinting almsgiving at the church door on Sundays to the poor of Dublin, 'the hundredheaded rabble of the cathedral close'. As to Swift's madness, it had been established in 1882 that Swift suffered from Ménière's Disease, a diagnosis further elaborated and confirmed by the late Dr T. G. Wilson in the *Irish Journal of Medical Science*, June 1939. This showed that the giddiness and vertigo, as well as the deafness, from which the Dean suffered were due to a physical disturbance in his ear. Swift expired, as Dr Johnson said, 'a driv'ler and a show'; he went out not with a bang but a whimper.

These instances of Joyce's arbitrary use of material from his own notebook and other sources show that he failed to use that material in the way that he had originally planned and, further, that he treated both this material and other works and phrases culled from obscure sources to revisions that rendered them well-nigh unintelligible.

The themes of Irish origin in *FW* which I have identified in Part II of the present volume will be found to depend for authentication of their explication on widely dispersed page references: a particular theme seems to be deliberately fragmented and forced into irrelevant contexts by some such method of redisposition, explained in Chapter 20 (Bruinoboroff), as was utilised in dealing with the titles, first lines and the names of the airs used in Thomas Moore's *Irish Melodies*. Joyce saw nothing amiss in this literary carpentry. 'The important thing is not what we write, but how we write', he told Arthur Power (*Conversations with James Joyce*).

It seems that Joyce needed a 'text' from some other person's speech or writing to energise the stylistic rendering of his own prose, that this was a constantly recurring necessity and that it is probably the real explanation of his scattering the *disjecta membra* of his stock of quotations hither and thither throughout his book. If one estimates what would be left in *FW* if all the borrowing from other books were excised, one is faced with the conclusion that the operation would result in a very lean book to which Burton's comment in 'Democritus to the Reader' (*Anatomy of Melancholy*) would be quite applicable : 'They lard their lean books with the fat of others' works'. (Burton, in turn, might well be accused of having fattened his text with Shakespeare's 'Falstaff sweats to death / And lards the lean earth as he walks along'.)

Considerable portions of *Finnegans Wake* therefore clearly consist of miscellaneous passages and phrases drawn from a variety of source material, divided up and dispersed throughout early drafts of the primary *Wake* text. Indeed, the whole of the book is homogeneous to the extent that all its contents appear to be similarly composed from a medley of heterogeneous material. In many cases particular material was provided by friends and admirers, Joyce deciding how much of it was to be used and in what parts of the book. Le Fanu's *The House by the Churchyard* and Mark Twain's *Huckleberry Finn* are regarded as important sourcebooks. In August 1937 Joyce wrote to Frank Budgen asking him to mark noteworthy passages in Le Fanu's book and adding, 'In this way I can get an idea of the book in an hour or so.' About the same time he wrote to his son's stepson, David Fleishman, requesting that he perform a similar service with *Huckleberry Finn*, adding, 'I never read it and have nobody to read it to me.' Mr Atherton has a special section, 'The House by the Churchyard' in his *The Books at the Wake* (pp. 110-13) showing that this is one of the major sources for the material of *FW*.

Joyce's reference to the Vatican (*FW* 152) as 'chalkfull of masterplasters' might excusably be borrowed as a succinct and inimitable description of the pieces in his own masterpiece. The common reader could understand at a glance the clever rewriting of a proverbial saying in 'You cannot make a limousine lady out of a hillman minx' (*FW* 376) and the man of letters or literary critic would not have much difficulty in descrying a reference to the awards of Nobel Prizes to Yeats and Shaw in 'for Will-of-the-Wisp and Barny-the-Bark two mangold nobles to sweeden their bitters' (*FW* 211) or to those wonders of the modern world, 'the flushpots of Euston and the hanging garments of Marylebone' (*FW* 192). But, by and large, both the elucidation of the plot or *schema* of the book and the intellection in detail of its prose remained to be tackled by 'that ideal reader suffering from an ideal insomnia' (*FW* 120)—a phrase borrowed in part from Huysman's *A Rebours*, 'une communion entre un écrivain magique et un idéal lecteur'. To the ordinary littérateur and the common reader alike the logomanic prose would present an impassable barrier.

Eugene Jolas, the principal publisher, in his Paris magazine, *transition*, of the first instalments of *Work in Progress*, did not bespeak any support from such Philistines. His 'Manifesto' for 'The Revolution of the Word' contained twelve articles which ended,

11. The writer expresses. He does not communicate.
12. The plain reader be damned.

He published all the instalments issued between 1927 and 1930 in *transition* and in his 1932 'Homage' to Joyce he wrote that the English language here reaches heights not achieved since Shakespeare. Joyce, however, was not Shakespeare, much less the Super-Shakespeare he ambitioned to be. He could never have a hand the multitudinous seas incarnadine and stop when it made the green one red. It may therefore be of interest to see what established literary writers and book reviewers of repute had to say about these extracts from *Work in Progress* issued under the aegis of a publisher who considered that it was no function of the artist to communicate and that he had merely to express.

As early as 1924 Joyce's brother, Stanislaus, rejected these experimental writings, calling them 'wearisome rigmarole'. In 1928 H. G. Wells, who had previously expressed his 'unstinted admiration' of his previous book, informed Joyce that he could not follow his new banner. In reviewing *A Portrait*, Wells had said that it reminded him of Swift and Sterne. With Wells this had become a cliché : largely self-educated, he has recorded that he had purged his own juvenile bombastic style 'by copious draughts of Swift and Sterne'. The association of the two names with his own style may have been responsible for Joyce's regular coupling of them in *FW* but he may also have had, as usual, a *varia lectio* in mind, *sterne* (Ger.) 'stars', to associate Swift with Stella and Vanessa.

Ezra Pound, who brought Joyce to Paris and who was largely responsible for the publication of *A Portrait of the Artist as a Young Man* and, indirectly, for Sylvia Beach's publishing *Ulysses*, as well as for the initial publicity which led to Joyce's becoming an international literary figure, dismissed *Work in Progress* as 'circumambient peripherization'.

In 1931 Michael Stuart, writing on Mr Joyce's Word Creatures', saw the tendency in Ulysses to create 'universals' carried much further in *Finnegans Wake*, where they became the 'characters', having no individual life-stories of their own. My exegeses reveal a sufficient array of factual commentary on individual personalities, scenes and events to indicate that the opposite was the way Joyce wrote. The trouble is that they need such exegeses to unveil them. Part of the task he set himself was to be the centre of the universe he was creating and the historical universalisations were overwritten on his auto-biography, on basic local historical and fictional characters and on large quantities of material filched from Anglo-Irish, English and other literatures to add to the content of the original draft an overcoat of literary and historical universality.

In 1932 Desmond Mac Carthy said the work was 'naturally incomprehensible' but conceded that by the third or fourth reading 'one begins to discover a vague sense in it'. L. A. G. Strong, writing about 'Two Tales of Shem and Shaun', diagnosed that 'Mr Joyce, in his passage from literature to music has passed into a No-man's-land which belongs to neither'.

In 1933 Robert Cantwell said, 'we are watching the greatest living master of prose breaking up the language in which he won our respect'. In 1934 Ronald Symond referred to *Work in Progress* as 'multi-coloured chaos'.

The publication in 1939 of the complete work under the title of *Finnegans Wake* did little to provide the clarification which some readers of the instalments already published had been expecting. The breaking out of war a few months afterwards may, as Joyce thought, have deflected some attention from the book and abbreviated the notices that did appear, but it was foolish to expect in any circumstances that this enigmatic volume should receive an immediate welcome.

Paul Rosenfeld wrote that the book was 'cold and cerebral in comparison with that of a veritable "radical" like Gerald Manley Hopkins'. Louise Bogan's verdict was, 'There are better gods than Proteus'. The *Times Literary Supplement* remarked that Mr Joyce was of course abundantly justified if he was content with the satisfaction of art for art's sake and a splendid audience of one. Sir Harold Nicolson's contemporary *obiter dictum* (*Diaries and Letters 1930-39*, p. 401) was that *Finnegans Wake* was 'a very selfish book'.

In *The Observer*, Oliver Gogarty wrote : 'This archmocker in his rage would extract the Logos, the Divine Word or Reason from its tabernacle and turn it muttering and maudlin into the street. . . . This is the most colossal leg-pull in literature since McPherson's *Ossian*. Mr Joyce has had his revenge.' Gogarty's mis-spelling of Macpherson as 'McPherson' reminds one that Joyce managed to turn the author and the title into 'makefearsome ocean'.

G. W. Stonier, in the *New Statesman*, pointed out that 'The mistake is to read him as though he were writing the same languages as Mr Agate, Sir Hugh Walpole and Mr Charles Morgan : he is not . . . He writes for those who are tired of our ready-made literary cadences'.

On the young Malcolm Muggeridge the effect of the whole was of 'impenetrable and despairing darkness'.

Morley Callaghan queried Joyce's intention : 'is it an attempt to produce the reality of dream or is he just using that structure . . . to orchestrate words for their own sake?'

Richard Aldington said that common honesty compelled him to state that he was unable to explain either the subject or the meaning (if any) of Mr Joyce's book.

In the *Irish Times* the conclusion was that although after *Ulysses* Joyce had had no more to say, in *Finnegans Wake* he went on saying it.

The review by Harry Levin which appeared in 1939 and which Joyce considered to reveal more understanding than most was subsequently expanded into the 'Finnegans Wake' section of his book, *James Joyce*.

This cross-section of contemporary criticism indicates that the reaction to *FW* on the part of reputable writers and critics, who might be expected to appraise its artistic merits and intelligibility with greater insight than would the generality of the reading public, was, at worst, unfavourable and at best, apart from Joyce's closest followers, tinged with considerable doubt as to what the author was at. Joyce had mistaken the extent to which the average critic or the common reader was able or willing to follow him into the artificial wilderness of his subjective phantasies and private mythologies. Although a considerable portion of the book is preoccupied with its own composition and publication, the author does not really offer a serious or intelligible apologia :

> The proteiform graph itself is a polyhedron of scripture. There was a time when naif alphabetters would have written it down the tracing of a purely deliquescent recidivist, possibly ambidexterous . . . and presenting a profound rainbowl in his (or her) occiput . . . In fact, under the closed eyes of the inspectors the traits featuring the *chiaroscuro* coalesce, their contrarieties eliminated, in one stable somebody similarly as by the providential warring of heartshaker with housebreaker and of dramdrinker against freethinker our social something bowls along bumpily, experiencing a jolting series of prearranged disappointments, down the long lane of (it's as semper as oxhousehumper!) generations, more generations and still more generations. (*FW* 107)

This 'circumambient peripherization' does not get us very far, except for the phrase 'possibly ambidexterous' which may suggest that the author set about the rearrangement of his material with both hands, one starting from the front and the other from the end, hoping that the tunnels would meet in the middle. The 'prearranged disappointments' are only too evident in the text but these serve merely to muddy the waters still further. It is not really reassuring to be told at the end of this passage that the book is as simple as ABC when that is put in words signifying the hieroglyphic origins of the first three letters of the Hebrew alphabet—ox, house, camel, and when the word 'simple' is written 'semper', suggesting that the disappointments are perennial. Nor is there anything more reassuring in any other portion of *Finnegans Wake* or in Joyce's letters, except the suggestion that if any passage that seems to be difficult is read aloud its significance will then become perfectly clear. The unintelligibility or the irrelevancy in their contexts of various passages in *Finnegans Wake* have successfully resisted clarification by this method of exposition.

The analyses of the book undertaken here have succeeded in identifying its author's conception of himself as an Anglo-Irish writer in exile over against the public figure of the Irishman at home who distrusts and ostracises the artist and sends him to 'Cavantry', and whose political activities serve to illustrate contemporary Irish history (Chapters 15, 16, 17 above). A considerable amount of other material drawn from Irish literary, historical and legendary sources is detailed in the next four chapters (18-21). Various passages (including those explicated in Chapter 21) constitute in themselves literary criticisms, most of them being also masterpieces of virtuosity in the use of puns and parodies. Their impact is, however, lost or submerged in the effort to superimpose a universalised myth on the local themes and to equate Joyce himself, his family, the city of Dublin and the river Liffey, with an epitome of human life and the succession of generations from the Palaeolithic to the megalopolitan.

The river is personified to portray poetically the natural phenomena of change, the annually recurring miracle in vernal renewal of leaf and bloom, and the successive elements of rainfall, river-flow, evaporation, cloud formation, humidity and again, precipitation. The presentation in symbolic forms of these natural phenomena might well be described as an over-elaborated series of platitudinous truisms.

The parable of the Phoenix so aptly applied to the Easter Resurrection of Christ and the Easter Week Insurrection of the

Irish is only superficially expounded, as is the theme of the
Fall of Satan through pride, of Adam through disobedience and
of the apple or of Humpty Dumpty through the operation of
the law of gravity ('pomme full grave') (20) when these are
placed in juxtaposition in the jingling lines :

> *Cleftfoot from Hempel must tumpel, Blamefool Gardener's*
> *bound to fall;*
> *Broken eggs will poursuive bitten Apples for where theirs is*
> *Will there's his Wall.* (FW 175)

'Wall,' by the way, has a capital 'W', bringing us back, we
may suppose, 'by a commodius vicus of recirculation' to the Fall
of Finnegan off the wall which has been, of course, in erection
since Balbus was habitually engaged on it in the Latin Grammar,
or else off the wall of the tremendous edifice of *Finnegans Wake*
itself then in course of erection—'A Waalworth, a skyerscape
of most eyeful hoyth entowerly' (4). That one should get hurt
by a fall off the construction of the novel in which he is a
character, is, to say the least, a novel idea. That Finnegan arose
from the dead when whiskey was dashed on his face in the
course of his wake does not justify Joyce in his postulate that
a Fall implies a Resurrection. Humpty-Dumpty could not be
put together again and poetical as Joyce's phrase about the
Phoenix may be, we cannot literally believe that 'the fiery
bird disembers' (24).

There is an over-simplification of analogy and a super-
ficiality of thought in the manner in which these moral and
cosmic doctrinal universalisations are overlaid on the simple
domestic themes.

When Joyce set out in 1923 to write this massive missive to
Mother Ireland and to 'the wohld bludyn world' (593), he was
already, like Shelley's image of Byron—

> *The pilgrim of eternity, whose fame*
> *Over his living head like Heaven is bent.*

Byron awoke one morning to find himself famous. Joyce prophesies for himself in *Finnegans Wake* that he would find fame
'twixt a sleep and a wake' (192).

The cosmopolitan avant-garde who had acclaimed *Ulysses*
were even more enthusiastic over the 'new language' of *Work*

in Progress. They constituted a clique or claque in whose eyes Joyce could do no wrong. They hailed his new literary experiments as 'priestly work' on the naive premise that Joyce himself was a priest, not only in his work of artistic creation but also as a Catholic writer with an Irishman's natural bias against the English language. This fanciful idea seemed to have some support in Joyce's notions as a young man of artistic transubstantiation, redisposal of material to an artistic end. Joyce seemed to adopt this view in declaring his purpose—'if reams stood to reason and his lankalivline lasted he would wipe alley english spooker, multaphoniaksically spuking, off the face of the erse.' (*FW* 178)

Again he stated his intention to vie in language with the pioneers in nuclear physics so as to achieve the 'abnihilization of the etym' (353).

The result is, as has been already illustrated, a work with wide veins of marvellously comic content, parodies of inspired perversion and the representations of factual events in his personal life, the contemporary Irish scene and a variety of amusing treatments of Anglo-Irish literature. Overlaid on these and the so-called universalisations, but shot through both upper and lower strata are long stretches of writing about what an American might call 'most anything', and loosely strung together banalities, the wording of all of them gratuitously altered in spelling, as in the Spoonerism 'wious pish' (189) for 'pious wish', to take one example out of many alterations which were not worth while making.

The *claritas*, *consonantia* and *integritas*, together with the artistic objectivity bespoken for art in *A Portrait*, have all been abandoned. *FW* is a work made in the author's image and likeness, so introverted that its end meets its beginning, a consummation which he achieved with such difficulty that one might appropriately borrow Bloom's reflection on Stephen in *Eumaeus* to describe the process: 'high educational abilities though he possessed he experienced no little difficulty in making both ends meet'. He was an argotnaut to Kathartica in the seas of verbomania, his pirate's flag carrying the school and cross buns ensign, his booty the loot of the literatures, languages, music halls and 'slanguages', of the world.

Miss Weaver, who had her reservations about *FW* from the

first, gently expressed them in writing in January-February 1927, quoting Pound in support of the view that he was wasting his genius. Joyce was startled. 'It is possible Pound is right,' he wrote, 'but I cannot go back.' Later in the year he conceived the amazing idea of having James Stephens finish the book for him in the event of his being unable to do so himself. Stephens, Joyce believed, was like himself born on 2 February 1882, at the same hour of the day, and this in itself made him a personage of supreme importance. They had the same Christian name and 'Stephens' could be equated to Joyce's surrogate, Stephen Dedalus. Moreover the book would then have as co-authors J. J. & S., the name of a brand of Dublin whiskey manufactured by John Jameson and Son. Joyce was misinformed about Stephens's birthday which, as he was illegitimate, nobody knew for certain but in any event the train of thinking which led him to select his 'twin' as residuary legatee for the *damnosa hereditas* of the *FW* script would suggest that the driver's brainbox was running it off the rails. The fact was that Joyce was by that time unable to write any other kind of book. Jolas had said that the artist did not communicate. Joyce was bound to no such literary theory but psychologically he had become unable to communicate artistically with anybody other than himself. Early in his career he had taken for his role in life and literature that of the hunted deer. 'He even ran away with himself' (*FW* 171) and in writing *FW* he experienced the morose delectation of the autistic, still flashing his antlers on the heights from which, like Byron, he must look down on the hate of those below.

Sir Harold Nicolson *Diaries and Letters* gives an interesting impression of him, 4 February 1934, when he visited him in his apartment in the Rue Galilée, which, unknown to the writer, happens to constitute an extraordinary confirmation of Joyce's symbol of himself :

> . . . the impression of a very nervous and refined animal—a gazelle in a drawing-room. I suppose he is a real person somewhere, but I feel that I have never spent half-an-hour with anyone and been left with an impression of such brittle and vulnerable strangeness.

Nicolson had not had the opportunity of spending half-an-hour with Joyce's daughter, Lucia, for comparison.

Already in the 1920s Lucia was beginning to show signs of mental instability. In the 1930s her condition grew far more serious and Joyce after promoting various therapeutic devices such as the embroidery of letterines for deluxe volumes, at length consented to have Jung psychoanalyse her in Zurich. Jung would have liked an opportunity of also entering the mind of the master himself, but Joyce refused and in *Finnegans Wake* he observes, '. . . I can psoakoonaloose myself any time I want (the fog follow you all!) without your interferences or any other pigeonstealer'. (522) (The last word seems to refer to the psychoanalysts taking over the Holy Ghost's job.) For all this intellectual intransigence, his most faithful follower at this time, Paul Léon, who acted as his unpaid secretary conveyed to Miss Weaver, 23 March 1933, an account of his condition that was in effect a portrait of the artist as a sick man. 'He varies' Léon wrote, 'from states of great irritation and impotent fury to sudden lachrimose fits'. (*Letters*, III). Léon does not mention the occasional blood-curdling scream : this was usually a private act but it was once performed in the presence of Tom Kiernan who pulled the cold chain of silence on it in a London lavatory.

When Jung reported on schizoid symptoms in verses written by Lucia, Joyce insisted that this was evidence, not of madness, but of the new way of writing through a medium out of which future world literature would flower. Jung wrote afterwards that Joyce and his daughter were like two people going to the bottom of a river; she was sinking but he was diving, that Joyce used his art to control his schizophrenia. In other words he externalised his phantasies in writing to use it as a raft to keep himself mentally afloat. But while his writing may have proved of preventive or even therapeutic value to his mental condition, the effects of that condition on the resultant literary product as a work of art must be considered.

Joyce's original ambition in writing *FW* may have been to epiphanise himself as a modern Aristotle, the all-wisest Stagyrite who took all knowledge for his province. There soon developed, however, a compulsive element in his approach : he felt a need not alone to write everything but to write it all simultaneously. He succeeded to this extent, that if one could understand all the semantic and structural nuances of one page of *Finnegans Wake* then the sentence-structure of the whole book might become intelligible. This may explain in some degree the seemingly chaotic structure of the book, its author remorselessly intent on a faithful portrayal of his own talented but sick mind.

George Russell (AE) told Joyce at the end of their first meeting in 1902, 'You have not enough chaos in you to make a world.' Russell was probably right in this diagnosis. There is no chaos in *Chamber Music* or in *Stephen Hero* or in *Portrait of the Artist as a Young Man*, although critics of the latter work thought they detected signs of its falling asunder towards its close. Chaos first appears in *Ulysses*, in some of the later chapters, 'Wandering Rocks', 'Sirens', 'Cyclops', 'Circe' and 'Penelope', but it is contrived chaos, achieved by subjecting the episodes, characters and conversations to quick transformations of scenes and sounds, magical metamorphoses, stylistic alternations and (in Molly Bloom's case) mere mixed-up thinking. All this is achieved by the author's wordplay and by his playing with the identity of the characters beyond the point of credibility which they had presented in earlier chapters. The structured chaos of *FW* is that created by a mind retaining the capacity for expression but devoting it to the deliberate representation of disordered thinking, all this on the specious justification that this 'language of the night' must differ from the language of the day in *U*.

Professor Clive Hart in *Structure and Motif in Finnegans Wake* has offered a plan of this structure, a diagram of 'dreaming levels' throughout the book in the form of an endless line starting at the beginning of the text, 'riverun', to complete a circle covering Book I and the first three chapters of Book II, then proceeding to two internal concentric circles where the dreaming level sinks deeper, and then suddenly moving back to level one, making a great containing circle around the whole diagram.

One would like to think that Professor Hart's diagrammatic interpretation correctly represents Joyce's deliberate intention. It would indicate his determination to extend to all his work the symbolism he essayed when first he adopted 'Stephen Daedalus' as his pen name and then named 'Stephen Dedalus' as his fictional surrogate. It would establish *Finnegans Wake* not only as 'the last word in stolentelling' (*FW* 424) but also as an artistic structure in line with the labyrinth of Knossos in Crete which the original Daedalus is credited with having constructed for King Minos, the design of which has been reproduced on engraved stones in the megalithic structures of western Europe, Britain and Ireland and on isolated stones which have survived down to our own day, including the Hollywood stone removed some time ago from its site in the Wicklow mountains and now exhibited in the National Museum, Dublin. All the mazes, however, follow the conventional pattern of the Knossos labyrinth as pictured on a modern Cretan coin, in having seven concentric circles whereas Professor Hart's diagram shows only four ellipses. Furthermore, Professor Hart does not claim that his design can be traced to that of the Labyrinth : he says that it parodies mystical 'spirals of movement' as in Swedenborg's *Principia.*

Clive Hart's cartographic illustration traces the form and varying depths of the slumber through which the dream moves and shows that the dream is continuous whatever the depth of the sleep. In other words the contents of the whole book are represented as a dream. Such a study, as well as abstract linguistic and semantic analyses of the text, assist in clarifying the structure of the work but they do not show how it may be construed.

I have been concerned here with the content rather than the form and, within the limits I have set myself, it has been possible to identify and explicate considerable quantities of material. My explications of themes and identification of references relate primarily to the 'ground floor' or literal content of the main theme which has to do with Earwicker and his family, representing James Joyce and his family and his opposite number in Ireland. Thereafter my studies extended to mythic projections from the primary *personae* where these projections were based on identifiable characters in Irish history or legend or in Irish prophecies as in the case of St Malachy's list of future popes. I limited my investigations as far as possible to material not heretofore identified or adequately interpreted. Save where I could provide what I considered a more correct reference or more extended interpretation, I have avoided touching on Irish subjects already dealt with by Mr J. S. Atherton in *The Books at the Wake*, Mr M. J. C. Hodgart and Miss M. P. Worthington in *Song in the Works of James Joyce* and Mrs A. Glasheen in *A Second Census of Finnegans Wake*.

It is to be hoped that the factual and referential content of *FW* still remaining to be identified or explicated will be undertaken by appropriate specialists and published in easily accessible form. Authoritative exegeses on these planes are needed to provide a fully intelligible text for more comprehensive interpretation and also to deter or discourage illfounded generalisations about the main themes of the book or other misconstructions based on mistaken readings of words or references. Some commentators would bespeak such exegeses in the expectation of thereby finding a basis for a reappraisal which would give the book a totality of new meaning more significant than can now be discerned. My experience, based on the contents of those portions of the book to which I have given the closest study, would tend to discount any such expectation as fanciful. While detailed examination of the text may unveil further autobiographical items, personal thoughts and memories which the author, perhaps involuntarily, put on record and then endeavoured to conceal in verbal densities, the chief outcome will be a greatly enlarged referential corpus which will, however, continue to subserve the main themes with which we are already familiar—the naturalistic tale of the Chapelizod publican and his family overlaid by a universalised myth of creation, fall, guilt, exculpation and citybuilding with which is interwoven the world of nature personified in A.L.P. The persistent exegetist, who by this means attains a complete understanding of the linguistics and semantics as part of the structure of the book, will have attained a simultaneity of intellection which will enable him to absorb the multi-dimensional implications of the text at a single reading. This achievement, viewed from a merely mechanical standpoint, would not rate much higher than the skill of the accounts clerk of pre-computer days who could add up five or six columns of pounds, shillings and pence in one tot. Whether such reading would provide artistic satisfaction commensurate with the labour involved is a matter of speculation and would probably be ultimately a matter of taste, bearing in mind that much of the book, unlike *Dubliners*, is written in styles of 'deliberate meanness', employing artifices that deform all that they touch.

On another basis of interpretation one might perhaps consider an analogy between the potential transcendentalism of Bloom's end and that which might be ascribed to H.C.E. One possible destiny of Bloom was that of the 'aged impotent disfranchised ratesupported lunatic pauper' (*U* 646). Such a situation might be precluded by departure 'to the extreme limit of the cometary orbit . . . Whence . . . he would somehow reappear reborn above delta in the constellation of Cassiopeia and after incalculable eons of peregrination return an estranged avenger, a wreaker of justice on malefactors, a dark crusader, a sleeper awakened, with financial resources (by supposition) surpassing those of Rothschild or of the silver king.' (*U* 648-9) He would have the universal binomial denominations of Everyman or Noman. His tributes would be 'honour and gifts of strangers, the friends of Everyman, and a nymph immortal, beauty, the bride of Noman'. The 'Everyman' here referred to does not appear to be the medieval morality character. He is a symbol of all men as opposed to Noman who was Odysseus, Ulysses, Simon Dedalus deputising for Bloom. One would appear to be justified in regarding him as foreshadowing H.C.E. or rather H.C.E. in the aftermath of *FW* when the sleeper awakens. When one considers the Bloom who was in *U* and who may return, the exculpatory accused and triumphant avenger of 'Circe', a man of many parts, Emperor of the new Bloomoosalem, the Count of Monte Cristo of Joyce's juvenile reading, one may see H.C.E. as an amalgamation of Simon Dedalus and Bloom in Noman, linked in turn with the 'Cyclops' Citizen Cusack, 'nobodyatall with Wholyphamous' (73), 'a sleeper awakened' (*U* 49), Daedalus changed into Dedalus to accord with Ibsen's *When We Dead Awaken*, reappearing above delta (i.e. A.L.P.) not 'somehow' as in *Ulysses* but with the aid of the cosmic physics which, after an unsatisfactory and unenlightening interview with Einstein, an American journalist laconically dismissed as 'Light Caught Bending'. This, and not the gigantic caricature of his posterior as the landscape surrounding the main driveway of the Phoenix Park, may be the predestined, predicted but inexplicable orbit of Finnegan and his spaceship, *Finnegans Wake*, as postulated darkly in—

Bloody certainly have we got to see to it ere smellful demise surprends us on this concrete that down the gullies of the eras we may catch ourselves looking forward to what will in no time be staring you larrikins on the postface in that multimirror megaron of returningties, whirled without end to end. (*FW* 582)

Either the book is here projected as a projectile moving of its mere motion in a cosmic or 'vicous' circle of its own or else it is hurtled round in earth's nocturnal course with rocks and stones and trees, rolling impotently on as thou or I. Joyce's prophetic soul may have anticipated some adventitious lift to put it back into orbit when he predicted H.C.E. being 'rehearsed' 'later in the century' (*FW* 55) perhaps with the aid of a volume (*FW* 440) 'set up by Gill the father, put out by Gill the son, and circulating disimally at Gillydehooly's Cost.'

Meanwhile, in 1964, Gell-Mann, a distinguished research worker in the field of elementary particle physics, failing to find some fundamental idea or experimental fact which would unify his subject, postulated a particle which he called a quark, quoting 'James Joyce, *Finnegans Wake*, page 383'. The quark still eludes discovery despite intense technological research, including the use of the great accelerators. But could the technocrats not have also borrowed Joyce's 'wholemole millwheeling vicociclometer . . . autokinatonetically preprovided with a clappercoupling smeltingworks exprogressive process . . . [which] receives through a portal vein the dialytically separated elements of precedent decomposition for the verypetpurpose of subsequent recombination' (*FW* 614)? Or, for that matter, his 'collideorscape' (*FW* 143)? Long before Gell-Mann's time, Joyce, with his 'abnihilisation of the etym' had displayed 'moletons skaping with mulicules' (*FW* 353) and these, being male and female, should have provided the medium of unification predicted by the scientist. Indeed, they should also have provided the medium of the multiplication which the nuclear physics quarks have now in fact attained. It was not in the nature of a Joycean quark to subside submissively into the symbolism of a limbo in microphysics as a plus or as near as damn it to a minus or *vico verso*. It was not good for even a trinity of quarks to be alone and now they have increased and multiplied, each, as Bruno by his Nolan, confronted by his antiquark.

Three quarks were the seagulls' farewell salute to King Mark, surrogate of H.C.E., who is now diminished by the physicists to something many degrees below the level of visibility. H.C.E. would thus share the fate of Simon Dedalus who, leaving the stage in 'Circe', shrinks to the size of his dwarf simian acolytes. The idea of alternative destinies, infinitesimal instead of infiniteness, microcosmic for macrocosmic, might have intrigued Joyce. Mike or Mac.

Between his colonies in the microcosm and the Wandering Jew, his man in outer space, Joyce's trapeze, like a pulse, shuttles fierce on umbilical tightropes through all the worlds, recycling on ricorso to the natal spot of Baby Tuckoo in 41 Brighton Square, Rathgar. *Abi viator*, and reconsider your denunciation of the inconsequential Irish nomenclature which honours a $\triangle$ with a title of $\square$. Adjust your sights and observe that there is a fourth side, small but so significantly existential as to make the enclosed space a trapezium. A daring young man first saw the light there on 2 February 1882, the date providing data for a simple numerological horoscope which shows that Joyce's years of destiny were 1886, 1895, 1904, 1913, 1922, 1931 and 1940. Finally, for those prepared to place credence in Joyce's postulate of resurrection, 'the fiery bird disembers', the corresponding years for his resurrection would be 1949, 1958, 1967 and 1976, relying on 'sixes and seventies as eversure as Halley's comet' (54.7-8). The reference to the celestial phenomenon may permit us the secrets of the abyss to spy as far ahead as 1985 when we may perhaps see him come again in company with a namesake of Swift's pepette, Stella Crinita.

SELECT BIBLIOGRAPHY

Prose works by Joyce published in his lifetime:

Dubliners, London: Grant Richards 1914, Penguin Books 1973. New York: Viking Press 1970.

A Portrait of the Artist as a Young Man, London: Jonathan Cape (definitive text) 1968, Penguin 1966. New York: Viking Press 1968.

Exiles (a play), London: Cape 1952, Signet 1968. New York: Viking Press 1970.

Ulysses, London: Bodley Head 1960, Penguin 1969. New York: Random House 1961.

Finnegans Wake, London: Faber & Faber 1964, Faber Paperbacks 1975. New York: Viking Press 1957.

Works by Joyce published posthumously:

Stephen Hero (ed. Theodore Spencer; revised with Foreword by John J. Slocum and Herbert Cahoon), London: Cape 1956, Four Square 1966. New York: New Directions 1963.

The Critical Writings of James Joyce (ed. Ellsworth Mason and Richard Ellmann), London: Faber 1959.

Scribbledehobble (ed. Thomas E. Connolly), Oxford University Press, and Evanston: Northwestern University Press, 1961.

Books on Joyce and his works:

Anderson, C. G., *James Joyce and his World*, London: Thames & Hudson 1967. New York: Viking Press 1967.

Atherton, James S., *The Books at the Wake*, London: Faber 1959. New York: Viking Press 1960.

Benstock, Bernard, *Joyce-again's Wake. An Analysis of Finnegans Wake*, Seattle: University of Washington Press 1965.

Bowen, Zack, *Musical Allusions in the Works of James Joyce*, Albany: State University of New York 1975. Dublin: Gill and Macmillan 1975.

Budgen, Frank, *James Joyce and the Making of 'Ulysses'*, Oxford University Press 1934. Bloomington: University of Indiana Press 1959.

Budgen, Frank, *Myselves when Young*, Oxford University Press 1970.

Burgess, Anthony, *Joysprick*, London: André Deutsch 1973.

Byrne, J. F., *Silent Years*, New York: Farrar Strauss & Young 1953.

Campbell, Joseph and Henry Morton Robinson, *A Skeleton Key to Finnegans Wake*, New York: Harcourt Brace 1944. London: Faber 1947.

Colum, Pádraic and Mary, *Our Friend James Joyce*, London: Gollancz 1959.

Colum, Mary, *Life and the Dream*, London: Macmillan 1947. Garden City, New York: Doubleday 1947.

Connolly, Thomas E. (ed.), *The Personal Library of James Joyce*, Buffalo: University of Buffalo 1955.

Curran, C. P., *James Joyce Remembered*, Oxford University Press 1968.

Dahl, Liisa, *Linguistic Features of the Stream-of-Consciousness Techniques of James Joyce (et al.)*, Turku: Annales Universitatis Turkuensis 1970.

Ellmann, Richard, *James Joyce*, New York/London: Oxford University Press 1959.

Ellmann, Richard, *Ulysses on the Liffey*, London: Faber 1972.

Field, Saul and Morton Levitt, *Bloomsday*, London: Bodley Head 1973.

Freund, Gisèle and V. B. Carleton, *James Joyce in Paris*, London: Cassell 1966.

Gilbert, Stuart, *James Joyce's Ulysses: a Study*, London: Faber 1930. New York: Vintage Books, 1952, Viking Press 1966.

Gillet, Louis, *Stèle pour James Joyce*, Marseilles: Sagittaire 1941.

Glasheen Adaline, *A Second Census of Finnegans Wake*, Evanston: Northwestern University Press 1963.

Gorman, Herbert, *James Joyce, a Definitive Biography*, New

York: Farrar & Rinehart 1939, 1948. London: Bodley Head 1941, 1949.

Hart, Clive, *Structure and Motif in Finnegans Wake*, London: Faber 1962. Evanston: Northwestern University Press 1962.

Hart, Clive, *A Concordance to Finnegans Wake*, Minneapolis: University of Minnesota Press 1963.

Hayman, David, *A First-Draft Version of Finnegans Wake*, Austin: University of Texas Press 1962.

Healey, George Harris (ed.), *The Dublin Diary of Stanislaus Joyce*, London: Faber 1962.

Hodgart, M. J. C. and Mabel P. Worthington, *Song in the Works of James Joyce*, New York: Columbia University Press 1959.

Hutchins, Patricia, *James Joyce's Dublin*, London: Grey Walls Press; Australia, New Zealand: Invincible Press; Cape Town: M. Darling; Toronto: Falcon Press, 1950.

James Joyce's Letters, vol. I, ed. Stuart Gilbert, Faber 1957; vols, II and III, ed. Richard Ellmann, Faber 1966. New York: Viking Press 1966.

Joyce, Stanislaus, *My Brother's Keeper*, ed. Richard Ellmann, London: Faber 1966. New York: Viking Press 1966.

Kenner, Hugh, *Dublin's Joyce*, London: Chatto & Windus 1955. Boston: Beacon Press 1962.

Levin, Harry, *James Joyce, a Critical Introduction*, London: Faber 1944, 2nd edn. and Paperback 1960. Norfolk, Conn., New Directions Books 1960.

Litz, A. Walton, *The Art of James Joyce*, London/New York: Oxford University Press 1961, 1962.

Lyons, J. B., *James Joyce and Medicine*, Dublin: Dolmen Press 1973.

Magalaner, Marvin and Richard M. Kain, *Joyce, the Man, the Work, the Reputation*, New York: New York University Press 1956.

O'Brien, Darcy, *The Conscience of James Joyce*, Princeton: University Press 1968.

O'Connor, Ulick, *Oliver St John Gogarty*, London: Cape 1964.

O'Connor, Ulick (ed.), *The Joyce we knew* (Eugene Sheehy, William G. Fallon, Pádraic Colum, Arthur Power), Cork: Mercier Press 1967.

O Hehir, Brendan, *A Gaelic Lexicon for Finnegans Wake*, Berkeley: University of California Press 1961.

O Lochlainn, Colm, *Irish Street Ballads,* Dublin: Three Candles 1939, revised ed. 1946. New York: Citadel Press 1960.

Power, Arthur, *Conversations with James Joyce,* London: Millington 1974.

Ryan, John (ed.), *A Bash in the Tunnel. James Joyce by the Irish,* Brighton: Clifton Books 1970.

Strong, L. A. G., *The Sacred River,* London: Methuen 1949. New York: Pellegrine and Cudahy 1951.

Sullivan, Kevin, *Joyce among the Jesuits,* New York: Columbia University Press 1958.

Thornton, Weldon, *Allusions in Joyce,* North Carolina: University of North Carolina Press 1968.

Tindall, William York, *A Reader's Guide to Finnegans Wake,* London: Thames & Hudson 1969.

Bibliographical and other sources peculiar to the present volume

It would be impossible to itemise comprehensively the various sources of local knowledge drawn upon for information, identifications and exegeses peculiar to this book. There would be more of autobiography than bibliography involved in any such attempt. For example, I am indebted to the late Jasper Tully, editor of *The Roscommon Herald* and one-time member of the Irish Parliamentary Party, for the information that Wolfe Flanagan was the writer of the articles (and pamphlet) entitled *Parnellism and Crime.* It would be an act of supererogation to provide an extended list of citations such as this or to trace the origins of what remains in my memory of the fruits of personal contacts, travelling and reading of a lifetime. The list that follows is confined to works specifically used in providing material relevant to Joyce's works that, so far as I know, has not been included in books by any other commentators.

Bede, *A History of the English Church and People* (translated by Leo Sherley-Price), London: Penguin Books 1955.

Bodkin, M. M., *Recollections of an Irish Judge,* London: Hurst & Blackett 1914.

Graves, Robert, *The White Goddess,* London: Faber Paperback 1962.

Healy, Most Rev. John, *Ireland's Ancient Schools and Scholars,*

Dublin: M. H. Gill & Son; London: Burns & Oates; New York: Benzinger Bros. 1908.

Knox, Hubert Thomas, *Notes on the Early History of the Dioceses of Tuam, Killala and Achonry*, Dublin: Hodges Figgis 1904.

O'Brien, R. Barry, *The Life of Charles Stewart Parnell*, London: Nelson, 1910. New York: Harper & Bros. 1898.

O'Flaherty, Roderic, *Ogygia* (E. trs. from original Latin) by Rev. James Hely, A.B., Dublin: M'Kenzie 1793.

O'Kearney, Nicholas, *The Prophesies of St Colmcille and Malachy*, Dublin: Duffy 1932.

O'Rahilly, Thomas F., *Early Irish History and Mythology*, Dublin: Dublin Institute for Advanced Studies 1946.

Smythe, Colin, *The Prophesies of St Malachy and St Columbkille*, Gerrards Cross, Bucks, 1969.

INDEX